Welfare Policy and Poverty

Edited by
Mel Cousins

IPA
INSTITUTE OF PUBLIC
ADMINISTRATION
50 Years
CELEBRATING PUBLIC SERVICE
1957 – 2007

Combat Poverty
Agency *working for a*
poverty-free Ireland

First published in 2007
by the
Institute of Public Administration
57–61 Lansdowne Road
Dublin 4
Ireland
www.ipa.ie

and

Combat Poverty Agency
Bridgewater Centre
Conyngham Road
Islandbridge
Dublin 8
Ireland
www.combatpoverty.ie

ISBN: 978-1-904541-63-9

British Library cataloguing-in-publication data
A catalogue record for this book is available from the British Library

The views expressed in this text are the authors' own and not necessarily those of Combat Poverty Agency.

Publications and printed matter will be made available, on request, in a range of formats, including audio tape, large print, Braille and computer disc.

Cover design by Red Dog Graphic Design Consultants, Dublin
Typeset by Computertype, Dublin
Printed in Ireland by Betaprint, Dublin

Contents

Foreword

In 1986 the Commission on Social Welfare published a comprehensive report on the operations of the social welfare system including how it related to the taxation system and other social services. It made a number of important recommendations to the then Minister for Social Welfare on the implementation of an anti-poverty plan and it undertook an analysis of the distribution of national resources across different income groups with regard to taxation, social welfare, education, health and housing.

At its inaugural meeting in 1983 the Minister requested that the Commission give priority to considering the establishment of an organisation to combat poverty. The Commission responded to this request and proposed that such an organisation should have a remit to advise the Minister on specific measures to combat poverty in the community.

Subsequent to this recommendation, the Combat Poverty Agency was established as a state advisory agency to develop and promote evidence-based proposals and measures to combat poverty in Ireland. It was set up under the Combat Poverty Agency Act 1986, which sets out four general functions: policy advice, project support and innovation, research, and public education. Since its establishment, Combat Poverty has sought to promote a just and inclusive society by working for a poverty-free Ireland.

Two decades after the Commission on Social Welfare, the social and economic context in Ireland has changed dramatically. From a country where the limitations of the revenue available to the exchequer severely restricted welfare policies, and where public concern centred on the problems of unemployment and emigration, Ireland has become one of Europe's economic success stories. During this period, various structural reforms were introduced which helped to lift many people out of poverty.

Recognising that the existence of poverty is an impediment to growth, both socially and economically, another major development has been the increased role of the European Union in putting poverty and social exclusion at the top of the policy agenda, resulting in the coordination of these policies across the member states. This commitment by the governments of the member states results from the agreement in Lisbon, in 2000, to develop systems of social protection and social inclusion which underpin the transformation of the EU into a 'knowledge economy'.

However, despite unprecedented economic growth, the achievement of full employment and substantial improvements in living standards for most people, Ireland still faces considerable challenges in ensuring the welfare of all its citizens. For many, economic growth has not been matched by improvements in their standards of living and there remains a segment of the population that is unable to escape from circumstances of severe disadvantage and exclusion.

Although there has been a significant reduction in consistent poverty over the past two decades, it still affects 7 per cent of the population. These people, numbering some 289,000 in 2005, are living on very low incomes and are deprived of basic necessities such as adequate heating, clothing and/or food. The number of people at risk of poverty has also remained high. Based on the agreed EU measurement for relative poverty (60 per cent of the national median income – €193 per week in 2005), close to one in five people living in Ireland are surviving on low incomes.

This book marks the twentieth anniversary of two key milestones in the struggle to eradicate poverty and social exclusion from Irish society – the report of the Commission on Social Welfare and the establishment of the Combat Poverty Agency. It examines the progress made and the changes experienced over the past two decades in a number of key policy areas such as children, older people, people with disabilities and health. Reflecting the transformation of Irish society, it also deals with issues that did not exist twenty years ago, such as the integration of immigrants and the emergence of an intercultural society.

The Combat Poverty Agency wishes to thank all the contributors to this book for sharing their experiences and expertise. Together they have delivered a comprehensive insight into the key issues concerning poverty and social inclusion within the current policy agenda in Ireland and identified lessons for the future. Thanks are due in particular to Mel Cousins for his role in shaping this book and his dedication in bringing it to fruition.

As Combat Poverty's twentieth anniversary year draws to a close, we hope that this book will advance thinking and stimulate debate on how the Irish welfare state can evolve to achieve the target of a poverty-free Ireland.

Combat Poverty Agency

Acknowledgements

I would like to thank a number of people without whom this publication would not have been possible. First and foremost I must express my sincere thanks to the authors who contributed excellent chapters working to rather short deadlines. A number of people in the Combat Poverty Agency contributed to the publication in the conception of the original idea, its development into this book and by commenting on particular chapters including Helen Johnston, Jonathan Healy and Kevin O'Kelly. In particular, I would like to thank Bevin Cody for her indispensable input and support.

Mel Cousins

Chapter 1

Introduction

Mel Cousins

Introduction

The objective of this book is to provide an overview and analysis of key issues concerning public policy on poverty and social inclusion in Ireland and to draw policy lessons for the future. This chapter sets out the book's conceptual framework.

Building an inclusive society

Policies to combat poverty and social exclusion and to build an inclusive society are recognised as critically important at both national and international levels. Ireland was an innovator in adopting a strategy-based approach to combating poverty with the publication of the *National Anti-Poverty Strategy* (NAPS) (Ireland, 1997). This document, which followed an extensive consultation process, provided an analysis of the level and causes of poverty, discussed the measures taken to address poverty and social exclusion and set specific targets to be achieved through policy measures.[1]

---

[1]   The NAPS was revised in 2002 (Ireland, 2002a and 2002b) and integrated with the EU national action plan on social inclusion process.

Subsequently, in 2000, the EU also endorsed a strategic approach to poverty reduction with the adoption of national action plans on poverty and social inclusion. The EU has recently established three overarching objectives for social protection and social exclusion policies and three specific objectives in relation to the eradication of poverty and social exclusion:[2]

(a) Social cohesion, equality between men and women and equal opportunities for all

(b) Effective and mutual interaction between different policy objectives

(c). Good governance, transparency and the involvement of stakeholders in designing, implementing and monitoring policy

(d) Access for all to the resources, rights and services needed for participation in society

(e) Active social inclusion for all

(f) Well-coordinated social inclusion policies.

Ireland's most recent social partnership agreement – *Towards 2016* – also recognises the importance of measures to build an inclusive society (Ireland, 2006). A key policy focus over the lifetime of this agreement involves 'the development of an inclusive and sustainable economy and society' and the social partners are committed to the achievement of 'a

---

[2] Arising from a decision of the EU Council in March 2006, this process brings together strategies in the areas of social inclusion, pensions and healthcare: http://ec.europa.eu/employment_social/social_inclusion/objectives_en.htm

participatory society and economy with a strong commitment to social justice'.

Ireland has recently published its *National Action Plan for Social Inclusion 2007–2016* (NAPinclusion) (Ireland, 2007a), which builds on commitments in the National Development Plan 2007–2013 (Ireland, 2007b) and in *Towards 2016* and is discussed in later chapters.

The importance of setting targets and reviewing progress

An essential part of a policy to combat poverty and social exclusion is the setting of targets and indicators and the monitoring of progress to achieve the objectives set in strategy documents. This is recognised at both national and European (Social Protection Committee, 2006) levels, where specific targets and indicators of progress have been established in a range of different policy areas. An important part of the implementation of the national action plans on social inclusion is the monitoring of progress towards the meeting of objectives (see objective c). And, as part of *Towards 2016*, the social partners agree that it is important to set real and achievable targets for social inclusion measures and to set out specific policy measures to review progress.

It is now very timely to review the progress which Ireland has made towards reducing and, where possible, eliminating poverty and social exclusion. 2007 marks the tenth anniversary of the publication of the original *National Anti-Poverty Strategy* and the closing date for the achievement of the targets set in that document (and revised in 2002). It is also the twentieth anniversary of the Commission on

Social Welfare and it is therefore appropriate to review developments in welfare policy given the dramatic changes in Irish society over that period.

This publication will review key policy measures taken to combat poverty and social exclusion in recent years. It will establish the extent to which progress has been made to achieve targets (or in line with indicators) set in the EU and the Irish strategy documents. It will also identify new issues which have arisen in recent years such as the challenges posed by and opportunities arising from the significant increase in the level of migration into Ireland. Finally, it will evaluate the positive and negative aspects of measures adopted (or not adopted) in particular policy areas and suggest what needs to be done to ensure the development of a truly inclusive society.

What is poverty and social exclusion?

The Combat Poverty Agency has always taken a broad and relative definition of poverty and social exclusion. This approach is also adopted in the definition of poverty underpinning the NAPinclusion (Ireland, 2007, p. 21):

> People are living in poverty if their income and resources (material, cultural and social) are so inadequate as to preclude them from having a standard of living which is regarded as acceptable by Irish society generally. As a result of inadequate income and other resources people may be excluded and marginalised from participating in activities which are considered the norm for other people in society.

There are many different ways in which to measure poverty and social exclusion including the 'risk-of-poverty' (or relative income poverty) approach adopted by the EU and the 'consistent poverty' measure used in setting targets for the Irish NAPS (see Chapter 2). The pros and cons of different measures have been discussed extensively elsewhere (see Social Welfare Benchmarking and Indexation Group, 2001; Maître et al., 2006) and it is not intended to reopen the discussion in this book. From a conceptual point of view, poverty and social exclusion are multidimensional and no single indicator can fully capture these complex phenomena. As Maître et al. (2006, p. 2) state, 'when dealing with a phenomenon as complex and multi-faceted as poverty, there is a strong argument for not relying on any single measure or indicator'. Rather, a range of tiered and interrelated poverty reduction targets may be more appropriate. From a practical point of view, a range of targets and indicators has already been established using one or other measure of poverty and this book draws on these different indicators to establish the extent to which policy measures have been able to achieve the targets set by policy-makers.

The broader context

One important context for this review of policy is the National Economic and Social Council's 2005 publication *The Developmental Welfare State.* This study is perhaps the most important social policy report the NESC has published in its thirty-year history and it sets out a clear and intellectually argued rationale for a specific approach to welfare.

While recognising Ireland's strong economic performance, the NESC (2005, p. xiii) starts from the position that:

Ireland's welfare state and social policies ... need to change further if they are to (i) address the deep-rooted social disadvantage of a section of the population that has shown little mobility off means-tested social assistance, (ii) support people at work as they seek to maintain and improve their participation in the economy, and (iii) set and reach wholly new standards in how people with disabilities and people in institutional care are supported.

The report argues that 'good economic performance and improved social protection are neither intrinsically opposed nor compelled to occur together in some automatic way' (p. xiii). Rather, the NESC claims that they can be made to support each other and that social policy is 'not simply an exercise in redistributing a surplus there to be creamed off after a successful economic performance' but can contribute to or detract from economic success (p. xiii). The NESC sees Ireland as a 'hybrid' welfare state combining aspects of other European models. However, one distinguishing feature is that Ireland uses a 'moderate to low proportion of national resources in providing services and a low proportion in providing cash transfers' despite its relatively wealthy status in EU terms (p. xvi; see also Timonen, 2003).

The NESC proposes a developmental welfare state consisting of three overlapping areas of activity: services (including education, health, childcare, eldercare, housing, transport and employment services), income supports and activist or innovative measures.[3] It sees access to a wide range of services as essential 'to attaining the workforce quality that

---

[3] Because the focus of this book is on national policy we do not focus, in detail, on the area described by the NESC as involving activist or innovative measures.

6

underpins a competitive, knowledge-based economy, to maintaining social cohesion and combating social exclusion' (p. xix). The Council argues that 'the development of a dynamic, knowledge-based economy has inherent social implications that can serve social justice and a more egalitarian society' and that a move to the developmental welfare state is integral to sustaining the dynamism and flexibility of Ireland's economy (p. xxiii).

The NESC's approach is clearly influenced by that of Polanyi (1944), who argued that rather than, as economic theory would suggest, society being subordinate to markets, a successful market economy is, in fact, impossible unless it is embedded in society. It also reflects much recent work which has emphasised the positive relationship between the economy and business and the development of the welfare state (for example Swenson, 2002; Mares, 2003; Iversen, 2005).

It is also important to place issues concerning poverty and social inclusion in the broader context of the developing discourse around equality and rights-based approaches. Poverty and social exclusion do not, of course, affect all sections of society equally. It has always been the case that particular groups, on the basis of, for example, gender, disability or ethnicity, have suffered from particular (and often cumulative) disadvantages. This emphasises the importance and value of the equality approach, which is recognised in the EU national action plan on social inclusion framework (objective a): 'to promote ... equality between men and women and equal opportunities for all through adequate, accessible, financially sustainable, adaptable and efficient social protection systems and social inclusion policies'.

From a legal point of view, Ireland has introduced quite comprehensive equality legislation (Equal Status Acts 2000 to 2004). It has also established a statutory Equality Authority which seeks to achieve positive change in the situation and experience of those groups and individuals experiencing inequality. This is achieved by stimulating and supporting a commitment to equality within the systems and practices of key organisations and institutions as part of the cultural values espoused by society and as a dimension to individual attitudes and actions. Nonetheless, there remains a challenge to ensure that principles set out in law are implemented in practice in all areas of anti-poverty policy.[4] This can be of particular importance in relation to policies for migrants and ethnic minority groups such as Travellers.

A third important contextual issue is the development of a more rights-based approach to anti-poverty policies. In many cases, groups suffering from poverty and social exclusion may also experience discriminatory attitudes both in society generally and in the provision of services. The establishment of legal rights to services can form an important means by which disadvantaged groups can overcome discrimination. Indeed, the importance of rights is recognised in the EU framework and one of the common objectives refers to 'access to all to the ... rights ... needed to participate in society' (objective d). In Ireland, some social services – such as the social welfare system – are almost entirely rights-

---

[4] As can be seen in the case of gender equality, where, for example, the establishment and implementation of equal pay legislation has still not achieved the objective of ensuring that men and women receive broadly similar remuneration (taking account of factors such as experience, qualifications etc.) (see Russell and Gannon, 2002, who find that a significant pay gap remains).

based. However, in other areas, services are provided on a more discretionary and budget-limited basis.

Ireland has adopted a number of important pieces of rights-based legislation, in addition to the Equal Status Acts, such as the European Convention on Human Rights Act 2003 and the Mental Health Act 2001.[5] However, national strategy documents on poverty and social inclusion remain somewhat ambiguous about the role of a rights-based approach in an anti-poverty strategy, preferring to focus on issues concerning quality of service delivery. See, for example, the recent NAPinclusion (Ireland, 2007), which makes frequent reference to 'access to quality services'.

Structure of the book

The book analyses key developments in anti-poverty policy in Ireland. In order to do so, individual chapters focus on particular policy areas. However, a number of key cross-cutting issues are addressed across chapters. In particular, we have tried to identify the impact of gender in relation to each of the specific policy areas covered and to make reference to gender data and developments of particular relevance from a gender perspective. In addition, questions concerning equality and rights-based approaches are discussed where appropriate. Finally, chapters make reference to the EU context insofar as this is relevant.

In Chapter 2, Jim Walsh provides an overview of trends in relation to poverty since 1987. Drawing on data from the

---

[5] Ireland has also ratified a number of international rights-based instruments, for example the UN Convention on the Rights of the Child.

Living in Ireland Survey and the EU Survey of Income and Living Conditions, this chapter provides a general overview of developments in relation to income distribution and poverty and deprivation trends in Ireland over the period in question, putting them in a European context.

Following the approach set out by the NESC in *The Developmental Welfare State*, the book adopts a lifecycle approach with individual chapters on income support as it concerns children, people of working age and older people. In Chapter 3, John Sweeney focuses on issues concerning children and income poverty and examines key questions concerning the structure of welfare support for children in Ireland. In Chapter 4, Mary Murphy looks at pivotal topics concerning people of working age from a poverty perspective, including the extent to which people in employment may be at risk of poverty, issues concerning unemployment, activation strategies to help people make the transition from welfare to employment and strategies to ensure that those in work can obtain quality employment. In Chapter 5, Tony McCashin examines current policies to provide income support for older people, the extent to which such policies are succeeding in their objectives and crucial questions concerning pension policy.

Given their importance from a poverty perspective, and given that quality services are a key objective of the Combat Poverty Agency's strategic plan (CPA, 2005),[6] the book includes chapters on education and healthcare. In Chapter 6, Roland Tormey looks at education and poverty, focusing on

---

[6] The Agency's current strategic plan (2005–2007) sets out three strategic objectives: distribution of income and jobs, access to quality services, and local and regional responses to poverty.

primary and secondary education and examining issues such as access to education and the impact of poverty and social class on educational outcomes. In Chapter 7 on healthcare, Cecily Kelleher considers key questions concerning healthcare and poverty including access to healthcare and the determinants of health outcomes.

In recognition of the importance of disability, and given the recent adoption of the Disability Act, it is important to examine the close relationship between disability and poverty. In Chapter 8, Eithne Fitzgerald looks at recent developments in relation to disability (including the implementation of the National Disability Strategy) and identifies key issues and challenges.

The issue of migration did not really feature in the 1997 NAPS or the 2002 revised NAPS, however recent migration levels mean that it must be addressed now as part of an overall review of poverty and social inclusion in Ireland. Given the very significant increase in migration into Ireland over the past decade, Jane Pillinger looks specifically at migration issues from a poverty and social inclusion perspective in Chapter 9.

The concluding chapter brings together the major themes explored in the book and identifies key challenges and possible options from a public policy perspective.

References

CPA (2005), *Working for a Poverty-Free Ireland*, Dublin: Combat Poverty Agency

Ireland (1997), *Sharing in Progress: National Anti-Poverty Strategy*, Dublin: Stationery Office

Ireland (2002), *Building an Inclusive Society: Review of the National Anti-Poverty Strategy under the Programme for Fairness and Prosperity*, Dublin: Department of Social, Community and Family Affairs

Ireland (2006), *Towards 2016: Ten-Year Framework Social Partnership Agreement 2006–2015*, Dublin: Stationery Office

Ireland (2007a), *National Action Plan for Social Inclusion 2007–2016*, Dublin: Office for Social Inclusion

Ireland (2007b), *Transforming Ireland: A Better Quality of Life for All*, National Development Plan 2007–2013, Dublin: Stationery Office

Iversen, T. (2005), *Capitalism, Democracy and Welfare*, Cambridge: Cambridge University Press

Maître, B., Nolan, B. and Whelan, C. T. (2006), *Reconfiguring the Measurement of Deprivation and Consistent Poverty in Ireland*, Dublin: ESRI

Mares, I. (2003), *The Politics of Social Risk*, Cambridge: Cambridge University Press

NESC (2005), *The Developmental Welfare State*, Dublin: National Economic and Social Council

Polanyi, K. (1944), *The Great Transformation: The Political and Economic Origins of Our Time*, Boston: Beacon Press

Russell, H. and Gannon, B. (2002), 'The Male/Female Wage Gap in Ireland', in *Impact Evaluation of the European Employment Strategy in Ireland*, Dublin: Department of Enterprise, Trade and Employment

Social Protection Committee (2006), *Portfolio of Overarching Indicators and Streamlined Social Inclusion, Pension, and Health Portfolios*, Brussels: European Commission

Social Welfare Benchmarking and Indexation Group (2001), *Final Report of the Social Welfare Benchmarking and Indexation Group*, Dublin: Stationery Office

Swenson, P. (2002), *Capitalists against Markets: The Making of Labor Markets and Welfare States in the United States and Sweden*, New York: Oxford University Press

Timonen, V. (2003), *Irish Social Expenditure in a Comparative International Context*, Dublin: Combat Poverty Agency

Chapter 2

Monitoring poverty and welfare policy 1987–2007

Jim Walsh[1]

Introduction

This chapter presents an overview of trends in relation to
poverty and welfare policies since 1987 and provides the
fundamental evidence base which will be further developed in
the thematic chapters. Poverty and welfare policies can be
seen as two sides of the one coin. Poverty trends are heavily
influenced by government welfare and tax policies which
influence the income levels of the population. Welfare and tax
policies are the most tangible government instruments to
respond to poverty trends and are central to the preparation
of anti-poverty policies, especially for groups outside the
labour market such as children and older people.

The chapter begins with a review of key developments in
poverty and welfare policy over the last twenty years. It
presents the findings on poverty trends since 1987, the date

---

[1] This chapter was written while on a visiting research fellowship at The
Policy Institute, Trinity College, Dublin.

of the first national poverty survey. These are compared with poverty levels in the EU, using common statistical indicators developed under the open method of policy coordination on poverty and social exclusion. The chapter also looks at the evolution of welfare rates over the last twenty years and analyses the distributive and poverty impact of tax and welfare policies, in particular under the ten years of the *National Anti-Poverty Strategy* (NAPS). Finally, the chapter draws a number of conclusions for poverty and welfare policy.

Key developments

Three key developments are identified in relation to monitoring poverty and welfare policy over the last two decades. In terms of poverty, the main developments are the initiation of regular poverty surveys and reports and the establishment of official measures of poverty. Regarding welfare policies, the key development is the establishment of official benchmarks for welfare adequacy. Underpinning these developments is an enhanced policy focus on poverty at both national and European levels, as reflected in the NAPS and the EU social inclusion process.

Regular poverty surveys and reports
The first poverty survey dates from 1987 and was followed by two extended surveys covering the periods 1994 to 2001 and 2003 onwards. These dedicated surveys have provided a comprehensive database for understanding the nature and extent of poverty in Ireland, for establishing a comparative framework on poverty levels across the EU and for informing the development of anti-poverty policies.

Official measures of poverty

The adoption of official measures (or social indicators) of poverty is a relatively recent development, dating initially from 1997 and later extended in 2001, and is directly linked to the identification of poverty as a public policy priority at both national and European levels. The Irish government first adopted an official poverty measure as part of the NAPS in 1997. The measure was derived in the first instance from the official definition of poverty contained in the strategy (Ireland, 1997, p. 3):

> People are in poverty if their income and resources (material, cultural and social) are so inadequate as to preclude them from having a standard of living which is regarded as acceptable by Irish society generally. As a result of inadequate income and resources, people may be excluded and marginalised from participating in activities which are considered the norm for other people in society.

The definition reflects a relative understanding of poverty, based on prevailing living standards. It also highlights the importance of measuring both inadequate income and a lack of resources. In line with this, the government-approved measure of poverty is a combination of low income and deprivation of one or more 'basic lifestyle items', first developed by the Economic and Social Research Institute (ESRI) in the early 1990s (Callan *et al.*, 1993; Nolan and Whelan, 1996). Basic lifestyle items include going without food, clothing and heating or experiencing debt due to ordinary living expenses, and low income was defined as a percentage of average income (both 50 and 60 per cent thresholds are used). This combined income and deprivation measure was officially termed 'consistent poverty' and used as the means to express the official government target to reduce poverty under the NAPS and its current successor, the *National Action Plan for Social Inclusion 2007–2016* (NAPinclusion).[2]

Consistent poverty is both a measure of poverty and an expression of a political commitment to tackle poverty. This has elevated the status of consistent poverty from a social indicator of poverty to being the litmus test of government progress on poverty. Monitoring of this indicator/target was the responsibility of the ESRI and later the Central Statistics Office (CSO). No other poverty measure was identified in the NAPS, although it contained other poverty targets relating to employment, education and income (housing and health targets were added in the 2002 review of the NAPS).

Alongside the designation of a national consistent poverty measure were developments at European level regarding the selection of agreed measures of poverty. These arose in 2001, when, as part of the EU open method of coordination on poverty, the European Council adopted a set of 'common statistical indicators' to monitor trends in poverty and social exclusion in member states across Europe.[3] The indicators were designed as a balanced and evolving portfolio selected on a number of normative principles and capturing the diversity of poverty and social exclusion, including income, education, employment, health and material deprivation.

---

[2] This was articulated as the global poverty reduction target, with the aim to reduce the numbers in consistent poverty to between 5 and 10 per cent and later to 2 per cent or less by 2007, 'as measured by the ESRI'. The latest formulation is to reduce consistent poverty to between 2 and 4 per cent by 2012, with the aim of eliminating consistent poverty by 2016, under the revised ESRI definition.

[3] The indicators were developed by the Social Protection Committee (2001), informed by a scientific study by Atkinson *et al.*, 2002.

A recently revised list of twenty-four indicators (building on a previous list of eighteen) is broken down into three categories: primary or lead indicators, secondary or supporting indicators and context or interpretation indicators. There is also provision for a further set of national indicators to reflect the exigencies of the social situation in member states (Social Protection Committee, 2006).

At the core of the EU indicators is the standard measure of relative income poverty, defined as the percentage of the population below 60 per cent of median income and officially referred to as the 'risk-of-poverty' rate. This unique nomenclature is used to imply that this is not a measure of poverty per se, but of the likelihood of poverty (Nolan, 2006a).[4] Median income is defined at the level of individual member states and not on an EU-wide basis. However, because the value of the 60 per cent median will vary over time and between countries, the indicator is to be accompanied by a statement of value in national and purchasing power standard currency. Variations of the risk-of-poverty rate are used for a number of other indicators.

There are two other financial indicators, both relating to income distribution: the income quintile ratio (ratio of total income received by the richest 20 per cent of the national population to that received by the poorest 20 per cent) and the Gini coefficient (summary measure of income equality ranging from 0 to 1). The non-financial indicators of poverty are of a more generic nature and relate to causes of poverty, including long-term unemployment, jobless households, early

---

[4] Risk of poverty is more traditionally used in the technical sense to refer to the proportion of any population group which falls below the relevant poverty standard (Callan et al., 1996b).

school-leaving, low educational attainment, reading literacy, employment of migrants and life expectancy. Two additional categories are material and housing deprivation and child wellbeing; the specific details of these indicators are still to be developed. Reporting on these indicators is the responsibility of Eurostat, drawing on a variety of data sources including the European Union Survey of Income and Living Conditions (EU-SILC).

The two official measures of poverty – consistent poverty and relative income poverty – have greatly influenced the understanding of poverty in the Irish context and of trends over time. However, there has also been a tension between the two measures, especially given the changing economic circumstances in Ireland and the widening divergence between the two measures as to the numbers in poverty (see below). The relative income/risk-of-poverty measure has been downplayed as a legitimate way to measure poverty by government and some social commentators. Criticisms focus on three aspects: it confuses poverty with income inequality, it is misleading in a situation where living standards (and welfare rates) are rising in real terms and it is not suited to comparing countries at different stages of development (Social Welfare Benchmarking and Indexation Group, 2001; Beblavy and Mizsei, 2006; Ireland, 2007). Thus, the NAPinclusion 2007–2016 views the risk-of-poverty measure as 'not ... [a] measure [of] poverty as such, but rather the proportion of people below a certain income threshold' (Ireland, 2007, p. 25). Income poverty, though an EU indicator of poverty, has far less status in Ireland than the national (consistent) poverty measure.

The consistent poverty measure has also attracted some criticism, notably in relation to its unchanged nature since

1987 and methodological issues arising from a change in survey format (from the Living in Ireland Survey [LIS] to the EU-SILC). It has been suggested that this resulted in a loss of credibility for the consistent poverty measure, leading one academic analyst to argue that the original measure has 'faded from use' (Collins, 2006). To address these and other concerns, the ESRI undertook a revision of the consistent poverty measure using EU-SILC data. The revision included a technical assessment of alternative deprivation items and a consultation process involving government and broader social interests. This process led to a 'reconfigured' deprivation measure, based on the enforced absence of at least two items from an enlarged eleven-item list (Maître et al., 2006).[5] The new measure was endorsed by government and used to express its poverty reduction target in the NAPinclusion 2007–2016. However, some anti-poverty groups have been unhappy with the new measure, especially its omission of the debt item. This process highlights the political dimension of the establishment of poverty measures.

Welfare adequacy benchmarks

An important policy development in the last twenty years has been the establishment of official benchmarks for adequate welfare payments. The starting point for the setting of welfare benchmarks is a value judgement that payments should be adequate to provide a living standard that is considered acceptable in contemporary society. How adequacy is to be assessed is a more difficult issue with a variety of approaches being adopted. From a policy perspective, welfare adequacy benchmarks are directly related to the measurement of

---

[5]   Five new indicators were added and two of the original set were dropped.

poverty in society and the growth of average incomes. Given overall budgetary constraints, the funding of welfare adequacy benchmarks also represents a trade-off with income tax rates, either in higher taxes or tax cuts foregone. Thus, a policy concern with welfare adequacy can become an important shaper of income distribution and work incentives.

Table 2.1 outlines the various official assessments of welfare adequacy over the last twenty years. These differ in their policy remit and their methodologies to formulate their recommendations.

The first assessment of welfare rates was undertaken by the Commission on Social Welfare in 1986. The Commission was a government-appointed expert body charged with undertaking the first systematic review of the social welfare system in Ireland. A central theme of the Commission was the necessity to establish a benchmark of welfare adequacy to replace the ad hoc and politically driven approach to the setting of welfare rates. Drawing on a variety of methodologies, the Commission recommended a minimum adequate welfare rate of between €63.50 and €78.20 per week (£50 to £60), with an immediate priority rate of €57 per week (£45). The Commission's recommendations have played an important part in debates about welfare adequacy and in official policy statements (Callan *et al.*, 1996a). The proposals were endorsed in a succession of social partnership agreements and programmes for government. The Commission recommended a payment of 0.6 of the personal rate for adult dependants. It did not propose an adequacy target for child income support, as it felt that additional work was required on that issue. Instead, it argued that the existing thirty or more rates of child dependant allowance be rationalised.

Table 2.1: Assessments of welfare adequacy

Year	Body	Approach	Proposal(s)
1986	Commission on Social Welfare (CSW)	Seven methods used to calculate an adequate income for a single adult, based on average earnings/income and various administrative thresholds	Minimum welfare payment of between €63.50 and €78.20 per week; payment for adult dependant of 0.6 of personal rate; child rates to be 'rationalised'
1996	Economic and Social Research Institute	No scientific way to establish adequacy. Updated CSW methodology along with new poverty measures to establish adequacy range	Minimum welfare payment of between €86.30 to €121.90 per week
1998	National Pensions Policy Initiative	Adequacy expressed as a proportion of average earnings	Personal rate for state pension of €121.90 per week or 34 per cent of gross average industrial earnings
2001	Social Welfare Benchmarking and Indexation Group	Adequacy related to percentage of average income/earnings. Child adequacy defined as a proportion of adult payment	Minimum personal rate of between 27 and 30 per cent of gross average industrial earnings; child income support between 33 and 35 per cent of minimum adult rate

In the mid-1990s, the government commissioned a review and update of the Commission's minimum welfare rates and an assessment of their impact on poverty, income inequality and work incentives. The review, carried out by the ESRI (Callan *et al.*, 1996a), provided a new estimate of a minimum adequate income ranging from €86.30 to €121.90 per week (£68 to £96). The new adequacy figures were not explicitly endorsed in subsequent government policy.

The next statement on welfare adequacy was made by the Pensions Board (1998) in its report on the National Pensions Policy Initiative. The focus here was on providing a 'reasonable' level of income for older people through the state pension. The Pensions Board chose the upper end of the ESRI minimum welfare rate as this would minimise the risk of poverty and provide income support in the most efficient way. This rate was expressed as a percentage of gross average industrial earnings (34 per cent). The Pensions Board confined its proposals to the state pension. Government welfare policies have never acknowledged this estimate as official policy. Rather, the government has set a succession of cash targets for the state pension, the most recent being €200 per week to be achieved by 2007 (Ireland, 2002a).

The most recent estimation of welfare adequacy was provided by the Social Welfare Benchmarking and Indexation Group, which reported in 2001. This group was established under the *Programme for Prosperity and Fairness* to address its objective to provide every person with sufficient income to live life with dignity, and comprised representatives of the social partners. Its remit was to develop a new 'benchmark' for welfare adequacy for both adults and children, taking into account economic and financial considerations. Influenced by the approach in the National Pensions Policy Initiative, the majority recommendation of the group was for a minimum welfare payment based on 27 per cent of gross average industrial earnings. It also presented the possibility of increasing this to 30 per cent in the longer term.

Subsequent to the report of the Social Welfare Benchmarking and Indexation Group, the government adopted a new welfare adequacy target in the revised NAPS (Ireland, 2002a). This articulated a minimum welfare rate of €150 per week (2002 values) to be achieved by 2007. This was the equivalent of 30 per cent of gross average industrial earnings at the time, though this link was not explicitly stated (CORI Justice, 2006).

These four official reviews of a minimum welfare rate have proved very influential in advancing the level of welfare payments, as will be demonstrated below.

Poverty trends 1987–2005

This section begins with the macroeconomic context for the evolution of poverty since 1987. This leads to an analysis of trends in poverty over time, using both the relative income (risk-of-) poverty and consistent poverty measures. Selected years are used to present the data: 1987, 1994, 1997, 2001, 2003 and 2005. The presentation of findings is preceded by a short discussion on the performance of the two measures over time relative to overall trends in income, welfare rates and deprivation levels. The information is presented for the total population and for demographic categories identified as being particularly vulnerable to poverty in official anti-poverty policies (children, older people, women and non-Irish nationals). This is followed by a profile of those in poverty using household composition, economic status and spatial categories. The section concludes with an examination of the composition of the population in poverty, focusing on the situation in 2005.

Macroeconomic background

The last twenty years have seen dramatic changes in the Irish economy and society. The 1980s were characterised by high unemployment, low economic growth and high levels of emigration. Since then, there has been a major transformation in the economy (see Table 2.2). Between 1987 and 2005, GNP increased by 216 per cent in real terms, with the bulk of this growth coming in the period from 1994. This rapid economic growth had a major impact on the labour market. The total numbers in employment increased from 1.1 million to 1.9 million, a rise of 800,000 (74 per cent), with 90 per cent of this increase occurring in the period from 1994 to 2005. The growth in employment was accompanied by a dramatic fall in unemployment, from 226,000 in 1987 to 65,000 in 2001. The change here is concentrated in the period 1994 to 2001, as since 2001 the numbers out of work have risen again, to 86,000 in 2005. The unemployment rate fell from 16.9 per cent in 1987 to a low of 3.9 per cent in 2001, before rising slightly to 4.4 per cent in 2005. As well as lower unemployment, employment growth has been accompanied by an increase of 50 per cent in the size of the total labour force. This increase has been fuelled by school-leavers, increased labour market participation by women and, most recently, by immigration (replacing the pattern of outward migration in the years 1987 to 1994). The latter phenomenon, together with a higher birth rate, has led to a population increase of over 500,000 since 1987 (up 16 per cent).

Table 2.2: Key economic indicators, 1987–2005

	1987	1994	1997	2001	2003	2005	% change
GNP (100 baseline)	100	135	182	258	286	316	216
Employment (000s)	1,111	1,221	1,380	1,722	1,794	1,929	74
Unemployment (000s)	226	211	159	65	82	86	−62
Unemployment rate (%)	16.9	14.7	10.3	3.9	4.6	4.4	−74
Migration (000s)	−23	−5	19	33	30	53	–
Population (000s)	3,547	3,586	3,664	3,847	3,979	4,131	16

Source: Central Statistics Office, www.cso.ie

What are the implications of this economic boom for household living standards? Figure 2.1 shows the changes in average incomes since 1987, adjusted for inflation (inflation for the period was 68 per cent).[6] Average equivalised incomes increased by 125 per cent in real terms (277 per cent in nominal terms) in the study period. Three phases of income growth can be observed: from 1987 to 1994 (7 years) average income grew by 34 per cent; from 1994 to 2001 (7 years) average income increased by 57 per cent; and finally, from 2001 to 2005 (4 years) incomes grew by 7 per cent. A comparison can be made with the growth in the basic welfare rate in this

---

[6] This is based on data from the various poverty surveys conducted over this period and refers to mean equivalised disposable income averaged over individuals, with the exception of 1987 which is averaged over households.

period (discussed in more detail below), which increased by
106 per cent in real terms (245 per cent in nominal terms),
slightly less than the growth in average income. The rate of
increase between the two has changed over time, with the
increase in the minimum welfare rate exceeding income
growth between 1987 and 1994. Thereafter, average
income increased more rapidly than the minimum welfare
rate, before growth rates converged again in the 2000s.
Overall, welfare rates, though increasing in real terms, have
lagged behind the rapid rise in incomes from work, tax cuts
and other sources.

Figure 2.1: Growth in average equivalised income and the
minimum welfare rate, 1987–2005 (%, constant prices)

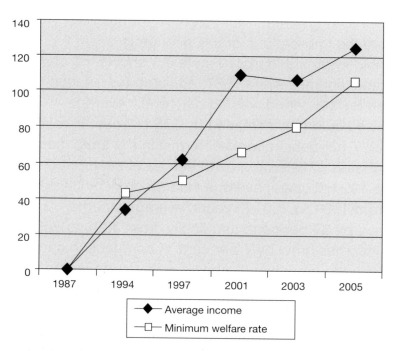

Sources: Central Statistics Office, www.cso.ie and Department of Social
and Family Affairs

Turning to the pattern of income distribution and how it was affected during the period of rapid economic growth, Table 2.3 begins by giving the income distribution across the population, broken down into five equal-sized groupings (quintiles) and ranked from poorest to richest. In 2005, the richest 20 per cent of the population had two-fifths of all income. The third and fourth quintiles had 17 and 23 per cent respectively. The bottom two quintiles had a combined total of 20 per cent of all income, made up of 12 per cent for the second quintile and 8 per cent for the first quintile.[7] At this level, there has been little change in income distribution since 1994. The share going to the bottom quintile has fallen by 0.7 per cent, while the fourth quintile has declined by 0.6 per cent. The gainers have been the second, third and top quintiles, but in all cases the increase was 0.5 per cent or less.

This analysis is further broken down, using tenths of the population and focusing on the top and bottom deciles only. Now the trend over time is more pronounced with the share of the bottom tenth declining from 3.8 per cent in 1994 to 3.2 per cent in 2005, a drop of 0.6 per cent (equivalent to one-sixth). The richest tenth increased its share from 24.4 per cent to 25.6 per cent, up 1.2 per cent over the period (equivalent to one-twentieth).[8]

---

[7] The average weekly disposable income per individual for the richest quintile in 2005 was €760, rising to €970 for the richest decile. At the other end of the distribution, the bottom one-fifth received €150 per week, falling to €122 for the poorest one-tenth.

[8] As Nolan and Smeeding (2005) note, household survey data may not fully capture trends at the top of the income distribution. Using Revenue data, they suggest that the share of total income accruing to the top 1 per cent in the late 1990s was twice the equivalent level in the 1980s.

Table 2.3: Trends in income distribution, 1994–2005 (shares in equivalised disposable income among individuals)

	1994/5 (%)	1997 (%)	2001 (%)	2003 (%)	2005 (%)	Change
Bottom quintile	8.6	8.1	8.0	7.9	7.9	−0.7
2nd quintile	12.0	12.2	12.9	12.8	12.3	0.3
3rd quintile	16.5	16.9	17.9	18.2	17.0	0.5
4th quintile	23.2	22.9	23.2	24.1	22.6	−0.6
Top quintile	39.7	40.0	38.2	37.0	40.1	0.4
Bottom decile	3.8	3.5	3.3	3.0	3.2	−0.6
Top decile	24.4	24.2	23.3	23.8	25.6	1.2
S80/S20*	5.1	5.0	4.5	5.0	5.0	–
Gini coefficient	33	33	29	31	32	–

* Income inequality data from Eurostat; first data are for 1995 and there is a break in the series between 2001 and 2003

Table 2.3 also presents the figures for the official EU measure of income inequality, the S80/S20 income quintile share ratio, which shows little change over the period from 1995 to 2005.[9] The Eurostat data for the Gini coefficient (a summary measure of income inequality) also indicate little change in inequality over the period for which data are available. Nolan (2006b) has recently concluded that income inequality was not dramatically changed by the economic boom. He found that Ireland is still in a substantial cluster of OECD countries with relatively high levels of income inequality but is not one of the most unequal OECD countries.

---

[9]   The limitations of the Eurostat data are discussed in Nolan and Smeeding (2005).

Trends in risk of poverty, 1987–2005

Performance of risk-of-poverty measure over time

For this analysis, we concentrate on a poverty cut-off point of 60 per cent of the median equivalised income.[10] The weekly value in euro of this cut-off point is illustrated in Figure 2.2 for the period 1987 to 2005, using constant 2005 prices. In 2005, 60 per cent of the median was the equivalent of €193 per week for a single adult.[11] The value of 60 per cent of median income increased by 127 per cent since 1987 and by 82 per cent since 1994 (actual weekly figures were €85 and €107 respectively for a single adult in 2005 prices). This increase in the threshold is in line with the growth in incomes as demonstrated above. The results emphasise the dramatic change in the real value of the median threshold in a short period. They also demonstrate the significance of using a relative threshold rather than one fixed in real income terms to measure poverty patterns in an economy undergoing a sustained period of growth.[12]

Another way to interpret the evolution of the 60 per cent of median income threshold is to relate it to prevailing social

---

[10] Income is defined as total disposable household income, after income tax and PRSI contributions are deducted. Income is adjusted for household size using an equivalence scale which attributes a weight of 1 to the first adult, 0.66 to each subsequent adult (aged 14 or more and living in the household) and 0.33 to each child (aged less than 14). The equivalised income is attributed to each member of the household and the median income is then identified.

[11] The equivalent value for a household of two adults and two children in 2005 would be €447.16.

[12] In Figure 2.2, the value of the 60 per cent median threshold between 2001 and 2003 records a small decline, which reflects technical changes in the measurement of household income between the LIS and the EU-SILC. However, as the poverty measure is based on 60 per cent of median income in both cases, this does not undermine the results.

Figure 2.2: Risk-of-poverty line, 1987–2005* (equivalent of 60 per cent of median equivalised income per individual, €, 2005 values)

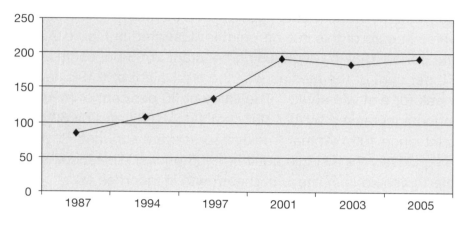

* For 1987, 50 per cent of the mean is used, which is roughly the same as 60 per cent of the median
Sources: ESRI LIS and CSO EU-SILC

welfare rates (see Table 2.4). This has two benefits: first, to give a value to the threshold vis-à-vis what the state considers is an adequate level of income; and second, to understand a key influence on the numbers of people who are likely to fall below this poverty threshold and how far below they are likely to fall. In 2005, the minimum welfare payment was equal to three-quarters of the 60 per cent of median income threshold, while the state pension was 86 per cent.[13] In previous years, welfare transfers have made up a small proportion of 60 per cent of median income. The lowest

---

[13] The link between welfare rates and the poverty threshold is more pronounced at 50 per cent of the median. In 2005, the state pension was in excess of this threshold, while the minimum welfare payment was only €1 below. This relationship would mean the numbers below this poverty threshold would be greatly diminished.

figures were in 2001, when the minimum welfare payment was equal to 63 per cent of the threshold and the state pension was equal to 72 per cent. Much higher proportions existed in the earlier period, with the respective rates equivalent to 86 and 118 per cent of the threshold in 1987.

Table 2.4: Welfare rates as a percentage of 60 per cent of median income, 1987–2005

	1987 (%)	1994 (%)	1997 (%)	2001 (%)	2003 (%)	2005 (%)
Minimum welfare rate	86	97	82	63	71	77
State pension	118	101	84	72	82	86

Source: Department of Social and Family Affairs (welfare rates)

Trends in risk-of-poverty measure, 1987–2005
Figure 2.3 examines the trends in the risk-of-poverty rate since 1987. The risk-of-poverty rate has hovered between 16 and 22 per cent over the last twenty years. Within this period, there have been some peaks and troughs. Between 1994 and 2001, the risk-of-poverty rate grew from 15.5 to 22 per cent, an increase of one-quarter. This coincided with a rapid increase in average incomes, while the relative value of welfare rates declined. In the 2000s, the rate fell back to 18.5 per cent, coinciding with a period of substantial welfare increases and less rapid growth in average income.

Figure 2.3 also records trends over the period for the demographic categories of children (under 16 years), older people (65 years or more) and women. A consistent 22 to 24 per cent of children were at risk of poverty between 1994 and 2005, slightly more than the average across all the population. In contrast, the risk-of-poverty rate for older

Figure 2.3: Trends in the risk of poverty, 1987*–2005 (% of individuals)

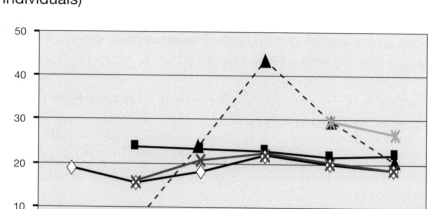

* The construction of the 1987 figure is different in two regards: the poverty threshold is 50 per cent of the mean and income is averaged over households. It is likely that a median threshold would have produced a lower level of poverty, perhaps around 14 per cent
Sources: ESRI LIS and CSO EU-SILC

people evolved quite dramatically over the same period. Beginning from a low of 5 per cent in 1994, the rate grew to a peak of 45 per cent in 2001. Since then, it has moderated back to 20 per cent, almost identical with the average figure.[14] These dramatic changes can be linked to the value of the state pension relative to the poverty threshold.

---

[14] The level of recorded poverty for older people is sensitive to the level chosen, for example at 70 per cent of median income a much smaller fall is apparent.

For women, the risk-of-poverty rate has increased over time from a low of 16 per cent in 1994 to a high of 23 per cent in 2001, before falling back to 18.5 per cent in 2005. The trend in female poverty is shaped by the pattern for older people, as there is a predominance of women among older people.

Data on the nationality of persons in poverty are available under the EU-SILC for 2004/5.[15] In 2005, 27 per cent of non-Irish nationals were at risk of poverty, as compared with 18 per cent of the national population. In line with the overall trends, the non-Irish national poverty rate fell by 2 per cent from 2004.

Profile of individuals at risk of poverty

Turning to the risk-of-poverty rate, analysis of various socio-demographic sections of the population can give insights into the consequences of poverty for families and locations, as well as the economic causes of poverty, and can help to identify changes over time. Figure 2.4 presents details on poverty rates by household composition for 1994 to 2005. Lone-parent households (one adult and one or more children) have consistently had the highest level of income poverty (between 36 and 50 per cent), over twice the average rate. Another group who experienced a high rate of income poverty is single-person households. Originally, this group had a low rate of poverty, but in the late 1990s/early 2000s this increased to over 40 per cent, before falling back to 30 per cent. Two-person households also experienced a disimprovement in their risk-of-poverty rate (reaching 30 per

---

[15] These estimates are considered tentative by the CSO because of concerns about the extent to which household surveys capture minority groups in the population, especially given large migration flows.

Figure 2.4: Risk of poverty by household composition, 1994–2005 (% of individuals)

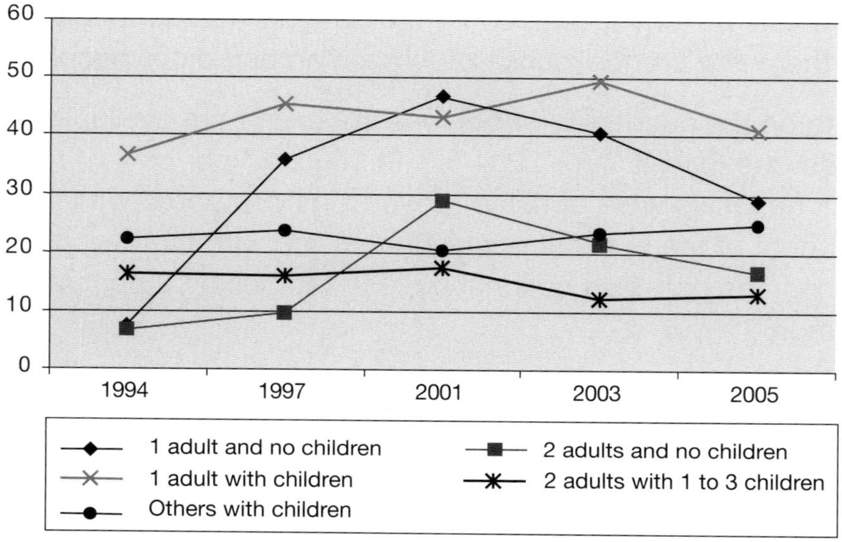

Sources: ESRI LIS and CSO EU-SILC

cent), before coming back in line with the average rate. In both these cases, the increase in poverty risk can be linked with the higher risk for older people, who represent a large component of such household categories.

The rate of income poverty for couples with children was generally in line with the average, though with some variation since 2001. Thus, smaller families (one to three children) have experienced a reduced risk of poverty, falling from 17 to 13 per cent. In contrast, the position of larger families (others with children) has deteriorated, with their risk of poverty rising from 20 to 25 per cent.

Trends in the labour force status of those at risk of poverty are presented in Figure 2.5. Over time, the lowest risk-of-poverty rate was consistently among those at work, which has remained below 10 per cent. People not at work due to unemployment or illness/disability had the highest risk-of-poverty rates, standing at 40 per cent in 2005. This was an improvement on the rates in the middle of the period, when they reached 60 and 65 per cent. Other higher risk groups are people engaged in home duties and students (28 to 30 per cent in 2005). The risk-of-poverty rate for the former increased dramatically between 1997 and 2001, before falling back somewhat by 2005. The rate for retired people has also worsened from its low base in 1994, doubling by 2005 to 20

Figure 2.5: Risk of poverty by labour force status, 1994–2005 (% of individuals)*

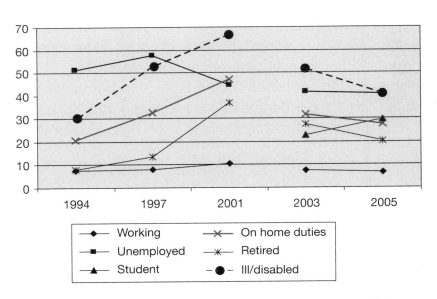

* Data for 1994 to 2001 are based on the labour force status of the household reference person, which is then applied to all individuals in the household. Data for 2003 and 2005 relate to each individual aged 16 or over
Sources: ESRI LIS and CSO EU-SILC

per cent. Overall, these patterns reflect a significant decline in the incomes of those not at work compared to those in employment, albeit with a gradual improvement towards the end of the period. However, people of working age but not in work still face relatively very high rates of risk of poverty, over five times the rate of those in work and up to twice the rate for those not in the labour force.

Trends in consistent poverty, 1987–2005

Figure 2.6 traces the trends in the consistent poverty measure, which combines low income with deprivation of basic necessities. Focusing on the period from 1994 to 2001, consistent poverty was halved, from 8 to 4 per cent. In 2003, under the new EU-SILC methodology, the recorded level of consistent poverty rose to 9 per cent, before decreasing to 7 per cent between 2003 and 2005. The decline in the rate of consistent poverty was replicated for children, older people and women, though with different end points. Child consistent poverty declined from a high of 14 per cent in 1994/1997 to 5.5 per cent in 2001, and again from 12 per cent to 10.5 per cent in 2005 (this is 1.5 times the overall rate).

Among older people, there was a small rise in consistent poverty over time, culminating in a rate of 4 per cent in 2005, half the average rate. The female rate of consistent poverty has closely traced the rate for the total population. It was 7.5 per cent in 2005, which was slightly ahead of the average and 1 per cent higher than the male rate. The rate of consistent poverty among non-Irish nationals was 13 per cent in 2005, twice that of the Irish rate; the rate fell from 15 per cent in 2004, suggesting that more recent migrants are less deprived than those who arrived in the country before them. There is a

36

Figure 2.6: Trends in consistent poverty, 1987–2005 (% of individuals; % of households for 1987)

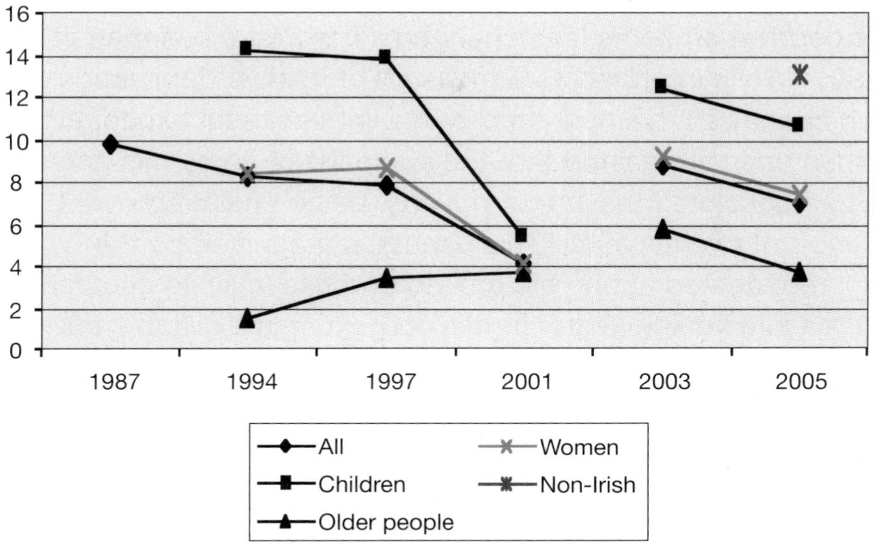

Sources: ESRI LIS and CSO EU-SILC

pronounced gender aspect in the poverty rate for non-Irish nationals, with almost 15 per cent of non-Irish national women in consistent poverty, compared to just over 11 per cent of non-Irish national men.[16]

A number of issues must be considered in interpreting trends in consistent poverty over time. First, the findings for the period from 2001 to 2003 are not comparable due to changes in survey design. The 2001 and 2003 figures are derived from two different surveys: the LIS and EU-SILC, whose design differences may influence the reporting of deprivation levels (Maître *et al.*, 2006). These methodological factors are considered to make comparison of the two sets of findings

---

[16] This gender difference is not apparent in the risk-of-poverty measure.

problematic and unreliable. Therefore, in interpreting trends over time, the period from 1994 to 2001 should be treated separately to the period from 2003 to 2005. Second, the list of deprivation items is unchanged since first developed in 1987. While intended as a measure of relative deprivation which may evolve over time in line with societal expectations, it has been suggested that the static list of items has acted as an absolute measure of poverty, being unaltered over a period of twenty years. This aspect is magnified by the unprecedented economic growth and rise in living standards in the intervening years. In this context, it is inevitable that deprivation on a set list of indicators will have greatly reduced. A third issue is whether the meaning and value associated with the various indicators may have changed over time. For example, the debt indicator is open to interpretation, as debt becomes a more acceptable feature of modern living.

Profile of individuals in consistent poverty
The household composition of individuals in consistent poverty is presented in Figure 2.7. As with the overall pattern, the rate of consistent poverty declined for all households between 1994 and 2001 and again from 2003 to 2005. The group with by far the highest rate of consistent poverty is lone-parent families (one adult and one or more children). Their poverty rate had a peak of 43 per cent in 1994, five times that of the average. This rate fell dramatically in 1997 to 20 per cent, but the improvement was not sustained, as the rate rose to 24 per cent in 2001 and in 2005, was 27 per cent (still four times the average). Other high-risk groups are one-person households and larger families, both of whom had rates of 10 per cent in 2005, a small improvement on their position in 1994. Smaller households recorded lower rates of

Figure 2.7: Consistent poverty by household composition, 1994–2005 (% of individuals)

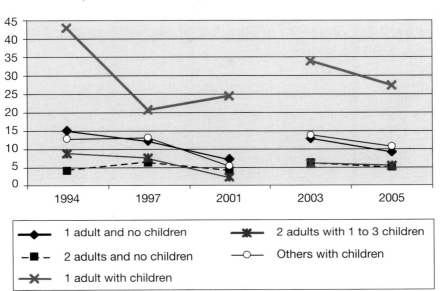

Sources: ESRI LIS and CSO EU-SILC

consistent poverty over time, even with the higher results under the EU-SILC. The lowest levels were found in two-person households without children, who were consistently close to or below 5 per cent.

The labour force status of those experiencing consistent poverty is outlined in Figure 2.8. Categories with a higher rate of consistent poverty (between 10 and 22 per cent in 2005) were the unemployed, people not at work due to illness/disability, students or those engaged in home duties. The rate of consistent poverty among all these groups has fallen over time, especially in the case of the unemployed, where it has declined from over 50 per cent to 21 per cent in 2005. Those at work or retired were the least likely to be in consistent poverty, at less than 3 per cent in 2005. Their positive situation has pertained for the last two decades.

Figure 2.8: Consistent poverty by labour force status, 1994–2005 (% of individuals)

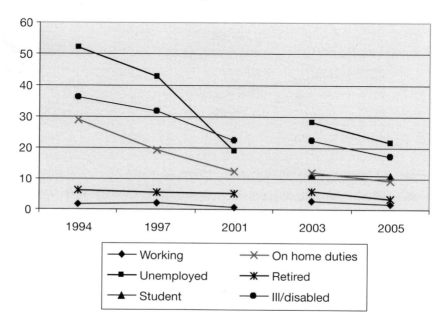

Sources: ESRI LIS and CSO EU-SILC

Looking at socio-spatial variables, the divide between those residing in owner-occupied homes and those in rented accommodation is greatly accentuated using the consistent poverty measure. Over one-fifth of persons in rented accommodation were in consistent poverty, which was seven times the risk among persons that own their home. A lesser divide is apparent in the risk of consistent poverty between the Border, Midland and Western (10 per cent) and the South East (6 per cent) regions, while there is minimal difference between urban and rural locations (7 and 6.5 per cent respectively). In terms of trends since 2003, consistent poverty has decreased across all socio-spatial categories with one exception: a small increase in the rate of rural consistent poverty, resulting in a narrower differential between rural and urban levels.

Composition of population in poverty 2005

The analysis now turns to look at the composition of the population in poverty, focusing on the situation in 2005 and comparing the findings of the two measures of poverty. In Figure 2.9, the composition of the population in poverty (risk-of- and consistent) by age is presented. The largest group in poverty under both measures is people of working age, with around 60 per cent of the total. Children (aged under 16) are the second biggest group, at between 27 and 34 per cent of the total, with the higher share recorded under the consistent

Figure 2.9: Composition of population in poverty by age, 2005 (%)

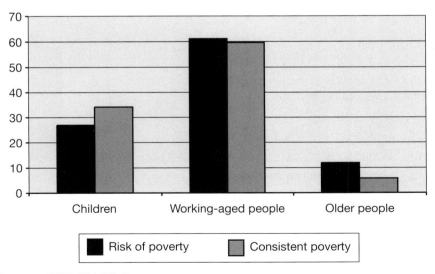

Source: CSO EU-SILC

poverty measure. Older people are the smallest category, representing 6 per cent of those in consistent poverty and 12 per cent of those at risk of poverty. If figures were broken down by gender, they would reveal that women account for slightly more of the population in consistent poverty (54 per cent) than men. The population at risk of poverty is divided 50:50 between women and men.

Figure 2.10 presents the make-up of those in poverty by household structure. The dominant household category is larger households with children at between 28 and 32 per cent of the total. (This compares with 21 per cent of the overall population.) Other household categories account for between 8 and 19 per cent of those in poverty. Lone-parent households, though having a very high risk of poverty, account for less than 15 per cent of those in poverty as they

Figure 2.10: Composition of population in poverty by household structure, 2005 (%)

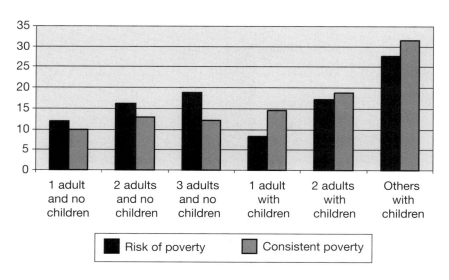

Source: CSO EU-SILC

are a small percentage of the total population. Lone parents represent a much higher share of persons in consistent poverty, which is the opposite of the situation for adult-only households.

Figure 2.11 presents the composition of the population in poverty by economic status. Excluding children under 16 years, the main economic grouping among those in poverty is people engaged in home duties, who represent 20 per cent of those at risk of poverty and 18 per cent of those in consistent poverty. People in work are also a significant category at between 10 and 15 per cent (though having a generally low rate of poverty). People not at work due to unemployment or illness constitute smaller proportions of those in poverty,

Figure 2.11: Composition of population in poverty by economic status, 2005 (%)

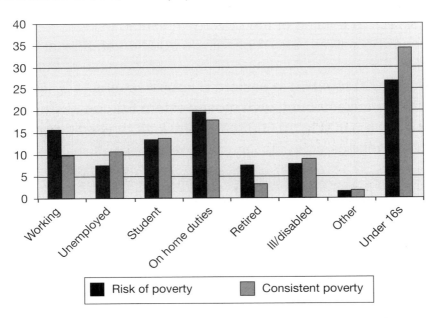

Source: CSO EU-SILC

reflecting the decrease in unemployment rather than a fall in their rates of poverty. In contrast, students are now one of the largest categories at 13 to 14 per cent, mainly arising from their relatively high poverty rate (1.6 times the average).

Finally, the make-up of the population in poverty can be looked at from a spatial perspective. The largest concentration of consistent poverty is to be found in rented accommodation, which accounts for two-thirds of the total (this compares with 22 per cent of the total population). This proportion of the population in consistent poverty is greater than the other and much larger spatial categories: urban areas and the South East region (64 and 61 per cent respectively).

Poverty in a comparative EU context

This section places Ireland's poverty rates in a European context, using the various indicators of poverty developed at EU level.[17] The value of the poverty threshold using purchasing power parity[18] per single adult on an annual basis shows considerable variation across member states, from a low of 2,000 to 4,000 in eastern European states to a high of 16,000 in Luxembourg, with most western European states around the 8,000 to 10,000 mark. The Irish threshold is in the middle rankings at 9,000.

Figure 2.12 displays the risk-of-poverty rate for the EU member states and shows that Ireland has one of the

---

[17] There are some differences in the definition of income and choice of equivalence scale between Irish and EU data, which amend slightly the results for Ireland presented earlier.

[18] The purchasing power parity (PPP) method is used to equalise the purchasing power of different currencies in order to facilitate cross-country comparisons.

highest risk-of-poverty rates. The average poverty rate for the EU-25 and EU-15 was 16 per cent. The comparable rate for Ireland was 20 per cent, 1.25 times the EU average and one of the highest of all member states. Other countries with high poverty rates were Greece, Spain, Portugal, Latvia and Poland. However, Ireland has a much higher living standard than these five countries. The lowest poverty rates were in Sweden and the Czech Republic at 9 and 10 per cent respectively. In terms of countries with comparable living standards, the closest poverty rate was the UK with 19 per cent. Otherwise, all better-off countries have poverty rates of below 15 per cent. Thus, we can conclude that while Ireland is not exceptional in having a poverty rate that is above the EU average, it is unusual (along with the UK) in combining a higher poverty rate with better-off living standards.

Figure 2.12: Risk-of-poverty rate, EU member states, 2005 or nearest (% of persons below 60 per cent of median income)

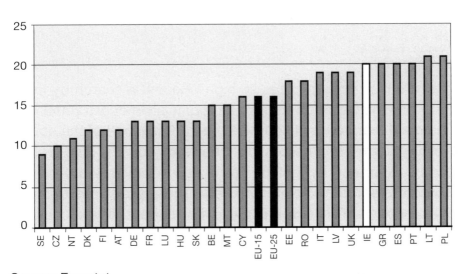

Source: Eurostat

Using a measure similar to the Irish consistent poverty level (combining the risk-of-poverty measure with a measure of deprivation), Figure 2.13 shows Ireland in a somewhat better light but still with a level of consistent poverty higher than several EU countries with a comparable level of wealth.

Figure 2.13: Percentage of individuals at risk of poverty and deprived, 2003 or nearest

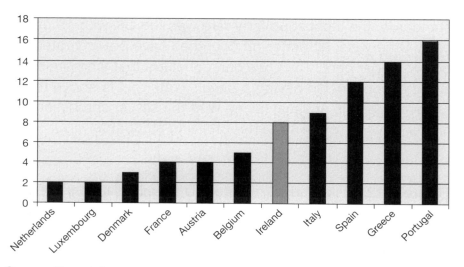

Source: Eurostat

Why are Irish poverty rates so high? Recent research by the ESRI has looked at a range of factors (Callan *et al.*, 2004). The main feature identified was the performance of the social welfare system in ameliorating the risk of poverty. This feature can be illustrated by looking at the risk-of-poverty rate in the EU before and after social transfers. The average pre-transfer risk-of-poverty rate in the EU was 43 per cent. After social transfers, this rate was reduced to 16 per cent, a reduction of 64 per cent. Ireland had a lower pre-transfer poverty rate at 40 per cent; social transfers lowered this rate to 20 per cent, reducing poverty by one-half. However, other richer countries achieved a poverty reduction effect of 70 per cent.

Tax and welfare policies 1987–2007

Switching focus to the impact of welfare policies on poverty over time, there follows a look at the evolution of welfare rates for adults and children. The analysis is then broadened to take in tax as well as welfare changes over the last twenty years, using the ESRI tax/welfare simulation model.

Evolution of adult and child welfare rates

The evolution of social welfare rates is outlined in Figure 2.14 for the key categories of basic personal payment, state pension and qualified adult allowance, together with the level of income support for children (combining child benefit, child dependant allowance and the clothing and footwear allowance). The basic welfare rate has quadrupled in the last twenty years from €43 per week in 1987 to €185 per week in 2007. Adjusting for inflation, the increase in real terms is 138 per cent. This increase has occurred incrementally over the period, though with two significant growth periods. The first was between 1987 and 1993 and coincided with the implementation of the recommendations of the Commission on Social Welfare. The second runs from 2003 to 2007, when welfare policy was focused on achieving the indexed target of €150 per week for the minimum welfare payment. The state pension also increased substantially over this period, though by a more modest 85 per cent in real terms.

Also of interest are the performances of the qualified adult allowance (QAA) and the rate of child income support (CIS). The QAA increased by 117 per cent in real terms in the twenty years. The value of CIS has grown by 120 per cent.

Figure 2.14: Change in welfare rates, 1987–2007 (%, constant prices)

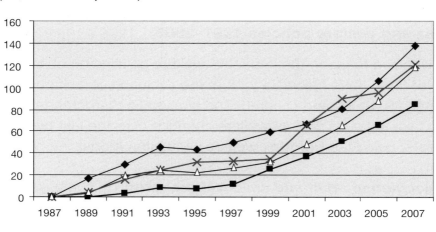

The evolution of CIS is the most dramatic of all welfare rates on two counts. First, increases have oscillated more than for other welfare rates, with superior increases in the mid-1990s and, in particular, between 1999 and 2003, when the total increase surpassed that of the basic welfare rate. Second, there have been major changes in the components of CIS, with a policy shift from selective child dependant allowances to universal child benefit. Child benefit has grown from €19.11 per month in 1987 to €160 per month in 2007, a rise of 360 per cent in real terms. Child dependant allowances, by contrast, are unchanged in real terms, mainly as a result of a policy decision to freeze the rates between 1994 and 2006. These variable rate changes have led to a re-structuring of CIS, with child benefit doubling its contribution to the total CIS package from 28 per cent in 1987 to 59 per cent in 2007.

Distributive and poverty impact of budgetary policy

Now, we broaden the analysis to take into account changes in tax policies and also to benchmark welfare (and tax) changes with increases in wages. The latter is important as otherwise welfare rates, while ahead of inflation, may not keep pace with wage growth, resulting in a relative decline in living standards for welfare recipients (Callan *et al.*, 2001).

The four periods of budgetary policy examined in Table 2.5 are closely linked to the periods in office of different governments. Each period covers five budgets, with the exception of the first period when six budgets were produced. The economic and political context of each period has its own distinctive features.[19]

---

[19] The first period, 1987 to 1992, was an era of modest economic recovery after the doldrums of the early 1980s. Policy was framed by two partnership agreements, the *Programme for National Recovery* and the *Programme for Economic and Social Progress*, while the two governments of this time were composed of Fianna Fáil (alone) and Fianna Fáil with the Progressive Democrats. The next period, 1993 to 1997, opened with an economic slowdown, before the economy picked up. The main partnership agreement was the *Programme for Competitiveness and Work*. The two governments of this era were both coalitions: Labour and Fianna Fáil for two years and Labour, Fine Gael and Democratic Left for three years. The third period, 1998 to 2002, was one of exceptional economic growth. The government was made up of Fianna Fáil and the Progressive Democrats. The two partnership agreements were *Partnership 2000* and the *Programme for Prosperity and Fairness*, and the *National Anti-Poverty Strategy* was also established. The final period, 2003 to 2007, began with a slowdown in economic growth, followed by a significant improvement in the later years. The government was unchanged, while the new partnership agreements were *Sustaining Progress* and *Towards 2016*.

Table 2.5: Distributive impact of budgetary policy, 1987–2007 (% change in disposable income by quintile)

	1987–1992 (%)	1993–1997 (%)	1998–2002 (%)	2003–2007 (%)
Bottom quintile	8.1	–0.7	8.7	18.1
2nd quintile	–2.5	0.1	12.3	8.5
3rd quintile	–1.7	2.4	13.0	3.3
4th quintile	1.6	2.6	14.1	2.0
Top quintile	4.7	1.2	11.9	1.0
Average gain	2.6	1.5	12.1	3.5

In the period from 1987 to 1992, the average gain from budgetary policies was 2.6 per cent. Benefit was skewed towards the bottom and top quintiles, with the middle 60 per cent of the population either losing or gaining a modest amount. The increases in welfare payments highlighted in the previous section were the main driver in the gain for the bottom quintile.

The next period provided smaller gains, in the order of 1.5 per cent. Here the emphasis was primarily on the third and fourth quintiles, with gains of approximately 2.5 per cent. The poorest group actually recorded a small loss in this period.

A major expansion in budgetary policy took place in the third period, with an average gain of 12.1 per cent. While all income categories benefited from this budget largesse, the middle-income groups did the best. This arose from the major reform in tax policy, including rates cuts and a switch to tax credits. There were also significant increases in child benefit, which favoured families across the income range.

The fourth period, from 2003 to 2007, saw a significant reduction in the scale of tax and welfare improvements to 3.5 per cent, though still greater than the first two periods. What is most defining in this policy period is the overwhelming focus on lower income groups, with the bottom 40 per cent of the population getting an average income boost of between 8.5 and 18.1 per cent. The gains for the rest of the population were more modest, between 1 and 3.3 per cent. This policy shift in favour of low-income groups can be seen as compensating for the more tax-oriented budgets at the end of the millennium.

We have a particular interest in the ten years from 1998 to 2007, which coincided with the ten-year NAPS as well as exceptional budget surpluses. These features warrant an in-depth analysis of the distributive impact of this budgetary era. In addition, the impact on poverty of budgetary policy is investigated. Figure 2.15 presents the combined distributive impact of the last ten budgets from 1998 to 2007, when the average income gain was 16 per cent. The outcome strongly favours low-income groups, with an increase of 28 per cent for the bottom quintile and 22 per cent for the second quintile. At the same time, middle and high income quintiles show significant gains of 13 to 17 per cent. As noted above, the gains for the poorest quintiles mostly accrued between 2003 and 2007, when welfare rates were increased by large amounts.[20]

Another perspective on budgetary impact is to examine the share-out of total budgetary resources (over €10,000 million) over the ten years. Income tax accounted for by far the greatest allocation of these resources, at 65 per cent. Less

---

[20] This policy change was first apparent in Budget 2002, with the poorest 40 per cent gaining up to 4 per cent, as compared to an average increase of 1 per cent. The average gains in the next three budgets were modest. It was primarily in Budgets 2006 and 2007 that significant gains were recorded by low-income groups.

Figure 2.15: Distributive impact and share-out of total resources under Budgets 1998 to 2007, against wage-indexed policies, by income quintile

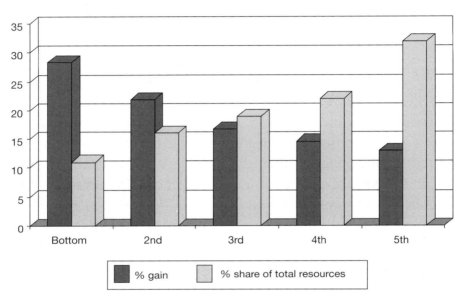

than one-fifth went on social welfare improvements, while 16 per cent was spent on child income support (almost all on child benefit). Looking at the distribution of total budgetary resources across income categories in Figure 2.15 reveals that the largest proportion of budgetary resources went to the top quintile of the population, who got almost one-third of the total. This higher share is at the expense of the bottom two quintiles, who received between 11 and 16 per cent. The amount provided for middle-income groups (third and fourth quintiles) is proportionate to their share of the total population. Using the EU measure of income inequality (S80/S20), the richest 20 per cent got almost three times the amount received by the poorest 20 per cent. This regressive outcome is still superior to the distribution of all income, where the top quintile has almost five times the income of the poorest quintile.

What are the implications of recent budgetary policy for relative income poverty? Figure 2.16 illustrates the poverty impact of Budgets 1998 to 2007, using three discrete median thresholds: 50 per cent, 60 per cent and 70 per cent. Overall, tax and welfare policy has achieved a significant reduction in the level of income poverty in the last ten years. The reduction at the 60 per cent line was 11 per cent across the total population, as compared with a wage-indexed policy.[21] At this threshold, the poverty gap[22] was also reduced, by 24 per cent. There was a greater impact on poverty among older people and children, with a reduction of around 15 per cent in both cases and the poverty gap falling by one-third. Poverty among women was cut by 10 per cent, in line with the norm, while the poverty gap was reduced by 20 per cent.

Results are also presented at 50 and 70 per cent of median income. At the lowest threshold, there was a 25 per cent reduction in poverty for the total population, while a decrease of 6 per cent was achieved at the 70 per cent threshold. This reflects the flat nature of welfare increases, with the greatest gain accruing to those at the bottom of the income range. The stronger reduction at the lowest threshold was more pronounced among older people, where income poverty was cut by over half at the 50 per cent line compared to 7 per cent at the highest threshold. Similarly, child poverty at the 50 per cent line decreased by 29 per cent and by 9 per cent at

---

[21] In absolute terms, the falls are 4.5 percentage points at the 50 per cent line, 1.5 percentage points at the 60 per cent line and 1 percentage point at the 70 per cent line.

[22] The poverty gap refers to the average distance in financial terms that individuals fall below the poverty line.

the 70 per cent line. Finally, among women, the reduction in poverty was 20 per cent at the lowest threshold and 6 per cent at the highest.

Figure 2.16: Effect on income poverty of Budgets 1998 to 2007, against wage-indexed policies (change in poverty rate at 50, 60 and 70 per cent of median income)

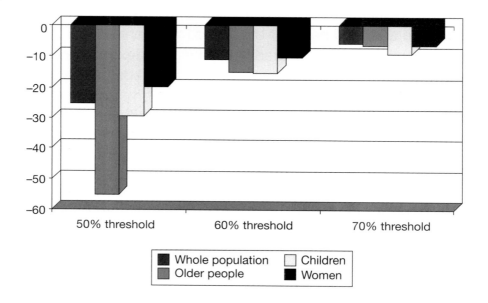

Overall, this analysis of budgetary policy highlights the following outcomes:

- Economic growth has a major bearing on the capacity of policy-makers to engage in discretionary tax/welfare expenditure

- Ambitious welfare commitments under the revised NAPS were the critical factor in targeting low-income groups

- The most generous budgetary period (1998–2002) in the last twenty years was dominated by tax reductions

- Political allegiances do not seem to be a determining factor in distributive impact

- Even the most pro-welfare era still gave three times more government resources to the richest quintile than to the poorest

- Tax/welfare policies can have a major impact on income poverty.

Conclusions

This analysis of poverty trends and tax/welfare policies highlights a number of key conclusions from the last twenty years. There is now a high level of poverty monitoring in Ireland, using both indigenous and international measures of poverty and supported by dedicated cross-national data-collection instruments. In Ireland, monitoring poverty has added political importance due to the setting of overall targets under the NAPS.

The income or risk-of-poverty levels remain largely unchanged over the last twenty years. However, this negative outcome must be tempered by the fact that the threshold has increased significantly in real terms. The pattern for consistent poverty is positive, with a reduction of 50 per cent between 1994 and 2001. This picture is complicated by the establishment of a new higher benchmark in 2003 under the EU-SILC. There is also concern about the absolute nature of the deprivation element of the measure.

In a comparative EU context, Ireland has higher than average levels of poverty. A key factor behind this outcome is the weak impact of welfare transfers on underlying poverty rates. However, analysis of recent budgetary changes suggests an intensification of the poverty impact of fiscal policies, which may take some time to work its way into EU comparisons.

Overall, we can see that there have been major welfare gains in the period under review, driven by policy targets and budgetary resources. Budgetary policy has been redistributive and pro-poor, though this has not been a consistent pattern. However, there has been a huge unseen leakage of resources through tax breaks and incentives (Hughes, 2005; Combat Poverty Agency, 2006). In conclusion, it is critically important that welfare rates remain central to the poverty debate as we can see that policy on welfare rates has made a significant difference to poverty levels.

References

Atkinson, T., Cantillon, B., Marlier, E. and Nolan, B. (2002), *Social Indicators: The EU and Social Inclusion*, Oxford: Oxford University Press

Beblavy, M. and Mizsei, K. (2006), 'Making Spurious Poverty Statistics History', *Development and Transition*, vol. 4, June

Callan, T., Keeney, M. and Walsh, J. (2001), 'Income Tax and Welfare Policies: Some Current Issues', in Callan, T. and McCoy, D. (eds.), *Budget Perspectives. Proceedings of a Conference Held on 9 October, 2001*, Dublin: ESRI

Callan, T., Keeney, M., Nolan, B. and Maître, B. (2004), *Why is Relative Income Poverty so High in Ireland?,* Dublin: ESRI

Callan, T., Layte, R., Nolan, B., Watson, D., Whelan, C. T., Williams, J. and Maître, B. (1999), *Monitoring Poverty Trends*, Dublin: Stationery Office and Combat Poverty Agency

Callan, T., Nolan, B. and Whelan, C. T. (1993), 'Resources, Deprivation and the Measurement of Poverty', *Journal of Social Policy*, vol. 22, no. 2, pp. 141–172

Callan, T., Nolan, B. and Whelan, C. T. (1996a), *A Review of the Commission on Social Welfare's Minimum Adequate Income*, Dublin: ESRI

Callan, T., Nolan, B., Whelan, B. J., Whelan, C. T. and Williams, J. (1996b), *Poverty in the 1990s. Evidence from the 1994 Living in Ireland Survey,* Dublin: Oak Tree Press

Central Statistics Office (2005a), *EU Survey on Income and Living Conditions (EU-SILC). First Results 2003,* Statistical Release, 24 January, Dublin/Cork: CSO

Central Statistics Office (2005b), *EU Survey on Income and Living Conditions (EU-SILC). 2004 (with revised 2003 estimates),* Statistical Release, 12 December, Dublin/Cork: CSO

Central Statistics Office (2006), *EU Survey on Income and Living Conditions (EU-SILC). 2005,* Statistical Release, 16 November, Dublin/Cork: CSO

Collins, M. L. (2006), 'Poverty: Measurement, Trends and Future Directions', in Healy, S., Reynolds, B. and Collins, M. (eds.), *Social Policy in Ireland. Principles, Practice and Problems*, Dublin: The Liffey Press

Combat Poverty Agency (2006), *Promoting Equity in Ireland's Tax System*, Dublin: CPA

Commission on Social Welfare (1986), *Report*, Dublin: Government Publications

CORI Justice (2006), *Socio-Economic Review 2007. Addressing Inequality*, Dublin: CORI Justice

Guio, A.-C. (2005), *Material Deprivation in the EU*, Statistics in Focus, Population and Social Conditions, 21/2005, Luxembourg: Eurostat

Hughes, G. (2005), 'Pension Tax Reliefs and Equity', in Stewart, J. (ed.), *For Richer, For Poorer; An Investigation of the Irish Pension System*, Dublin: Tasc

Ireland (2002a), *Building an Inclusive Society*, Dublin: Stationery Office

Ireland (2002b), *National Action Plan against Poverty and Social Exclusion 2003–2005*, Dublin: Stationery Office

Ireland (2007), *National Action Plan for Social Inclusion 2007–2016*, Dublin: Stationery Office

Layte, R., Maître, B., Nolan, B., Watson, D., Whelan, C. T., Williams, J. and Casey, B. (1999), *Monitoring Poverty Trends and Exploring Poverty Dynamics*, Dublin: ESRI

Maître, B., Nolan, B. and Whelan, C. T. (2006), *Reconfiguring the Measurement of Deprivation and Consistent Poverty in Ireland*, Dublin: ESRI

Nolan, B. (2006a), 'The EU's Social Inclusion Indicators and Their Implications for Ireland', in Healy, S., Reynolds, B. and Collins, M. (eds.), *Social Policy in Ireland. Principles, Practice and Problems*, Dublin: The Liffey Press

Nolan B. (2006b), 'Trends in Income Inequality in Ireland', Combat Poverty Agency seminar, 14 March: http://cpa.ie/research/seminars/presentations/2006-03-14_BrianNolan.pdf

Nolan, B. and Callan, T. (eds.) (1994), *Poverty and Policy in Ireland*, Dublin: Gill & Macmillan

Nolan, B. and Smeeding, T. (2005), 'Ireland's Income Distribution in Comparative Perspective', *Review of Income and Wealth*, vol. 54, no. 4, pp. 537–560

Nolan, B. and Whelan, C. T. (1996), *Resources, Deprivation and Poverty*, Oxford: Clarendon Press

Nolan, B., Gannon, B., Layte, R., Watson, D., Whelan, C. T. and Williams, J. (2002), *Monitoring Poverty Trends: Results from the 2000 Living in Ireland Survey*, Dublin: ESRI

Pensions Board (1998), *Securing Retirement Income*, Dublin: Pensions Board

Social Protection Committee (2001), *Report on Indicators in the Field of Poverty and Social Exclusion*: http://ec.europa.eu/employment_social/social_protection_commitee/docs/laeken_list.pdf

Social Protection Committee (2006), *Portfolio of Overarching Indicators and Streamlined Social Inclusion, Pension, and Health Portfolios*, Brussels: European Commission

Social Welfare Benchmarking and Indexation Group (2001), *Final Report of the Benchmarking and Indexation Group*, Dublin: Stationery Office

Whelan, C. T., Layte, R., Maître, B., Gannon, B., Nolan, B., Layte, R., Watson, D. and Williams, J. (2003), *Monitoring Poverty Trends: Results from the 2001 Living in Ireland Survey*, Dublin: ESRI

Chapter 3

Child poverty and child income supports

John Sweeney

Introduction

'A comprehensive assessment of the lives and well-being of children and adolescents in the economically advanced nations' (UNICEF, 2007) contains good and bad news for Ireland. Though we are still playing catch-up with other advanced countries in areas such as early education, childcare and child protection, the overall wellbeing of Ireland's children is ranked ninth of the world's twenty-one richest countries (ahead, for example, of France in sixteenth place and the UK in twenty-first place). Relative to children in other countries, Irish children perceive their lives positively, show a good preparedness and ability to cope with pressures, enjoy good family and peer relationships and are well served by their educational system. That is the good news. The bad news is that Ireland would have scored even better but for poor rankings on the dimensions of material wellbeing and health and safety (nineteenth in each). Relatively high percentages of children live in households with low incomes, no parent in employment and a paucity of educational and cultural resources. By international standards, Irish children are exposed to high levels of risk to their health and safety.

The UNICEF assessment is dictated by the methodology employed and is not intended to provoke. But we should be provoked. In the first place, to address what appear as our relative weaknesses more boldly and imaginatively. Ireland has achieved an expansion of employment unprecedented in the industrialised world, disposable incomes and government revenue have risen rapidly, *and* there have been major improvements in child income supports. Yet a large minority of the nation's children still do not have an acceptable standard of living. This chapter is about that challenge – exploring what must be done differently to extend material wellbeing to all children in Ireland so that, at least, this element in the framework of each child's development is assured. In second place, the UNICEF assessment should provoke us to value and protect what currently appear as Ireland's relative strengths. Individuals, families and communities in Ireland may be living through profound social and cultural changes but Irish children still enjoy a quality to the non-material dimensions of their lives that children in countries that have been richer for longer might envy.

The focus of this chapter on the role of child income supports in alleviating child poverty may – in some years' time – appear dated and reflect a dominant perspective on child poverty that, with hindsight, will be seen to have been characteristic of the 1987 to 2007 period. After all, children do not have incomes and the level of their household's income is only an indicator of a risk of child poverty and an ambiguous guide to their wellbeing. However, if new perspectives are to emerge and strengthen, it is probably necessary that the concentration on child income supports first occurs. Only when it is clear that relatively little more can be accomplished through them will fresh analyses and complementary policy developments – particularly of the services from which socially disadvantaged children benefit disproportionately – move centre stage in combating child poverty.

There *is* unfinished business with child income supports in Ireland. If the role of household income in combating child poverty should not be exaggerated, it should not be minimised either. The first section below, therefore, explores how low household income damages children. A second section briefly summarises what we now know about why a significant minority of households with children have seriously low incomes. The chapter then reviews how our current set of child income supports has been conceptualised and structured to support low-income families. At the heart of the chapter is a close-up look at the strengths and weaknesses of each of the main instruments that currently subsidise the costs of parenting. This is followed by suggestions on the direction that further reform should take and, finally, conclusions on child poverty and child income supports in Ireland.

How does low household income affect children?

A first set of relationships between low household income and poor childhood conditions must be acknowledged which are not, properly, a challenge to the levels of child income transfers and household incomes. Where low household incomes mean children live in crowded and poorly heated homes, are exposed to severe health and safety risks in their neighbourhoods, attend schools characterised by high levels of absenteeism and staff turnover, receive prompt medical attention only by attending hospital accident and emergency services, and so on, the primary response should not be to boost household incomes so that families can escape those homes, neighbourhoods, schools etc. The real challenge is to improve the standards of housing, neighbourhoods, schools and health services available to families on low incomes *while they are on low incomes.*

This is a major challenge to service-providers which they must, and by and large do, assume. Nothing is gained by having public policy feed a process whereby access to core services of a high standard is dependent on income. Publicly funded service-providers must therefore shoulder responsibility for breaking links between low family income and children's exposure to poor standards in housing, physical security, education and healthcare. Higher social welfare payments, more generous child income supports and better-resourced and integrated welfare-to-work policies are not the appropriate instruments for ensuring that all children have access to quality services.

If families with low incomes had access to quality services for their children, would their low incomes still be a legitimate concern of public policy? Child income supports are, ultimately, additions to household income paid to adults on behalf of children for whom they have responsibility. It should not be assumed that a child in a household where the equivalent income is below 60 per cent of the median is, on that evidence alone, in need. The child may even be the least likely member of the household to experience deprivation if parents successfully shield their children from the consequences of low household income, through self-sacrifice and the quality of the parent–child relationship. It is important, therefore, to 'avoid stigmatising low-income families with high levels of parenting skills' (UNICEF, 2005,

p. 6). The least ambiguous indicators of child poverty, in fact, are provided by non-monetary outcomes (low birthweight, sickness and accidents in childhood, neglect and abuse, poor 'school readiness', hazardous environments etc.). Where the data allow it, such final child outcomes are more reliable as evidence of child poverty than low household income, which remains an intermediate or instrumental factor.

It is important, therefore, that the convenience of framing a child poverty measure in terms of income does not 'skew the policy response excessively towards tax and transfer changes, and away from improving public services for children which might have a greater impact on their well-being over the longer term' (Brewer, 2003, p. 1). In fact, 'research cannot yet tell us whether directing extra resources to parents is better for children's well-being in the longer term than improving services for children' (p. 14).

Granted all this, it is nevertheless possible to distinguish three important ways in which low household incomes impact negatively on child members of those households. The first is simply that items which aid children's development, and which parents know would do so and want for their children, are unaffordable (for example medicines, children's furniture, space within the house to do homework, heating, school trips, a computer). Research makes clear that adequately resourced home environments significantly improve opportunities for children's development and justify prioritising low-income households with resources available for child income support. In other words, additional income is important at low levels of household income, while above a certain threshold additional income does little to improve the environment for children further. The best available data in 2007 suggest that a large minority of children in Ireland by international standards do not have sufficiently well-endowed home environments.[1]

A second route by which low household income impacts negatively on children is by undermining the quality of parenting they receive. Parents who struggle with debt, are themselves poorly fed, are unable to purchase medicines or to socialise beyond a minimum extent, must work long and awkward hours etc. are more likely to be tired much of the time, experience ill health or suffer depression. In the process they become less attentive or more authoritarian parents. Some striking research in Ireland finds that it is the degree of financial stress experienced by a mother rather than the level of household income itself which has the stronger influence on child wellbeing (McKeown and Haase, 2006). While closely related, the two are not one and the same thing. Among households with similar levels of income, the extent to which the mother was struggling to make ends meet had a strong and independent influence on the parent–child relationship and the mother's own health.[2]

---

[1] UNICEF (2007) uses 2001 data from the World Health Organization's survey on *Health Behaviour in School-age Children* and 2003 data from the OECD's *Programme for International Student Assessment* to conclude that Irish children have poor educational and cultural resources in their homes by OECD standards (placed nineteenth out of twenty-four countries). See, especially, its Figure 1.3b.

[2] McKeown and Haase comment: 'It is clear from [our analysis] that helping people to cope financially involves much more than money, however important that may be in particular cases. Helping people to cope financially also requires, as a pre-requisite, helping them to cope with themselves and the life events that they experience' (2006, p. 60).

A third route by which low household income impacts negatively on children hinges crucially on the children themselves. They also notice what money does directly for them. They too have direct economic concerns (preferred food, bedroom accessories, trips etc.) whose denial they find hard. More crucially, children too are social beings and feel acutely the judgement of their peers. They can be anguished when denied an item or activity that would strengthen their group belonging and when 'not having' marks them out as different. School, in particular, is a hugely important world to children in which not being able to afford what protects their status can cause deep unhappiness.

Why do some households with children have very low incomes?

Children do not have incomes and we consider a child to be below an income poverty line only after aggregating all sources of the household's income and reckoning the share of that which is specifically available to meet the child's needs (this, essentially, is what adjusting household income using an equivalence scale does). Child income poverty figures can appear to play tricks but once attention is paid to such factors as where the poverty line is drawn, the equivalence scale used, the years to which the data refer and the age group selected, most differences can be explained. The UNICEF report (2007) found that 6 per cent of Irish children lived in relative income poverty (using 50 per cent of median income in 2000), whereas the EU-SILC (CSO, 2006) estimated 21 per cent (using 60 per cent of median income in 2005), but the conclusion is the same: Ireland has one of the worst performances in the industrialised world on this score. What is even more challenging is that there has been only a modest fall of 3 to 4 per cent in these proportions despite the onset of the economic boom, the huge drop in unemployment, the major increases in child benefit and other improvements in the labour market and tax and social welfare codes. We should not be satisfied.

To answer what is going on, three sources of household income – and their interrelationships – need to be separately considered: earnings, adult social welfare receipts and child income supports.

Parental earnings

What parents earn is the most important determinant of whether children are reared in income poverty or not. Analysis of child poverty in 2000 (NESC, 2003) made it clear that parental non-employment was the single most important factor associated with child poverty, much more important than whether a child was being reared in a lone-parent or couple household. For example, children of lone parents in a job faced a poverty risk of 8 per cent but children with two non-employed parents faced a poverty risk of 33 per cent. While parental employment did wonders in reducing children's poverty risk, it by no means guaranteed it. Nearly one-half (46 per cent) of all children in consistent poverty had parents in employment. This type of evidence has been a clear invitation for some time to develop policy responses to child poverty that both encourage parents to cross from non-employment to work and provide a continuing element of in-work support where parents have low earnings.

It is clear which parents are having difficulty accessing employment and earning at a decent level in contemporary Ireland. They are primarily women. The surge in women's employment rates in Ireland is well documented but, for some groups, they remain exceptionally low by OECD standards. For example, the employment rate[3] of mothers in Ireland with two or more children aged under 16 is one of the lowest in the industrialised world (Cournède, 2006); the employment rate of older women (aged 55 to 64) is low, less than half of the rate in Sweden; and the employment rate of women who have not completed upper secondary education is one of the lowest in the EU (NESC, 2005b). It is, of course, important to be clear whether and under what conditions it is better for a mother with young children and/or with only limited earnings power to take up employment rather than to remain in the home. But either way the position adopted has major implications for the design and resourcing of child income supports. Cross-country differences in child poverty rates are related to differences in mothers' employment rates (Förster and d'Ercole, 2005).

The principal challenge of Ireland's high child income poverty has been well articulated by UNICEF (2005, p. 30):

A child poverty rate of 15.7 per cent (at the 50% of median line) puts Ireland close to ... the bottom of the child poverty league. But the problem of Ireland has been principally one of preventing income inequality from widening during a period of sustained economic growth and rising median incomes. A child poverty rate based on a percentage of median income will increase unless low-income groups share equally in the benefits of growth. Faced with this challenge, the appropriate response would seem to be a more active policy for developing the skills

---

3   In full-time equivalent terms, also called the 'effective labour supply'.

and opportunities of low-income parents to enable them to capture a higher share of the benefits of economic progress.

Adult social welfare payments

The level of the payments to which non-employed parents are entitled, whatever the reason they are not employed, also impacts strongly on the likelihood of their children falling below the income poverty lines. Over the period from 1994 to 2006, the proportion of children in Ireland living in jobless households fell by more than in any other EU-15 country (Eurostat). However, this still left 11 per cent of Irish children in jobless households in 2006, the third highest proportion in the EU, though Ireland was recording the area's third lowest unemployment rate. (Ominously, all of the reduction was achieved by 2000 after which there was a slight increase.)

Some of the parents of this 11 per cent of children may have bright futures in the workforce and need phased and systematic supports to move progressively from their current reliance on social assistance to decent employment. Life on means-tested assistance is not something they want to model for their children and their own wellbeing and parenting may improve through having a job. The challenges this presents to the current social welfare code – its assumptions, qualifying conditions, benefit withdrawal rates etc. – are being increasingly well focused.[4] However, some currently non-employed parents may simply not be in a

---

[4] It is a major theme in the NESC report, *The Developmental Welfare State* (2005b), in the *Government Discussion Paper: Proposals for Supporting Lone Parents* (Ireland, 2006a) and in the social partnership agreement, *Towards 2016* (Ireland, 2006b, section 31).

position to take up employment, at least in the medium term, because of poor health, an exceptional level of caring commitments, or other difficulties, and an income sufficient to raise their children with dignity will remain the responsibility of the state. For both sets of non-employed parents – those who can become self-reliant in the medium term and those who cannot – a higher adult payment has an important role to play in bringing their children above the income poverty lines. It has been cogently observed: 'Countries with the lowest (child) poverty rates are those in which children benefit a good deal from other transfers not necessarily directed to them' (Corak *et al.*, 2005, p. 35).

Each of the strategies employed to date – for example meeting the adequacy level set by the 1986 Commission on Social Welfare (a major benchmark up to 1997), raising rates by 'more than inflation' and to the degree that 'resources permit' (the discretionary strategy favoured by the Department of Finance), reaching '€150 a week in 2002 terms by 2007' (the benchmark adopted in the 2002 revised NAPS) – has its cogent logic, but not one of them guarantees that children in welfare-dependent households will be raised above the income poverty line.

Child income supports

Children's greater likelihood of being income poor compared to adults in Ireland has been much reduced since 1987 and improvements in child income supports can claim much of the credit for this. Before the large increases in child benefit that began in 2001 were completed, and on the basis of data gathered for twenty-two countries in July of that year, Ireland's cash transfers on behalf of children were found to be good by international standards (Bradshaw and Finch, 2002).

69

They were high relative to average disposable earnings, to recipient households' total disposable incomes and as a proportion of the overall level of social welfare spending. Indeed, in some family circumstances, the level of cash transfers in Ireland rated among Europe's best. When the value of state services on behalf of children (support for families in accessing childcare, health services, education and housing) was added to child income supports in this international comparison, however, Ireland's high ranking was abruptly reversed. For example, while Ireland's total package of supports for an unemployed lone parent with one child was the best of the twenty-two countries studied, it swung to last position when the lone parent was on average female earnings and paying for childcare (see also NESC, 2005b).

Observing that good levels of child income support by international standards are not resulting in low levels of child poverty by international standards brings us to the heart of the matter. Using even the same level of resources differently, could more be achieved? The remainder of this chapter explores the strengths and weaknesses of the instruments currently being used. Overall, Ireland is a prominent example of a general characteristic observed of child income support arrangements in the English-speaking world: 'We find that market incomes play a larger role than state transfers in accounting for the cross-national diversity of outcomes for disadvantaged children. The English-speaking countries other than the USA, for example, actually provide quite substantial income transfers to their most needy children. The living standards of these children, however, remain relatively low because of low labour-market incomes' (Bradbury and Jäntti, 2001, p. 88).

Origins and basic structure of Ireland's child income supports

Currently, five instruments transfer cash directly to households on behalf of children being supported in or from them. Ranked in order of the public expenditure incurred, they are child benefit (CB), the early childcare supplement, child dependant additions (CDAs), family income supplement (FIS) and the back to school clothing and footwear allowance (see Table 3.1).[5]

Table 3.1: Child income transfers: Public expenditure and child beneficiaries, 2006

	Annual cost 2006 (€m)	Estimated number of children benefiting	Estimated weekly value per child
Child benefit	2,040	1,087,000	€34.61 (lower) €42.69 (higher)
Early childcare supplement	353*	350,000	€19.23
Child dependant additions	295	349,930	€16.80
Family income supplement	94.5	43,788	€41.50
Back to school clothing and footwear allowance	25	160,000	€2.31 (2–11 yrs) €3.65 (12–22 yrs)

* Cost in a full year; introduced mid-2006

[5] Supplementary welfare allowance exceptional needs payments for children's items also transfer money to parents on behalf of their children but on an infrequent basis and a small scale.

Between direct spending and tax expenditures[6], the government spent the equivalent of 2.2 per cent of gross national income in 2004 (the last year for which full figures are available) on boosting the cash resources at the discretionary use of parents via cash transfers and tax reductions.

The development of policy

In broad summary, the more important policy changes since 1987 have been:

1986–1992	CDAs were substantially increased
1994	CDAs were frozen and CB given a large increase
1998	The calculation of FIS thresholds was moved to a net income basis (hitherto, gross income had determined eligibility)
2001	A major programme of increases in CB began
2006	The early childcare supplement was introduced
2007	FIS thresholds were recalibrated to increase support for large families
2007	CDAs were increased for the first time since 1994.

However, the basic contours of the system were conceptualised in the mid-1980s, and reconfirmed in the mid-1990s. This story is important to this chapter.

The 1986 report of the Commission on Social Welfare (CSW) examined child income supports in depth. It rejected two

---

6   Four tax credits reduce the tax-take from individuals as a direct consequence of their responsibility for rearing children – the one-parent family tax credit, the home-carer's tax credit, the widowed parent's tax credit and the incapacitated child tax credit – while child benefit is exempted from income tax.

extreme positions: on the one hand, that the state is responsible for the full costs of rearing children, regardless of their families' resources; and on the other, that child income support provided by the state should be given only to a small group of low-income families. Instead, it believed that the state should make 'a contribution' to the income of all families but 'full provision' for children in families wholly reliant on social welfare (p. 293).

The instrument through which the state makes 'a contribution' to the costs of rearing all children is CB (then termed children's allowance), which is funded out of general taxation. The CSW did not address the question of the proportion of the cost of rearing a child that *should* be socialised in this way (nor has this issue been systematically addressed in any subsequent Irish study). It recommended only that the then rate 'be improved' in real terms, noting that it had been allowed to decline from its peak in 1982.

The instruments through which 'the State should provide the *full cost of rearing children* for families dependent on social welfare payments' were CDAs and CB (p. 201). The CSW did not try to establish the cost of rearing a child directly but deduced it instead by applying the appropriate equivalence scale[7] to what constituted a minimally adequate weekly income for an adult. The same approach was taken in 2002 when the revised NAPS (Ireland, 2002) expressed its target for CDAs and CB combined as 33 to 35 per cent of the lowest adult social welfare payment.

---

[7] The CSW noted the absence of Irish research on the appropriate equivalence scale for Irish conditions.

The CSW accepted that each instrument had inherent strengths and weaknesses in helping poor families. On the one hand, increasing CDAs gave greater priority to low-income families and, thus, successfully 'selectivised' child income support. However, if the rates became 'very high', they would create a work disincentive for large families. The CSW emphatically rejected that CDAs at that time were exercising a significant disincentive effect.[8] On the other hand, CB created no work disincentive, was an independent income for mothers and adjusted the post-tax incomes of households in recognition of children being reared in them.[9] However, CB spread child income support thinly across all families at a 'substantial' cost to the exchequer. On balance, the CSW favoured 'the continuation of a significant element of child dependant allowances' with, 'in the long term, a modest relative shift towards [CB] and away from child dependant allowances' (p. 298).

The CSW did not back the intention in a 1985 government plan (*Building on Reality*) to merge CDAs and CB into a single, taxable child benefit. It believed the large presence of children in the population and the extent of poverty among them made meeting the full cost of rearing a child for families on social welfare through taxable CB alone too expensive. It chose to back instead the new FIS, just being introduced, as a third instrument that would provide support for workers on low earnings who were not entitled to CDAs (because they were not in receipt of welfare) but whose families needed

---

8   A strong critique of the huge variety of rates at which CDAs were paid led to an extensive rationalisation and simplification of the payment structure in subsequent years.
9   With this last observation, the Commission rehearsed the position against taxing CB taken by the Commission on Taxation in 1982.

more support than CB alone. The CSW was not enthusiastic in according FIS this role. Its introduction, it noted, had added 'a layer of complexity to child income supports' and 'made more difficult (their) proper long-term evolution' (p. 300).[10] The CSW recommended that, as the rate of CB improved over time and marginal tax rates came down for low-paid employees, FIS should eventually be dispensed with.

In summary, the scenario envisaged from 1986 onwards was of three instruments providing support to three groups of families: CB as a first tier reaching all families; and then CDAs and FIS forming a second tier for low-income families split into two groups, those reliant on social welfare receiving CDAs along with their CB and those on low earnings receiving FIS as well as CB. Twenty years later, the essential contours of Ireland's child income support system continue to match this description.

Ten years after the CSW, an Expert Working Group on the *Integration of the Tax and Social Welfare Systems* (1996) reviewed the whole system and explored some major alternatives. It was concerned that CDAs and FIS were creating significant work disincentives: CDAs creating an 'unemployment trap' because families only got them as income if they remained unemployed; FIS creating a 'poverty trap' because the withdrawal of the benefit as earnings rose added to rising tax obligations to absorb a major part of any increase in earnings.

The context to the 1996 report was significant. The unemployment rate in 1995 was 13.5 per cent, the same rate

---

10 The CSW cited the National Planning Board's (1984) evaluation of FIS as 'a further ad hoc adjustment to an already complicated and anomalous social welfare code' (p. 287).

as in 1990, and seemed to be responding little to the improvement in the economy. For much of the period since 1986, and contrary to the CSW's recommendation, priority had been given to increasing CDAs rather than CB.[11] A concern that CDAs had become a work disincentive led to a 1994 decision to freeze their value. The impact of doing so was softened with a major increase in CB (35 per cent) and a commitment to move towards a child benefit supplement 'that would be paid to social welfare recipients and low to middle income families' (then Minister for Finance Ruairí Quinn, Budget 1995). In the event, increases in CB alone were relied upon to compensate recipients of CDAs for the continuing erosion of their value and the child benefit supplement did not materialise.

Much of the analysis of the 1996 report centred on the calculation of replacement rates and it was clear that CDAs were causing these to be particularly high for welfare recipients with children.[12] CDAs at the time were also costing the exchequer more than CB (105 per cent of expenditure on CB), making it prohibitively costly to envisage raising CB to compensate for the abolition of CDAs, even though doing so would eliminate all disincentive effects.

Led by the principle that in-work income (net of tax and costs) should be higher than unemployment income (inclusive of secondary benefits) for people with children, the Expert Group examined some major alternatives to the child income

---

[11] From 1986 to 1992, the lowest CDA was increased from £8.70 to £12.50 per week (an increase of 44 per cent); in contrast, the lower CB rate was raised from £15.05 to £15.80 (an increase of 5 per cent).

[12] By 1995, for example, CDAs alone accounted for 28 per cent of the total income of an unemployed couple with three children.

support system in place. Two are particularly relevant to this chapter. A first alternative was to subsume CDAs and FIS into a higher rate of CB that would be taxable ('integrated child benefit', in effect the *Building on Reality* proposal of 1985). This was not recommended, however, because it 'would significantly increase public expenditure and income taxation, and many of the benefits would accrue to people on higher earnings rather than to those for whom employment incentives are an issue' (p. 43).

A second alternative also subsumed CDAs and FIS but this time into a child benefit supplement (CBS) paid only to families with income below a certain threshold regardless of where their income came from (employment or social welfare).[13] The Expert Group examined a modest example of how such a CBS might work[14] and concluded that it would be progressive (direct resources to where they were most needed) and flexible (could be made costly or inexpensive by adjusting its key parameters). However, it saw two significant drawbacks. As more people would receive a CBS than currently received CDAs or FIS, more in the population would, therefore, have a benefit withdrawal rate added to their marginal tax rate over a range of income. Secondly, a CBS would pose significant administrative challenges because of which it 'would take up to two years to implement' (p. 45).

---

[13] This, also, was an aspiration in an agreed programme for government (Ireland, 1995).

[14] The report considered the case of a CBS that was the same amount as a CDA at the time and withdrawn at a rate of 30 per cent once weekly family income passed £200 (which corresponded then to the average weekly earnings of women). This meant, for example, that a family with three children lost all eligibility for the payment when their income reached 120 per cent of gross average industrial earnings at the time.

In the final analysis, the 1996 report did not recommend fundamental reform but instead proposed a range of partial measures that could be implemented immediately to smooth the transition from welfare to work (for example retention of secondary benefits for a period, retention of CDAs for thirteen weeks for the long-term unemployed, retention of part of the main welfare payment on a declining basis, higher earnings disregards). It made several pertinent observations on the balance to be struck between piecemeal and fundamental reform, however, that remain useful and relevant to the contemporary challenge of improving Ireland's child income supports:

- Benefit withdrawal rates cannot be avoided 'in any social welfare system [where] earning money implies losing entitlement to benefit' (p. 7). Either high benefit withdrawal rates are imposed on a relatively small part of the population, or lower tax/withdrawal rates are faced by a much larger section of the population.

- Making supports universal (like CB) avoids imposing benefit withdrawal rates on small or large subgroups in the population but only by imposing higher tax rates on the whole of it. A society which provides an extensive range of supports and services, without either income testing or user charges, must levy taxes at a higher level to ensure such 'free' access.

- Effective social protection, which respects people's capacity and need for self-reliance, requires that its different strands develop in an integrated fashion and not in parallel. The Expert Group essentially wrestled with the unforeseen by-product of what, in isolation, were necessary social developments – the protection of the real incomes of people out of work and tax reductions for workers on low earnings: 'Several policy objectives being pursued in parallel on their own merits [contributed] to unemployment and poverty traps' (p. 21).

• There is a path dependence in how instruments of social protection develop: '[Our] options are discrete options, not steps towards a single solution; in other words, it is not a question of beginning with the least expensive option and hoping to move from there towards the more expensive options' (p. 137). Once an instrument is adopted, it creates constituencies that press for its extension and improvement, which makes a return to basic alternatives to it more difficult.

The current instruments of child income support

Child dependant additions (CDAs)[15]
As explained, CDAs are additions to the weekly social welfare payments of adults made on behalf of children living with them. Until 1994, their lowest value (per child) was equivalent to 22 per cent of the lowest adult social welfare payment. This had fallen to 10 per cent by 2006, a consequence of the 1994 decision to freeze their value. Budget 2007 ended this freeze and raised them to €22 a week, the equivalent of 12 per cent of the lowest adult welfare payment (see Table 3.2).

---

[15] 'Qualified child increases' is now their official term but, in deference to past practice embodied in the reports reviewed, here the term 'CDAs' is used. The word 'allowance' is often used instead of 'addition', even in the text of Sustaining Progress and NESC reports, but even more incorrectly. 'Addition' and 'increase' communicate more accurately that they are supplements to payments made to adult recipients on behalf of their child dependants.

Table 3.2: CDAs as a percentage of the lowest adult welfare payment, 1994–2007

	1994	1997	2000	2003	2006	2007
CDA (lowest rate) (€)	16.80	16.80	16.80	16.80	16.80	22.00
Lowest adult social welfare rate (€)	77.47	85.73	98.43	124.80	165.80	185.80
CDA as a percentage of the lowest adult rate (%)	22	20	17	13	10	12

Approximately 350,000 children benefited from CDAs in 2006, or about one in three of the CB population. The number of children for whom CDAs are paid has been declining, not because fewer adults are in receipt of social welfare,[16] but because welfare claimants in general have shared in the wider societal trends towards smaller families and more one-person households.

The shift in the composition of welfare recipients receiving CDAs deserves to be highlighted (see Table 3.3). In 1994 (just before the economic boom), one-half of all CDAs were paid along with unemployment benefit and unemployment assistance. By 2004, this had dropped to 16 per cent at a time when 48 per cent of all CDAs were being paid along with the one-parent family payment. The child dependants of lone parents came to outnumber those of unemployed people by

[16] Growing numbers in receipt of the one-parent family payment and the disability allowance in particular have offset falls in the numbers receiving unemployment benefit or unemployment assistance (NESC, 2005a, p. 53).

more than three to one. In addition, child dependants of people in receipt of a welfare payment for illness, disability or caring and of supplementary welfare allowance increased markedly.

Table 3.3: Number of equivalent full-rate CDAs and distribution by adult recipients, 1994 and 2004

| Adult recipient | Equivalent full-rate CDAs | | | |
| | 1994 | | 2004 | |
	Number	Distribution (%)	Number	Distribution (%)
Lone parent (inc. widow/er)	104,743	28	150,286	48
Ill, disabled, carer*	47,710	13	63,601	20
Unemployed	188,030	50	48,457	16
Supported employment**	16,042	4	18,803	6
Supplementary welfare allowance	12,900	4	24,405	8
Pensioner, pre-retired	9,578	3	4,914	2
Total	379,003	100	310,476	100

* 1994 figure includes child dependants of recipients of disabled persons' maintenance allowance
** Child dependants of smallholders are the only supported employment category for 1994; back to work allowance, back to enterprise allowance and back to education allowance are additional categories for 2004
Source: DSFA (annual), *Statistical Information on Social Welfare Services*

This shift in the composition of the CDA population reinforces the analysis above that a careful distinction needs to be made between non-employed parents with reasonable prospects of accessing employment in the medium term and those without such prospects. A conservative estimate would suggest that at least 30 per cent of all children on whose behalf CDAs were being paid in 2004 had parents who could not be expected to take up employment.[17]

The back to school clothing and footwear allowance (BSCFA) is an additional cash-transfer for children paid once a year on behalf of a large subset of the CDA population (160,000 children benefited from it in 2006, equivalent to 46 per cent of the CDA population). It is intended to support families on low incomes with the cost of their children's clothing and footwear at the start of the school year. In effect, it functions as an end-of-summer lump sum supplement to a large subset of families receiving CDAs. This subset must have incomes below specified thresholds (hence, PRSI-based CDAs are likely to be excluded) and children aged 2 to 17 years ('school going', though 18 to 22 year olds in full-time education also qualify). In expenditure terms, the BSCFA is a minnow – its €25 million cost constituted just 1 per cent of total spending on child income support in 2006 – but the increase in its value (by 80 per cent for 2 to 11 year olds and 136 per cent for 12 to 17 year olds over the period from 1994 to 2004) while CDA rates were frozen means it is now a significant supplement to CDAs for a large subgroup of the CDA population.

The strengths and weaknesses of CDAs can be summarised as follows.

Strengths
• It can be assumed that practically all the poorest children in the state have CDAs paid on their behalf. A large part of the expenditure on CDAs, therefore, is effectively targeted.

---

[17] These are children whose parents are claiming for three or more children, or receiving a pension, pre-retirement allowance, carer's allowance or blind pension.

- Most children on whose behalf CDAs are paid are resident in the state. This means there is little or no 'leakage' produced by migration in so far as the contribution of CDAs to reducing poverty within the state is concerned.[18]

- The BSCFA is received only by families on low incomes and functions, in effect, as a lump sum, providing an annual boost to the CDA families with the lowest incomes.

Weaknesses
- Not all families who receive CDAs have low incomes. Those paid along with insurance-based benefits (35 per cent of all CDAs in 2003, see DSFA, 2004) are not means-tested.[19] This means there is some deadweight in using even CDAs as an anti-poverty instrument. (The decline in the proportion of the CDA population who receive the income-tested BSCFA suggests this element of deadweight may be increasing.)

- Expenditure data on CDAs are not routinely provided (though data on the numbers of children are).[20] This contributes to their relatively low profile as a child income support.

---

[18] CDAs payable with payments covered by EU law on social security (Regulation 1408) are exportable.

[19] No CDAs are paid if spouses/partners have incomes above a limit in certain instances (principally unemployment benefit and disability benefit where a spouse's or partner's income was above €350 in 2005 cancelled the right to CDAs).

[20] The key source of data on welfare receipt is the annual publication of the Department of Social and Family Affairs, *Statistical Information on Social Welfare Services*.

- If parents receiving CDAs leave social welfare for employment, the CDAs are withdrawn and there is no automatic transition to FIS or to any other form of in-work child income support. The evidence is that only a small number make the transition to FIS (see below).

Family income supplement (FIS)

FIS is a subsidy to the weekly net wage of employees with children where family net income falls below a specified threshold.[21] Employees must be working at least nineteen hours per week, though this can be in conjunction with hours worked by their spouse or partner. 'Family income' is the joint income of the spouses/partners, net of tax and PRSI. The amount of the subsidy paid is 60 per cent of the gap between the actual family income and a threshold related to family size. The withdrawal rate, therefore, is also 60 per cent. Employees themselves must take the initiative to apply for FIS and have to enlist the cooperation of their employer in doing so.

Total expenditure on FIS has been rising rapidly, fuelled principally by a higher spend per child (up from a weekly €15.86 on average in 1994 to €41.50 in 2006) and to a lesser extent by a rise in the number of eligible children (up by more than one-third since 1994). Lone parents have come to account for more than one-half of its recipients – up from 15 per cent in 1994 – while the proportion claiming for three or

---

21 Until 2006, the basis on which the threshold was set could be discerned: it approximated to 1.66 times what a couple with the same number of children would receive on unemployment assistance (UA). As of 2006, the basis of its calculation is less clear; expressed as a mark-up on the same family's entitlement under UA, the mark-up now rises with family size (see Appendix Table A3.1).

more children has fallen steadily. It is not clear how much the steep rise in recipients since 2004 is due to significant numbers of migrants becoming eligible.

FIS's double objective – to encourage employment and support children – means its support is weighted significantly towards the one-child family, even after a recalibration of its income thresholds in 2006 reduced the bias considerably. In 2006, the maximum weekly payment per child that a family with three children could potentially receive was €48, whereas a one-child family could receive €103.[22] In earlier years, the payment to the one-child family had been almost three times the per child payment to the three-child family (see Appendix Table A3.1).

FIS enjoys a high profile as the state's main in-work income support for families with children. This high profile, however, is difficult to justify by either the number of children benefiting or its effectiveness in ensuring that employment is a route out of poverty for parents who take up employment. Given the continued growth in relatively low-paying employments that has been an integral part of Ireland's expanding labour market since 2000, the number of children being helped by FIS still appears low and constitutes evidence that low take-up on the part of eligible families and types of employment that make families ineligible (self-employment, employment for under nineteen hours per week) continue to be serious limitations.

The strengths and weaknesses of FIS can be summarised as follows.

---

[22] These are the maximum possible payments. Actual payments will reflect the application of the income test to the circumstances of individual applicants.

Strengths
- FIS is generous. The average weekly payout per qualifying child is significantly higher than that provided by CB or CDA.

- FIS attempts only a limited responsiveness in its level of payment to changes in a family's circumstances. This both increases income security for recipients and reduces administration costs. Once granted, FIS is paid for fifty-two weeks and remains the same even if weekly earnings increase (or decrease). If another child is born, the FIS payment is increased as soon as the Department of Social and Family Affairs is notified.

- FIS is particularly generous towards lone parents. Its thresholds in their case are a multiple of what a couple, not a single person, would receive on unemployment assistance.

Weaknesses
- FIS has a stubbornly low take-up rate.

- Low-paid employees must take the initiative to apply for FIS and enlist the support of their employer – and of their spouse's employer where s/he is also employed – to do so.[23]

- While FIS is intuitive on one level (the earnings of low-paid workers need to be supplemented if their in-work income

---

[23] The application form has fifty-five questions. Applicants must have a bank or building society account; they must provide two recent payslips, their P60 and their tax credit certificate; they are asked if they are cohabiting and, if ever married, the date of the marriage; they are required to give full details of all their income sources and of all income sources of their spouse or partner.

is to be greater than their out-of-work support), the amount people stand to receive is difficult to explain.

- FIS does not cover all parents in employment on low earnings. Self-employed workers and employees who work less than nineteen hours are not entitled to it.

- It is significantly more generous to small families than to large ones.

- FIS has a high withdrawal rate (60 per cent). This improves its targeting and reduces the number of people higher up the earnings ladder who receive a partial payment, but it generates a significant poverty trap.

- FIS can be paid in respect of children not resident in the state. The large numbers of EU migrants entering lower paid jobs since 2004 make it likely that a growing number of the children being supported by FIS are outside the state.

Child benefit (CB)
CB is a monthly cash transfer to households with children from which practically every child in the state benefits.[24] Third and further children receive a higher payment (23 per cent higher in 2006) than first and second children, and multiple births also attract higher support. Any person habitually

---

24 The introduction of the Habitual Residence Condition in 2004 means recently arrived families (including of returned Irish emigrants) have to show that they are habitually resident in the state. There is a presumption that they are not habitually resident until two years have elapsed but a person may be able to show that they are habitually resident in a much shorter period. In addition, children of asylum seekers whose claims are being processed and of illegal immigrants may not be receiving CB.

present in the state and with responsibility for a child can apply for CB. The payment is exempt from income tax[25] and is usually applied for by, and paid directly to, the mother. It is the main instrument through which the state socialises the costs of rearing children and is, primarily, an exercise in horizontal redistribution – from households without children to households in which children are being reared.

Reflecting demographic developments in the state, the number of families receiving CB is rising while the number of children has changed little. This is because falling family size has offset the rising rate of family formation.

The rate of payment of CB was significantly increased in 1995 but truly substantial hikes did not occur until 2001 and 2002 (see Table 3.4). This has been in response to several concerns, namely to reduce work disincentives for families reliant on social welfare, to support working parents with the cost of childcare and to recognise the value of work in caring for children in the home.[26] While these several objectives have been stated in support of the decision to prioritise CB, a reference level for the rate of CB has not been adopted. It is still not clear what proportion of the costs of rearing a child it is intended the state should socialise.

Budget 2006 introduced a new payment of €1,000 annually to be made on behalf of every child under six years. Though

---

[25] The Department of Finance estimates that, in the tax year 2004, CB's exemption from income tax cost €343 million (up from €127.4 million in 1999/2000). This was approximately the same as total expenditure on CDAs in 2002 (€323 million).

[26] Children's tax allowances were abolished in 1986. They had given recognition indirectly to people's caring roles in the home by reducing their spouse's tax liability.

Table 3.4: Monthly CB rates, 1994–2007

	Lower (€)	Higher (€)
1994	25.40	31.75
1995	34.29	40.64
1996	36.83	43.18
1997	38.10	49.53
1998	40.01	53.34
1999	43.82	58.42
2000	53.98	71.12
2001	85.73	109.22
2002	117.60	147.30
2003	125.60	157.30
2004	131.60	165.30
2005	141.60	177.30
2006	150.00	185.00
2007	160.00	195.00

termed an 'early childcare supplement', the payment is not conditional on parents incurring formal childcare costs. It is, in effect, distinguishable from CB only in its restriction to children aged under six and it being paid quarterly rather than monthly.

The strengths and weaknesses of CB can be summarised as follows.

Strengths
- CB is easy for people to understand. It is easily grasped that support is available and how much that support is. The qualifying condition (rearing a child) has no stigma attached to it.

- The process of application is once-off and simple. An application form must be filled in and a prompt response follows the provision of the essential information.

Arrangements are underway whereby the registration of a child's birth will automatically result in an application form for CB being sent without waiting for a parent first to request it.

- CB is the same for people in employment and people on social welfare, for people parenting alone and for couples. People may exit or enter employment, exit or enter welfare receipt and exit or enter 'couple relationships' without their entitlement to CB being affected.

Weaknesses
- Because CB is paid on behalf of almost all children in the state and regardless of parental income, it is an expensive programme. At the same time, it is unable to claim a significant impact on any one of its triple objectives. Even after the substantial increases since 2001, it is far from sufficient to prevent poverty on its own, to cover the costs of formal childcare on its own or to be considered to constitute – on its own – a wage for caring.

- As a poverty-alleviation measure, CB is not efficient. This is because it is paid wherever children are present and irrespective of children's actual needs. It was estimated in 2006 that 18.4 per cent of total expenditure on CB was received by the poorest 20 per cent of families in the state, while 42.4 per cent was received by families in the top half of the income distribution.

- The alignment of CB with all children in the state has been blurred by two recent developments. The large numbers of EU nationals working in the Irish economy mean it is now paid on behalf of a non-negligible number of children not resident in Ireland.[27] The introduction of the Habitual Residence Condition has made its payment on behalf of the children of 'third country' nationals living in Ireland no longer automatic.

A direction for reform

Reflecting on why and how the current child income supports have developed, and seeing the strengths and weaknesses of each instrument, begs the question of whether, and if so how, the system can be improved. There are rumblings in the undergrowth. The NESC, for example, 'believes that the continuing high levels of child income poverty constitute a very poor return to the State and society from the major increase in spending on child income supports which has taken place' (2005a, p. 155). It goes further: 'the continuation of existing policies is not desirable in the medium-term'. The NESC proposes two clear objectives for child income support policy over the coming years: (i) give priority to children in low-income households in allocating additional resources, and (ii) treat low-income families equitably. The second objective is more difficult. The search is on, in effect, for an instrument that would channel support only to children in low-income households, reach all such children and be triggered solely by low family income. There are interesting examples of such instruments in other countries (particularly in Australia, Canada and the UK) from which significant lessons can be learned.

---

[27] The value of Ireland's CB is significant from the perspective of several of the new EU member states; for example, its value for two children in 2006 (€150 * 2) was greater than monthly earnings on the minimum wage – adjusted for purchasing power – in Latvia (€240) and Lithuania (€292) (Eurostat, 2006).

The operation of a targeted, second-tier payment is illustrated in Figure 3.1. Where family income is below a certain threshold, the family receives a maximum payment per child in addition to CB (the chart assumes – for illustration purposes only – that the payment is the same again as CB). Unlike CB, however, this second-tier payment is not universal but is withdrawn accordingly as family income is higher than the set threshold (the chart assumes a 20 per cent withdrawal rate). At high levels of family income, therefore, families do not receive the payment at all but only CB. As the chart illustrates, three key parameters largely determine the impact and overall cost of such a payment: the threshold to family income below which the full payment is made, the level of the full payment and the rate at which the payment is withdrawn.

Figure 3.1: The basic parameters of an income-related, second-tier child payment

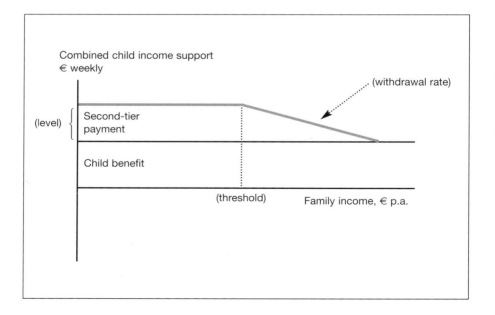

It is easy to describe such a second-tier payment but the administrative difficulties are formidable. For example, it requires, vitally, that, somewhere in the public administrative system, information on the level of income in all households with children is routinely, comprehensively and reliably captured.

Conclusions

This chapter opened by pointing to the continuing serious problem of children being reared in households with low money incomes. There have been major improvements in this area since 1987. There has been a significant rise in the real incomes of families reliant on social welfare and the poorest children in the state today have a significantly higher standard of living than their counterparts twenty years ago. However, in light of Ireland's hugely improved economic and employment situation, and the major investment that has taken place in child income supports which are now at a good level by international standards, the numbers of children below the different income poverty lines in Ireland remain disappointingly high.

In part, this is a challenge to the current structure of child income support in Ireland and an invitation to redesign it, if necessary by creating a new instrument. In particular, a policy shift that privileged CB as the best instrument for channelling income support to low-income families has run its course and a fresh willingness and capacity to prioritise low-income families is now needed and beginning to emerge. FIS has been made more generous and its pro-child rather than pro-employment credentials strengthened, and the first increase in CDAs since 1994 took place in 2007. However, a step-change in the willingness to prioritise children in low-income families, this author argues, would mean acknowledging that flaws remain basic to CDAs and FIS and that it is imperative to tackle the administrative challenges of finally introducing a second-tier child income support that treats all low-income families equally. This would be neutral as to the composition of families' incomes (social welfare, self-employment or employee earnings), paid in full when family income is low, withdrawn gradually as family income rises and not paid at all to families with high incomes.

However, while there is unfinished business with regard to the structure of child income support in Ireland, child income support will less and less be where the action is over the coming years if, or hopefully as, further inroads are made into reducing child poverty. On the one hand, child income support is now at a good level by international standards; on the other hand, child poverty is increasingly associated with jobless parents. Our mindset should now shift, from trying to ensure that the costs of rearing children do not pull households into poverty, to ensuring that jobless adults do not pull children into poverty. The two approaches are complementary of course, but their emphases are different. The first focuses on ensuring children do not heighten the poverty risk facing a household, the second on the poverty risk facing working-aged adults.

The level of adult welfare payments has always been important to children's financial circumstances. Currently, in small families (less than three children), the adult welfare payment typically accounts for a much larger component of family income than child income transfers do. This means adult welfare rates have considerable leverage in those situations to raise children out of income poverty. It is more difficult, however, to make the case for major increases in welfare payments to people of working age in a full employment economy than it is to raise income support 'on behalf of' children. Child poverty campaigners then enter the complex debate of how to raise welfare payments to working-aged adults substantially without creating dependency. Ideally, the higher payment should instead generate a dynamic that motivates and requires the adult recipient to become more self-reliant (NESC, 2005b). Significant further inroads into child poverty, therefore, are likely to hinge particularly on success in removing the obstacles that face low-skilled women in accessing education, training or employment, and on the unfolding of the Department of Social and Family Affairs' new social and economic programme for delivering more intensive engagement on an individual basis with all people of working age in receipt of social welfare.

While the structure of child income supports and the levels of and arrangements governing adult welfare payments are areas where changes will contribute to further reducing child poverty, it is necessary to keep household income in perspective. Some parents' mental or physical health, addictions and/or lifestyles make their children extremely unlikely to benefit from additional income transfers to the household. In these circumstances, the household's need for income has to be seized as a 'developmental opportunity' for challenging and empowering the parents to move forward in their lives, as a result of which their children stand to benefit in an irreplaceable way. On a broader level still, there is the need to learn from, and act on, the research into child wellbeing (including what makes children resilient despite socio-economic disadvantages). This underlines the crucial influences on child development and child wellbeing of non-monetary factors, namely the quality of the bonds they have with their parents, the quality of their neighbourhoods etc. It would be a tragedy if, while Ireland successfully climbed the international rankings for how well the material wellbeing of children is cared for, Irish children's overall wellbeing fell, as more of them became victims of stressful home situations and less child-friendly environments.

References

Bradbury, B. and Jäntti, M. (2001), 'Child Poverty Across the Industrialised World: Evidence from the Luxembourg Income Study', in K. Vleminckx and T. Smeeding (eds.), *Child Well-Being, Child Poverty and Child Policy in Modern Nations,* Bristol: The Policy Press

Bradshaw, J. and Finch, N. (2002), *A Comparison of Child Benefit Packages in 22 Countries – A Summary of the Child Benefit Package for Each Country*, York: University of York

Brewer, M. (2003), *What Do the Child Poverty Targets Mean for the Child Tax Credit? An Update*, Briefing Note no. 41, London: Institute for Fiscal Studies

Commission on Social Welfare (1986), *Report*, Dublin: Government Publications

Corak, M., Lietz, C. and Sutherland, H. (2005), *The Impact of Tax and Transfer Systems on Children in the European Union*, New York: UNICEF

Cournède, B. (2006), 'Removing Obstacles to Employment for Women in Ireland', *Economics Department Working Papers*, no. 511, Paris: OECD

CSO (2006), *EU Survey on Income and Living Conditions (EU-SILC) 2005*, Dublin: Central Statistics Office

DSFA (annual), *Statistical Information on Social Welfare Services*, Dublin: Department of Social and Family Affairs

DSFA (2004), *Review of the Back to School Clothing and Footwear Allowance Scheme*, Dublin: Department of Social and Family Affairs

DSFA (2006), *Government Discussion Paper: Proposals for Supporting Lone Parents*, Dublin: Department of Social and Family Affairs

Eurostat (2006), *Statistics in Focus. Population and Social Conditions*, no. 9, Luxembourg: Eurostat

Expert Working Group (1996), *Integration of the Tax and Social Welfare Systems*, Dublin: Stationery Office

Förster, M. and d'Ercole, M. M. (2005), 'Income Distribution and Poverty in OECD Countries in the Second Half of the 1990s', *OECD Social, Employment and Migration Working Papers*, no. 22, Paris: OECD

Ireland (1985), *Building on Reality*, Dublin: Stationery Office

Ireland (1995), *A Programme for Renewal*, Dublin: Stationery Office

Ireland (2002), *Building an Inclusive Society*, Dublin: Stationery Office

Ireland (2006), *Towards 2016: Ten-Year Framework Social Partnership Agreement 2007–2016*, Dublin: Stationery Office

McKeown, K. and Haase, T. (2006), *The Mental Health of Children and the Factors Which Influence It: A Study of Families in Ballymun*, Dublin: Ballymun Development Group for Children and Young People: www.youngballymun.org

NESC (2003), *An Investment in Quality: Services, Inclusion and Enterprise*, report no. 111, Dublin: National Economic and Social Council

NESC (2005a), *NESC Strategy 2006: People, Productivity and Purpose*, report no. 114, Dublin: National Economic and Social Council

NESC (2005b), *The Developmental Welfare State*, report no. 113, Dublin: National Economic and Social Council

UNICEF (2005), 'Child Poverty in Rich Countries', Report Card 5, Florence: Innocenti Research Centre

UNICEF (2007), 'Child Poverty in Perspective: An Overview of Child Well-Being in Rich Countries', Report Card 7, Florence: Innocenti Research Centre

Appendix

Table A3.1: Calculation of FIS

2006

Number of children	FIS income limits*	Income unemployed** (€) [UA+QAA+CDA]	Ratio (1)/(2)	Maximum FIS payment	FIS support per child (€)	Support for additional child as % of support for 1st child	Total FIS payment as % of income if unemployed (UA)	Range of earnings over which 60% withdrawal rate operative (€)
	(1)	(2)	(3)	(4)	(5)	(6)	(7)	(8)
1	465	292.6	1.59	103.44	103.44	–	0.35	172.40
2	510	309.4	1.65	120.36	60.18	0.58	0.39	200.60
3	565	326.2	1.73	143.28	47.76	0.46	0.44	238.80
4	630	343.0	1.84	172.20	43.05	0.42	0.50	287.00
5	705	359.8	1.96	207.12	41.42	0.40	0.58	345.20
6	775	376.6	2.06	239.04	39.84	0.39	0.63	398.40
7	845	393.4	2.15	270.96	38.71	0.37	0.69	451.60
8+	905	410.2	2.21	296.88	37.11	0.36	0.72	494.80

Table A3.1: Calculation of FIS (contd)

2004

Number of children	FIS income limits*	Income unemployed** (€) [UA+QAA+CDA]	Ratio (1)/(2)	Maximum FIS payment	FIS support per child (€)	Support for additional child as % of support for 1st child	Total FIS payment as % of income if unemployed (UA)	Range of earnings over which 60% withdrawal rate operative (€)
	(1)	(2)	(3)	(4)	(5)	(6)	(7)	(8)
1	407	241.0	1.69	99.60	99.60	–	0.41	166.00
2	433	257.8	1.68	105.12	52.56	0.53	0.41	175.20
3	458	274.6	1.67	110.04	36.68	0.37	0.40	183.40
4	483	291.4	1.66	114.96	28.74	0.29	0.39	191.60
5	515	308.2	1.67	124.08	24.82	0.25	0.40	206.80
6	541	325.0	1.66	129.60	21.60	0.22	0.40	216.00
7	562	341.8	1.64	132.12	18.87	0.19	0.39	220.20
8+	584	358.6	1.63	135.24	16.91	0.17	0.38	225.40

* Net family income, that is gross pay minus tax, employee PRSI, health contribution and any superannuation
** Based on social welfare rates as of 1 January of corresponding year. Earnings disregard not reckoned with

Chapter 4

Working-aged people and welfare policy

Mary Murphy

> ... an Ireland where all people of working age have
> sufficient income and opportunity to participate as fully
> as possible in economic and social life ...
>
> (Ireland, 2007, p. 40)

Introduction

The maxim 'a job is the best route out of poverty' and the
language of 'working-aged' are now firmly rooted in anti-
poverty and social inclusion discourse. Elsewhere, however,
this concept of 'working-aged' has been ideologically
contested. To suggest that someone of working age can work
may also be interpreted as suggesting they should work. As
Levitas observes, the language of working age constructs
social exclusion as 'non-participation in the labour market'
(2001, p. 451). She concludes there are anti-poverty
implications when a priority focus on labour market
attachment exists without parallel strategies to enhance
welfare generosity for those who remain without employment
or to examine wider ethnic and gender structural inequalities
in that labour market and implications for care and other

unpaid work. A policy that aspires to all working-aged social welfare claimants having an attachment to the labour market has, therefore, very important anti-poverty, rights and gender implications. These will be discussed throughout this chapter.

The chapter is divided into two parts. The first examines how the concept and definition of 'working-aged' has evolved and then explores recent key changes, continuities and challenges for particular subgroups of the 18 to 65 (or working) age group: the traditional 'unemployed', people with disabilities and different groups of women including lone parents, qualified adults (wives and partners of social welfare claimants) and carers. This part concludes by defining the working-aged population and examining the changing composition of the working-aged at risk of poverty. The second part of the chapter examines the policy responses to joblessness. The focus is on five distinct but overlapping policy areas: welfare adequacy, making work pay, improving the quality of employment, enhancing family-friendly employment and activation strategies. The chapter concludes by considering the institutional reforms necessary to achieve the *National Action Plan for Social Inclusion 2007–2016* (Ireland, 2007) targets and whether such targets offer hope to people of working age.

What is working-aged and who is working-aged?

The definition of who is considered to be within the scope of 'working-aged' has changed over time. Seventy was considered the upper limit of the legal working age for many years, but this was reduced to 66 years in 1973. It is likely in future years that, on equality grounds, this older age barrier to work will be removed. The 12 years of age considered the minimum legal working age in 1926 had risen to 16 years by 2006, however Irish policy focuses on 18 years as the lower age for inclusion in working-aged policy and this chapter defines working-aged as between 18 and 65 years. Just as the age definition has changed over time so too has the scope of who is considered to be part of the working-aged population. Recently both women and people with disabilities have been more fully embraced within the concept of working age.

The size of the working-aged population also changes with the size of the total population. It had risen from 1,300,000 in 1926 to 2,600,000 people in 2006. This group comprises over 2,100,000 in employment and a further 601,979 adults of working age claiming social welfare payments (Ireland, 2007). People of working age who are recipients of social welfare payments are at risk of poverty and have been the primary focus of various national employment action plans and anti-poverty strategies. The 2002 revised NAPS (Ireland, 2002) introduced a range of indicators about economic activity in the adult working-aged group. This reflected progression to a broader working-aged strategy and was consistent with the EU open method of coordination of social inclusion and employment policy. The different experiences of key subgroups of working-aged social welfare claimants – unemployed, people with disabilities, lone parents, qualified adults and carers – are now reviewed in turn. This part ends by reviewing the shift in composition of the working-aged at risk of poverty.

The unemployed

As in every country, the definition and measurement formulae for calculating who is without work in Ireland are socially constructed political choices. The choice of how to define and measure unemployment has been contested throughout the last twenty years. 'Unemployment' in the mid-1980s applied only to those available for and seeking full-time work and appearing on the 'live register', an administrative record of those receiving some form of unemployment compensation. This precluded, by definition, many women seeking only part-time work who could not provide childcare cover for their children. It also left invisible those ineligible for an insurance or means-tested unemployment payment or credit and unable to 'register' as unemployed. Failure to access the live register had consequences: these people could not access labour market programmes to help them find work, education or training. Over time the use of the live register to measure unemployment was debated.

A Labour Force Survey measurement based on the International Labour Organization's (ILO) definition of unemployment – recently actively seeking work of at least one hour per week – is now generally accepted as a more accurate definition of who is immediately available for work. However this definition excludes those who have not recently actively sought employment and so under-estimates the numbers of 'inactive' unemployed. The principal economic status (PES) definition, based on a self-assessment definition of unemployment, includes those presently inactive but who, given encouragement and supports, could work.

The INOU (2007) argues that the 4.5 per cent unemployment rate in 2007 (based on the ILO definition of unemployment but updated by live register trends) is not a true reflection of unemployment. It argues a PES definition (approximately 10 per cent in 2005) would be more accurate. A recent OECD development which measures 'latent' labour force supply (or labour force reserve) was applied by the NESF (2006) to estimate that approximately 75,000 Irish people are not included in the formal definition of unemployment. From a gender equality perspective, all these definitions are problematic in that they define employment and job-search activity according to male norms and render women's unemployment patterns less visible.[1]

From the perspective of unemployment, the differences between 1987, 1997 and 2007 Ireland are striking. Like many EU countries in 1987, Ireland was a bleak place. In the early to mid-1980s, global industrial restructuring meant significant job losses in key urban, low-skilled employment. By 1985, 230,000 were on the live register. The scale of unemployment and social misery cannot be understood without taking into account the very high annual levels of emigration which peaked at around 50,000 in 1986. Despite such high levels of emigration, live register unemployment peaked at 300,000 in January 1993 before declining to its lowest point of 135,000 in May 2001 (it had risen to 155,000 by January 2007).

Those households who find themselves unemployed have always experienced a high incidence of both relative income and consistent poverty. Relative income poverty rates decreased from 51.4 per cent in 1994 to settle stubbornly at around 40.6 per cent in 2004 (CSO, 2005). The very real hardship associated with unemployment is demonstrated by

---

[1] Only those seeking full-time work and entitled to compensation for unemployment can be on the live register. Only those actively seeking work can be counted in the ILO definition and, because the PES allows only one definition of a personal identity, those with the primary identity of homemaker, even if seeking work, do not label themselves as unemployed.

the numbers who suffered consistent poverty: 19.2 per cent in 2004 when the rate for the population as a whole was 6.8 per cent (CSO, 2005). The risk of poverty translated into real and significant psychological distress with the unemployed suffering seven times higher mental distress than those employed, even when those employed where in low-paid, temporary job contracts (Whelan, 1994). For women, the impact of poverty was even greater with the pressure of managing money and debt problems leaving them with higher levels of stress and ill health.

While the agricultural restructuring of previous decades impacted most heavily on rural communities, global economic restructuring has impacted on all Irish society but was felt most keenly by working-class families in small towns and in the inner-city and working-class suburban areas of cities. Given the scale of unemployment in the late 1980s and early 1990s, government responses were largely limited to containing the immediate ills of unemployment and poverty and the focus was on maintaining the real value of welfare payments. 1988 saw the first community-based social employment schemes[2] and in 1992 the government established the first twelve local 'area-based partnerships' of community and statutory service-providers, which focused on integrated service delivery in areas hardest hit by unemployment. The impact of long-term unemployment, experienced by over 40 per cent of live register claimants, was examined by the NESF (1994). This report recognised the barriers and obstacles to employment and led to the

---

[2] Later replaced by the community employment development programme, which was in turn replaced by the community development scheme.

establishment of the Local Employment Services Network (LESN) targeted at those finding most difficulty accessing employment.

Government macro responses to unemployment, largely channelled through social partnership, led to economic growth but it was a type of jobless growth. The trend turned in the mid-1990s and significant job creation led to record job growth in the late 1990s. The challenge became addressing labour market structural blockages and removing the obstacles to unemployed people taking up these jobs. In 1996, emigration trends turned and, for the first time since the 1970s, Ireland experienced net immigration. Innovative back to work allowances and tax reforms aimed at the lower paid improved the return from paid employment and LESN supported people who had previously lost all hope of ever getting paid work again to get back into employment.

In this optimistic environment the first *National Anti-Poverty Strategy* (NAPS) placed employment as the central route out of poverty and established relatively ambitious targets to reduce both unemployment and long-term unemployment (Ireland, 1997). Steady erosion of unemployment led to a revision of such targets in 2002 to decrease unemployment among vulnerable groups to the national average, to eliminate long-term unemployment by 2007 and to achieve a 70 per cent economic participation rate (and 60 per cent for women) by 2007 (Ireland, 2002). These targets were not changed in the NAPinclusion (Ireland, 2007) even though the economic participation targets are largely accomplished. The target to eliminate long-term unemployment has not yet been achieved, the 1.3 per cent long-term unemployment rate represents almost 30,000 people or one-quarter of all unemployed. Access to employment or economic inclusion

remains very uneven; Travellers for example have employment rates of only 17 per cent and over 40 per cent unemployment (Ireland, 2007).

People with disabilities

Disability not only impacts on the likelihood of finding work but also on the likelihood of finding decently paid work (Gannon and Nolan, 2004). People with disabilities have a 37 per cent employment rate and over 190,000 working-aged people with disabilities are without paid employment (Ireland, 2007). In 1986, the figure of 80,000 claiming disability benefit was considered above the norm for this type of payment and a concerted effort to tighten controls and access to the payment had reduced numbers to 42,000 by 1994 (albeit numbers claiming the longer term invalidity pension rose by 14,000 over the same period). A health board administered disabled persons' maintenance allowance was reformed in 1996 to disability allowance administered by the Department of Social and Family Affairs, and numbers claiming this have grown from 34,500 in 1996 to 62,800 in 2002 to over 79,000 in 2005. While growth in the labour force and general population will lead to increased numbers claiming disability payments, both FÁS (2004) and the NESC (2005) comment that the value of decreasing unemployment has been offset by increases in numbers claiming disability and lone-parent payments and that the average length of these claims is a cause for concern.

People with disabilities experience a significantly high risk of poverty. They also experience a significantly higher risk of consistent poverty: in 2004 terms, 21.7 per cent experienced deprivation compared to 6.8 per cent of the total population (CSO, 2005). Men with disabilities experience a 52.9 per cent risk of poverty while women with disabilities experience a 38 per cent risk of poverty (CSO, 2005). While *Towards 2016* (Ireland, 2006) commits to including people with disabilities in the national employment action plan, the NAPinclusion (Ireland, 2007) has a more limited ambition and adopts a short-term target of only 7,000 people with disabilities accessing employment by 2010. In the longer term it aims to increase the employment participation rate of people with disabilities by 8 per cent to 45 per cent by 2016. This clearly leaves the majority of working-aged people with disabilities vulnerable to poverty.

Lone parents

Until recently, Irish policy, located in a strong breadwinner welfare regime, firmly supported lone parents as mothers not workers. Irish policy, by providing a specific payment to enable full-time caregiving (like Norway, New Zealand and Australia), strongly recognised the social right to give and receive care (Slevik, 2005). The 1994 lone-parent allowance shifted this policy by introducing disregards for income, travel and childcare to facilitate employment and participation in active labour market programmes. 1997 reforms renamed the allowance 'one-parent family payment' (OPFP), introduced more work incentives but maintained the choice to parent full time. Since then policy and discourse have shifted towards a stronger employment focus and in 2006 formal proposals were made to introduce a work obligation for lone parents (DSFA, 2006b). *Towards 2016* commits to including lone parents, like people with disabilities, in the remit of the national employment action plan.

While Irish lone parents have less economic participation than women in general (47 per cent compared to 60 per cent), when compared to married women with children their participation rates are more or less equal (Rahaleen, 2006). However, despite this level of work participation, 80 per cent of Irish households headed by lone parents are in receipt of some form of social welfare payment and lone parents in receipt of OPFP are at the most extreme risk of poverty in the state. In 2004, compared to a national average of 6.8 per cent, 31.1 per cent of lone parents experienced consistent poverty and over 40 per cent were likely to experience debt (CSO, 2005). Children and adults in lone-parent households experienced a 48.3 per cent risk of relative poverty compared to a national average of 19.4 per cent. Female lone parents experienced a slightly higher risk of poverty than male lone parents.

As with disability payments, negative comment has been made about the growth in the numbers of lone parents claiming social welfare and in the average duration of such claims. Recently numbers have stabilised, with only a 0.3 per cent rise of 263 lone parents from 2004 to 2005, however the total number of lone parents now exceeds numbers on unemployment or disability allowances.

Qualified adults (wives and partners)

There were 119,223 qualified adults in the Irish social welfare system in 2005 (DSFA, 2006a). There is no age breakdown of this group available but 62,447 live with an old age social welfare recipient and are likely to be of pension age or at the older end of the working age range. Nonetheless, given that over 124,801 children in such households are fully dependent and 83,348 children are partially dependent on social welfare, households with qualified adults should be a key target for a social inclusion strategy. Arrowsmith (2004) argues that investment will meet the direct social and employment needs these adults have in their own right but their activation may also trigger their spouses' or partners' activation.

Qualified adults appear to have a lower employment participation rate than lone parents. They are involved in peripheral labour market activity (cleaning, care and hospitality sectors) and limit employment to remain within qualified adult means test thresholds (Murphy, 2003). The labour market needs of qualified adults and other women married to or cohabiting with social welfare claimants or low-paid male workers were examined by a social partnership working group (Ireland, 2000). However, despite some technical income disregard changes in 1996 and facilitation of a 'swap' in entitlement to labour market programmes between spouses, there was little structural change to facilitate such women to access employment (Murphy, 2003). Qualified adults are included in the broad vision of reforms proposed in the 2006 DSFA *Proposals to Support Lone Parents* and Budget 2007 reformed qualified adults' income disregards to make them consistent with jobseeker's allowance disregards. However qualified adults are not afforded the same visibility or priority in working-aged discourse as lone parents (Murphy, 2007). There is more societal and political ambiguity about obliging married working-aged mothers to access paid employment. A second group with little visibility are spouses of low-paid workers, who tend to return to only low-paid, part-time employment (Russell *et al.*, 2004) and who need access to appropriate quality labour market supports if they are to progress to decent employment.

Carers

The needs of low-income couples can be very complicated. While they share characteristics such as class, education, ethnic group and age, they also appear to share co-dependent health, disability and addiction issues. Health barriers of one partner affect the other partner. Many of the 25,000 Irish qualified adults living with an illness/disability-related recipient are likely to have significant unpaid care obligations. Given the complicated and inconsistent relationship between spouses' social welfare income disregards and taxes, the financial implications of employment are complex and harder to negotiate. With or without such barriers, care of children or adult relatives and associated domestic barriers are the primary obstacles to work for many working-aged women.

Policy must realistically take into account what needs to be done to enable access to employment but also to make employment more accommodating of the reality of caring obligations. Up to 1990, income support for care of relatives was addressed by a very limited prescribed relative's allowance. This was replaced in 1990 by a carer's allowance, which was then gradually improved in scale and scope over the 1990s and early 2000s so that by 2005 almost 25,000 claimed carer's allowance and 870 claimed carer's benefit. Budget 2007 changes allow social welfare claimants who are caring full time for a relative to claim a half-rate carer's allowance in addition to their own social welfare. This is likely to be attractive to many low-income working-aged women and could distract from the longer term, paid-employment route out of poverty. Policy, recognising the long-term poverty trap associated with caring, now also allows carers to maintain attachment to the labour market by working ten hours per week in paid employment. While in some ways all such changes are laudable, it has to be asked whether women (by far the primary recipients of carer's allowance) are being pushed towards a triple burden of childcare, adult care and paid employment and how this is related to the mental and physical health of these women.

Shift in composition of working-aged at risk of poverty

One of the more remarkable trends in Ireland over the period from 1986 to 2006 was the shift in the composition of types of households at risk of poverty (see Table 4.1). Over time, as unemployment decreased, the likelihood of unemployment being a risk factor for households experiencing poverty diminished. In 1994, 41 per cent of families experiencing poverty were unemployed; by 2000, the corresponding figure was 9.8 per cent. The reduction of unemployment as a risk factor for poverty between 1994 and 2004 occurred in parallel to increases in the risk of poverty for other groups of the working-aged – people with disabilities, lone parents, carers and asylum seekers without permission to work (CSO, 2005).[3] Lone parents comprise only 4 per cent of the total population but 15 per cent of the consistently poor population. Other working-aged groups also suffer significant risk of poverty, for example 13.1 per cent of migrants and 21.6 per cent of the traditional unemployed, compared to an average risk of 6.5 per cent (Ireland, 2007). Over the decade 1995 to 2005, numbers claiming disability and one-parent family payments increased as unemployment payments decreased. This meant

---

[3] Retired people's risk of poverty increased from 30 per cent in 1994 to over 56 per cent in 2000 before falling back to 47.3 per cent in 2004. The lack of economic opportunity and participation when working age leads directly to poverty in retirement is discussed further in Chapter 5.

that the overall numbers of working-aged welfare claims remained relatively static, even though the composition of those claiming welfare shifted. While the level of working-aged claiming benefits seems high, it is roughly comparable to other countries such as the UK and Sweden (Cousins, 2005).

Table 4.1: Composition of Irish working-aged, 1985 and 2000

	1985	2000
Working-aged on welfare	555,000	500,000
as a % of population	26	20
of which		
Unemployed (%)	55	30
Disabled (%)	6	20
Lone parents (%)	5	18
Other (%)	34	32

Source: NESC, 2005

Policies to promote access to employment for working-aged claimants

The shift in the composition of the working-aged poor caused both international and national commentators to switch attention from the problem of 'unemployment' to the problem of 'joblessness' in the larger working-aged population. *The Developmental Welfare State* (NESC, 2005), the most recent construction of Irish social policy, moved the debate away from unemployment towards the concepts of working-aged and joblessness. The challenge for social inclusion policy is no longer to end unemployment but to achieve economic inclusion. The decision to rename unemployment payments 'jobseeker' payments symbolically reflects this new policy consensus. But more substantial policy changes are required to realise the ambition of economic and social inclusion for all. The remainder of this chapter reflects on each of the following working-aged policy challenges.

- *Defining the target group* – Who are the target group for working-aged policies under the social inclusion strategy (Ireland, 2007)?
- *Welfare adequacy* – What needs to be done to ensure that those who cannot access work will have alternative routes out of poverty?
- *Making work pay* – How can we ensure that the focus on the working-aged will impact positively on poverty for all people of working age and their families?
- *Quality of employment and work–life balance* – How can we ensure that labour market policy is gender-sensitive and respects social rights and care choices?
- *Flexibility and activation* – How can we promote a more active system and what institutional changes are required to shift from a system that prioritised managing high unemployment to a quality system promoting higher economic participation?

Defining the working-aged target group
The first challenge is defining the larger population of working-aged compared to the previously narrow unemployed target.[4] The numbers of working-aged persons

---

[4] While there is an overlap between those economically active and those claiming social welfare, not all the social-welfare-claiming section of the working-aged population (approximately 45 per cent of whom are men and 55 per cent women) are actively seeking work or even want to work. Government working-aged social inclusion targets refer to the numbers of working-aged totally dependent on social welfare income. This excludes those in part-time or government-supported (contd)

that the government wishes to target to promote lifelong labour market attachment could be as high as half a million.[5] There is no clear definition of who the government considers to be within the scope of the latest social inclusion targets, which makes it difficult to monitor such targets (Ireland, 2007). It also makes it difficult to assess whether there are sufficient numbers of decent jobs available or whether the government has invested in the scale of resources necessary to provide this number of people with sufficient quality supports to access decent employment adequate to the task of lifting them out of poverty? The NAPinclusion (Ireland, 2007) suggests, for example, supporting 50,000 in case management. It is not clear how this target is related to the target of reducing by 20 per cent the number of those whose total income is derived from long-term social welfare payments by 2016.

---

4   (contd) employment from inclusion in the target and also excludes 118,000 qualified adults depending on social welfare income and women living on low incomes and at risk of poverty (many of these women wish to have some form of labour market attachment).

5   In 2004 (DSFA, 2006a), for example, the numbers unemployed were 131,539 but there were an additional 470,947 of working-aged and a total of 602,486 of working-aged depending on social welfare. One proxy or method for estimating the target of long-term social welfare claimants is the number of working-aged depending on social assistance and means-tested social welfare payments. Of these the main payments are one-parent family payment (80,103), disability allowance (72,976), unemployment assistance (3,840), pre-retirement allowance (11,228), widow's allowance (15,284), deserted wives' allowance (1,458), farm assist (8,350), supplementary welfare allowance (30,748) and carer's allowance (23,030). Of the social insurance payments, the most discussed targets are unemployment benefit (57,699) and disability benefit (58,726). This would give a total of 433,442.

Welfare adequacy

Social welfare income remains the primary anti-poverty tool for working-aged people without paid employment. If the most recent NAPinclusion (Ireland, 2007) strategy's target of reducing the numbers of working-aged claiming social welfare by 20 per cent is successful, it will still leave 80 per cent of the present social-welfare-dependent working-aged (up to 400,000 people) on welfare. The traditional Irish principle of social security design was to keep payments relatively ungenerous in order to promote and maintain the incentive to work. This raises the policy issue of social welfare adequacy.

Relatively low social welfare rates are a direct cause of the high risk of poverty presently experienced by people of working age (Callan, 2006). In 2004, for example, working-aged social assistance and benefit payments were worth approximately 65 per cent of the poverty threshold (60 per cent of average disposable income). When compared to Northern Ireland or the UK (where payments are set at only 40 per cent of the poverty threshold), the Irish rate seems relatively generous. However compared to Nordic rates (Norway 70 per cent, Sweden 89 per cent, Finland 121 per cent and Denmark 147 per cent), Irish rates are relatively low.

Substantial increases in Budgets 2005, 2006 and 2007 brought the lowest adult social welfare payments to approximately 30 per cent of the gross average industrial wage.[6] However the 2007 combination of child and adult

---

[6] Despite increases over the last number of budgets, analysis by OPEN (2006) shows the combination of social welfare supports for one-parent families (at €248.18 per week in 2006) to be up to €25 per week below what was required to be above the 2006 poverty line (estimated to be €273.62 per week).

social welfare payments is still only 90 per cent of what is required to lift one-parent families above the poverty line. Callan (2006) reflects that, while support to take up employment needs to be a key anti-poverty policy, adult social welfare rates are also critical for tackling adult and child poverty. Benchmarking and indexing social welfare minimum income standards needs a more central place in anti-poverty and social inclusion strategies. In the context of defining poverty as the 'inability to participate in normal activity', the minimum income standard has to be set at a rate that not only addresses deprivation-based poverty but also addresses relative income poverty. Goal five of the 2007 NAPinclusion – which sets a target to maintain, as resources allow, the value of the present weekly payment (€185.60 in 2007) – is a relatively weak anti-poverty adequacy target. It is a contingent target which commits to updating a still inadequate payment by an unstated indexation methodology.

Making work pay

The focus on work activation assumes of course that a job is the best route out of poverty. Overall evidence suggests this is indeed the case – only 1.7 per cent of those in employment experience consistent poverty (Ireland, 2007). However the extent to which people in employment may be at risk of poverty is a concern for policy-makers. The 'working poor' comprise a distinct group of employees experiencing relative poverty. EU data show that in the EU-25 up to 7 per cent of the employed population (14 million people) lived in households with income below the poverty line in 2001. Of the EU-15, 11 million workers or 20 million people (6 per cent of the population) lived in households with income below the poverty line, working poverty impacting on over one-third of those at risk of poverty (Vermeylen, 2004). In Ireland the percentage of working poor increased from 3.2 per cent in 1994 to 7.4 per cent in 2000 and 9.8 per cent in 2004 (CSO, 2005).

In trying to understand the policy challenges involved in making sure employment is indeed a route out of poverty, it is necessary to differentiate between 'low pay' and 'working poor'. Vermeylen (2004) defines the working poor as 'individuals who are employed or self-employed and whose household disposable income is less than 60% of national medium income'. This should be distinguished from the definition of the low-waged as 'workers earning less than two-thirds of (hourly, weekly, yearly) medium earnings' (Nolan and Marx, 2000). Ireland has one of the smallest overlaps between low pay and poverty of any EU country. Most low-waged workers live in non-poor households and this protects the individual on a low wage from experiencing poverty. Indeed income from low wages takes up to one-third of low-paid men, one-fifth of low-paid women and over 50 per cent of low-paid separated, divorced or widowed women out of the poverty net (Nolan and Marx, 2000).

Other low-waged workers are heads of households with no other adult working and/or with child dependants. Their individual wages are insufficient to take these households out of poverty. Lone parents are particularly vulnerable in this regard as childcare reduces the possibility of full-time work. Low-paid married men with children and non-working spouses are also a high-risk group. Factors influencing the likelihood of being working poor include employment status, age, sex, education level, contractual status and working time arrangements. Those working in non-standard employment (neither permanent nor full time) are most at risk of being working poor.

Nash (2004) and McCabe (2006) review the economic implications of non-standard employment and highlight how such jobs are concentrated in low-paid, low-skilled sectors and how such workers have less access to training, pensions, health insurance or sick pay cover. Even taking into account human capital differences, non-standard workers still had lower income than standard workers. Non-permanent, part-time workers fared the worst. Women in non-standard employment had a higher risk of poverty and financial strain than their male counterparts, with permanent part-time workers having the highest risk. Ensuring that part-time paid employment lifts people from poverty needs to be part of any gender-sensitive social inclusion strategy. Recent changes have enhanced social security and the labour rights of part-time workers and the NAPinclusion (Ireland, 2007) commits to consider recognising the validity of part-time work choices. This recognises that women have little choice but to work part time (it is often the only way they can financially and ethically reconcile care obligations and economic participation). However the challenge is not only to recognise such work as a valid choice but also to ensure that it is an effective route out of poverty.

Improving the quality of employment
Given the skills and education levels of many working-aged poor, low-paid jobs are likely to be the only short-term realistic employment option. While the establishment of a minimum wage had important anti-poverty advantages, a policy that sought to eradicate low wages fully would impact on employment supply and diminish the very jobs for which unemployed people can compete. The problem needs a more focused solution. More hours may need to be worked, but too many dependants may be relying on income from low-paid

employment. Policy requires measures targeted at working-poor households. Childcare provision needs to enable spouses to access employment and lone parents to increase hours of employment, this means appropriate and affordable childcare (Coakely, 2005). It also means maximising take-home-pay by further improvements in family income supplement or targeted in-work tax-breaks such as in-work refundable tax credits[7] or enhanced child income support such as child benefit supplement or taxable child benefit.

Education and training policy can play a long-term role by enhancing the skill levels of low-paid workers and their children and enabling them to break free of occupational segregation. Women's labour market preparation is dominated by employment programmes with lower progression outcomes and therefore more focus needs to be given to skilled training options. There is no tracking of the types of employment people are accessing through the national employment action plan process. While Indecon (2005) concludes that most unemployed are exiting the live register to low-paid jobs, we in fact know little about the employment and wage trends of those exiting the live register. A direct target to limit the increase in numbers of low-paid workers would be a welcome addition to any social inclusion strategy, as would a commitment to monitor trends in this regard.

Focusing on the working-aged as a policy group has significant gender and equality implications. Attention needs to be paid to the quality of employment in this regard. Brunton

---

[7] CORI (2007), for example, points to the government's failure to devise policies to help low-income families who are at risk of poverty but who do not benefit from mainstream tax changes as, due to their low incomes, they are effectively outside the tax net.

(2006) advises that work 'spillover' into family life can be positive or negative. Work can interact negatively with other parts of life when there is a mismatch between ideal hours and real hours.[8] Positive spillovers (or job satisfaction) lead to an improved home life.[9] The lack of control and choice associated with imposed work requirements, combined with a low-quality job, seem likely to provoke more negative than positive spillovers.

Enhancing family-friendly employment

To date the anti-poverty debate has been largely framed around work requirements without focusing on what needs to be changed in the worlds of care and work to accommodate people's caring and employment needs. The accommodation of a care ethic in labour market and employment policy is key for women. Without restructuring the world of work to accommodate care, women are likely to end up in non-standard and part-time employment, such employment is not a route out of poverty (Nash, 2004). Coakely (2005, p. 3) reflects that Irish mothers' decisions are mediated primarily by childcare responsibilities, they negotiate the world of work from the financial, practical and emotional starting point of a 'moral economy' and prioritise parental responsibility over financial gain. Duncan (2003) argues that failing to account for this ethic of care leads to a 'rationality mistake', where policy-makers over-focus on the financial considerations of making

---

[8] Negative outcomes arise when people feel overworked, parentally stressed, unhappy with their lifestyle choice, too tired and distracted to pay attention to things at home, have scheduling conflicts and their home life is interrupted by work demands and calls.

[9] Positive outcomes include wider social networks and enhanced personal psychological functioning through self-direction, job control and personal autonomy.

work pay at the expense of accommodating the reality of care (Lyons and Lynch, 2005). A welfare-to-work policy informed by an ethics of care would facilitate adult workers to care, encourage family-friendly work practices and facilitate adequate parental leave over the lifetime of the child in a way that addresses family-based gender inequality. Household functions are not shared equally in Ireland, with women working an average twenty hours per week more than men on unpaid household tasks (McGinnity et al., 2005). Initiatives to increase the number of working-aged in paid employment need also to increase the number of hours men spend in unpaid tasks and encourage or compel men to change their behaviour or broaden the scope of their household activities (Williams, 2004).[10]

One of the major obstacles to achieving better work–life balance or family-friendly policy is the attitudes of employers who fear that greater flexibility for employees will threaten economic competitiveness. The evidence from Nordic countries shows high levels of compatibility between competitiveness and work–life balance. However such is the national reverence of competitiveness that even the principle of 'an opportunity to balance work and family commitments' in the NAPinclusion has been deliberately qualified and made contingent on being 'consistent with employers needs' (Ireland, 2007, p. 40). Employers, rather than providing flexible employment, are increasingly requiring employees to be more flexible to suit employers' needs (Murphy, 2007; Duggan and Loftus, 2006). In the absence of satisfactory

---

[10] In 2005, Spain introduced a statutory obligation which obliges men who marry in civil ceremonies to pledge to share domestic responsibilities and the care and attention of children and elderly family members.

voluntary progress through the National Framework Committee on Work–Life Balance, consideration should now be given to a stronger legislative approach and a regulatory framework for work–life balance (Irvine, 2007).

The NAPinclusion qualifies the principle 'that every person with caring responsibilities should have access to appropriate supports to enable them to meet these responsibilities' by adding 'in addition to employment and other commitments' (Ireland, 2007, p. 40). Full-time family commitments are not on offer in this social inclusion strategy. A labour market strategy that obliges work participation is not necessarily gender or child sensitive and there are potentially negative consequences for child and family wellbeing from over-concentrating on work solutions to poverty (O'Brien, 2004). Various social rights (to care for or to be cared for, to child and family wellbeing, to minimum income) could be threatened by an over-zealous or unbalanced approach to employment-based social inclusion. Strong legal safeguards are needed to protect these rights and to ensure fair processes of decision-making (Murphy, 2007).

Class and ethnicity are defining features of working-aged people's lives (Armstrong, 2006). In Ireland there remains a strong societal ethos of respecting (and facilitating through the tax system) support for full-time mothering. This raises the issue of whether it is fair that state supports are being used to subsidise different working-aged choices for different classes of women and men. Class is also a defining feature influencing care and parenting choices. Middle-class childrearing norms are more enabling of maternal employment; working-class childrearing norms (perhaps recognising different opportunity costs) place more emphasis on direct mothering, 'being there' and home-based parenting and childcare options. There are also class differences in the experience of what it means to juggle motherhood and work. Armstrong (2006) differentiates middle-class women with capital resources who negotiate flexibility from working-class women who are required to be flexible. Indeed middle-class women's flexibility often depends on the flexibility of working-class women.

Ethnicity also defines present policy approaches to access to employment as asylum seekers are still denied the right to work. Compared to the national average, migrants have slightly higher economic participation rates but experience more than double the rate of consistent poverty. Given that working-aged migrants are likely to comprise a growing proportion of the working-aged poor, policy and institutional responses need to be sensitive to emerging ethnic trends and needs and to ensure diversity and equality training.[11]

Flexicurity
The ebbs and flows of unemployment are to some extent a function of the international political economy. The threats and opportunities posed by globalisation and global-level industrial restructuring are a constant feature of academic and policy discourse and set the context for Irish labour market and anti-poverty strategies (Scharpf and Schmidt, 2000). The national social inclusion strategy is embedded in the national paradigm of maintaining international competitiveness (Connolly, 2006). This strong national policy

---

[11] The evaluation of the UK New Deal for Lone Parents (Holland, 2005) showed those without English as a first language were least likely to enter employment after work-focused interviews. FÁS (Molloy, 2007) estimates that 50 per cent of people using its employment services in 2006 were non-Irish nationals with one-quarter from Poland.

framework was first established in the *Programme for National Recovery* in 1987 and reinforced in subsequent social partnership strategies, the most recent of which is *Towards 2016* (Ireland, 1987, 2006). As the global economy shifts to a new international mode of production, the Irish economy must be adaptable, flexible and increase its skill base to participate in a new knowledge economy. The NAPinclusion (Ireland, 2007, p. 40) recognises this need for a 'sense of personal security in a changing work environment'.

Various international institutions (Commission of the European Communities, 2006) have introduced the concepts of 'flexicurity' and 'active inclusion' into the anti-poverty debate. Flexicurity is a Danish concept which seeks, in the context of globalisation, to make labour markets more flexible and in return to provide high levels of social security for those in and out of work. As illustrated in Figure 4.1, it requires three interrelated and interdependent policies: active labour market measures, generous public welfare and flexible labour markets.

Figure 4.1: Flexicurity golden triangle

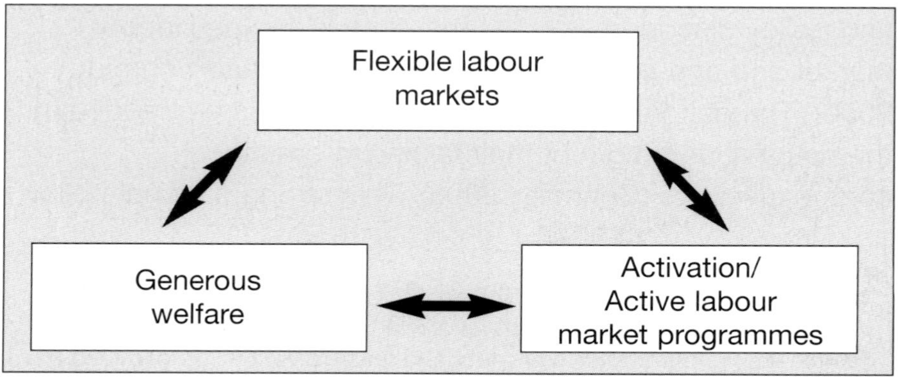

Source: NESC, 2005

How near is Ireland to a functioning model of flexicurity? While Ireland has one of the most flexible labour markets in the world, this flexibility has so far not been compensated for with a generous welfare system involving adequate social welfare rates or quality universal public services. This combination of strong flexibility and limited security means Irish policy is a considerable distance from a fully functioning flexicurity model. The Irish experience of activation and active labour market measures is more mixed but has not yet reached the level of conditionality exercised in Nordic activation policy and implied by flexicurity (Kirby and Murphy, forthcoming). The danger for people of working age who are at risk of poverty is that, in attempting to develop 'an Irish model of flexicurity', haste will be made in achieving higher levels of activation or conditionality without achieving the compensatory generous welfare system. The next section reviews what has been happening with Irish activation policy and addresses what institutional and policy changes are required to effect a more fully functioning working-aged activation policy.

Activation strategies

Active labour market expenditure is a long-standing feature of the Irish welfare state. Since the early 1990s there has been a new focus on 'performative inclusion', which stresses employment as the best route out of poverty (Dukelow, 2004). This focus has shifted public investment towards active labour market spending. Irish spending on active labour market programmes (ALMPs) increased from an already comparatively high 1.46 per cent of GDP in 1985 to 1.53 per cent in 2000, this represents a significant real spending increase given the scale of economic growth over that period (Kirby and Murphy, forthcoming). Between 1994 and 2001, Irish spending on ALMPs was 7.2 per cent of public social expenditure or more than double that of the EU average of 3.3 per cent. These ALMPs were primarily delivered by FÁS through a mix of employment services, training and employment programmes. In the early 1990s, the Department of Social and Family Affairs (then called the Department of Social Welfare) began to develop employment support services to facilitate people into jobs (Dukelow, 2004; McCashin, 2004) and introduced a number of employment subsidies or income supports to enable transition into employment. These included the innovative and widely acclaimed back to work allowance schemes.

The scale of spending on activation measures is more impressive than the actual progression outcomes achieved through activation policy. O'Connell and McGinnity (1997) conclude that while specific skills training and employment subsidies had impressive employment outcomes, general training had only weak, and community employment even weaker, employment outcomes. Denny et al. (2000) and Indecon (2002) stress the importance of active labour market programmes having labour market linkages. Over time, activation policy has become more progression-oriented and linked to participation obligations. Halpin and Hill (2006) review how participation in ALMPs is associated with entry to and exit from poverty and find that employment schemes (but not training schemes) are associated with a greater risk of entry to poverty and a lower chance of exiting poverty. This is explained by a selection effect, the poorest are most likely to have less general employment chances and are more likely to enter an employment scheme.

McCashin (2004) and Boyle (2005) argue compulsion is remarkably absent in the Irish policy regime. Empirical evidence, however, supports the conclusion that policy shows significant supportive *and* punitive changes which combine to push welfare claimants towards employment (Dukelow, 2004; Kirby and Murphy, forthcoming).[12] Historically, job-search conditions always applied to unemployment assistance payments and since the mid-1990s stricter work availability tests have been applied to all unemployment payments. The 1987 jobsearch programme was followed by 1992 legislation increasing and broadening the scope of sanctions. From 1996 onwards, fears of labour shortages sparked vigorous debate about the need for more conditionality. This resulted in a new Live Register Management Unit focused on 'a more effective application of conditionality' (Dukelow, 2004, p. 22). New regulations to tighten work availability and job-seeking guidelines were introduced in 1997 and 1998.

The 1997 national employment action plan was introduced through the European employment strategy's open method of coordination. Since then there has been a policy of systematic engagement with unemployed claimants and a significant level of live register exit (Indecon, 2005). However Irish social policy discourse continues to emphasise 'supportive conditionality' and 'sensitive activation' and policy still deviates from a strong model of conditionality in its reluctance to extend conditionality to lone parents, spouses of male claimants, and people with disabilities. Since 2005, however, there is a marked shift in discourse. The NESC

---

[12] Up to forty significant punitive or supportive changes took place over the period from 1986 to 2005, some of which had a substantial impact on the quality of social protection experienced by the claimant. Negative changes included freezing child income support, limiting duration of payments, means-testing insurance payments and restricting part-time workers' access to insurance payments.

(2005, p. 178) proposes all social assistance payments enable 'a life time attachment to the labour force' and the DSFA (2006b) proposes to apply work requirements for working-aged lone parents and qualified adults.

Targets and institutional reforms

If the NESC and DSFA proposals are ultimately implemented, Irish policy will be much more 'active'. However the NAPinclusion (Ireland, 2007) does not clearly or fully commit to extending the national employment action plan process to lone parents and people with disabilities. There remains a considerable journey to go on the path to a comprehensive welfare-to-work strategy or a social policy compatible with a competitive economy (Sweeney and O'Donnell, 2003). Many groups voice concerns about the levels of supports available to the unemployed and other working-aged claimants (INOU, 2006) and question the relevance of FÁS services to the working-aged Irish population (Rahaleen, 2006). Significant regional variations in employment levels can only be addressed with focused, localised, integrated employment strategies (NESF, 2006; Duggan and Loftus, 2006).

This raises the question of what national and local institutional arrangements are required to implement tightly integrated, local labour market programmes aimed at all or subgroups of the working-aged. Finn (2000, p. 53) observes that 'large scale, uniform, inflexible, benefit and employment and training systems are ending', local agencies now work in partnership with community groups in decentralised one-stop-shop gateways with more organisational accountability about responsiveness. OECD ministers have urged 'integration of benefit administration, job brokering and referral to active measures' (Finn, 2000, p. 54). More flexible local delivery or differentiation in policy implementation requires enhancing the capacity of local institutions and networks to work to a common agenda (NESF, 2006). Local partnerships in the EU are often local authority based or led but the weak system of local government in Ireland raises questions about local capacity to plan and implement local labour market activation programmes. *Towards 2016* and the NAPinclusion highlight the potential social inclusion role of the county development boards but there remain considerable local challenges to activate this latent potential (Ireland 2006, 2007).

Nicaise (2005) observes that, if anti-poverty outcomes are to be secured, activation policies need to focus on social integration, quality jobs and an ethic of care. Whether Ireland adopts a narrow work-first approach or a broader social inclusion approach to activation will be determined, not by the international political economy, but by national political mediation. The institutional spaces where such labour market and anti-poverty policies are mediated have themselves changed over the years. An innovative feature of the Irish policy system is a national social partnership policy-making structure which includes groups representing different communities of working-aged people living in poverty. The 1997 NAPS underscored this principle of consultation and stressed the importance of consultation with people living in poverty (Ireland, 1997). An effective implementation strategy requires actively listening to and learning from people in poverty about how they experience the delivery of both statutory and voluntary services. The more recent focus on working age brings a new relevance to the debate about the social integration needs of working-aged people living in poverty. Representative organisations are challenged to see the groups they represent not as individual communities of interest, such as women, disabled, Travellers or unemployed, but as working-aged people with parallel rights to both economic and social inclusion.

Conclusions

How can the government ensure it has a broad social inclusion strategy rather than a narrow work-first strategy for working-aged people? A rights-based approach will seek to safeguard the right to social inclusion and ensure it is not made contingent solely on economic participation. If it is accepted that work is not the only route out of poverty then it should also be accepted that more focus needs to be placed on securing and maintaining welfare adequacy for people of working age. Income support policies need to be used in a creative and targeted fashion to make work pay and to enhance the likelihood that economic inclusion will lead to effective routes out of poverty and into social wellbeing. A tracking mechanism is required to monitor whether work is in fact impacting positively on poverty. Pay is not the only criteria by which the quality of employment can be measured. A gender mainstreaming approach would ensure that the world of work is adapted to include an ethic of care and better work–life balance. In-work training is needed to ensure workers in low-paid employment have opportunities for progression and that all workers have opportunities for the level of upskilling and reskilling necessary to keep pace with the changing needs of this global economy.

The greatest policy challenge however is delivering a meaningful and integrated service that makes sense to the end user. This requires more national and local coordination than Irish institutions have been able to deliver. The focus therefore needs to be on institutional reforms that can deliver a quantum leap in the capacity to deliver one-stop-shop-type services which address comprehensively the range of needs of people trying to return to employment. These institutional reforms are required at both national and local levels. National reforms will require a rethinking of the institutional relationship between FÁS and the Department of Social and Family Affairs. Local reforms, recognising the traditional weaknesses of local government and what has been achieved through area-based partnerships, will need to use existing structures, such as the county development boards, as more effective spaces to achieve coherent and comprehensive local labour market strategies.

Without such institutional reforms, even the right policies will not be effectively implemented. Without the appropriate policies and implementation strategies, the social inclusion target for those of working age could be read as much as a 'threat' as an 'opportunity'. There remains a danger that the NAPinclusion (Ireland, 2007) strategy target to reduce the numbers of working age depending long term on social welfare by 20 per cent by 2016 could be as much a cost-saving target as a meaningful anti-poverty target. The first step in securing effective outcomes for the working-aged is putting in place a national framework for a social-inclusion-led activation strategy. This framework requires strong political leadership capable of delivering the scale of institutional reform required to generate integrated service delivery to people of working age.

References

Armstrong, J. (2006), 'Beyond 'Juggling' and 'Flexibility': Classed and Gendered Experiences of Combining Employment and Motherhood', *Lancaster University Sociological Research Online*, vol. 11, no. 2

Arrowsmith, J. (2004), 'A Review of What We Know About Partners of Benefit Recipients', London: Department of Work and Pensions: www.dwp.gov.uk

Boyle, N. (2005), *FÁS and Active Labour Market Policy 1985–2004,* Studies in Public Policy no. 17, Dublin: The Policy Institute

Brunton, C. (2006), *Work, Family and Parenting,* Wellington: Centre of Social Research and Evaluation, Ministry of Social Development

Callan, T. (2006), 'Child Poverty and Child Income Support', presentation to Combat Poverty Agency research seminar series, 27 November

Coakely, A. (2005), *Mothers, Welfare and Labour Market Activation,* Research Working Paper no. 05/04, Dublin: Combat Poverty Agency

Commission of the European Communities (2006), *Concerning a Consultation on Action at EU Level to Promote the Active Inclusion of the People Furthest from the Labour Market,* COM (2006) 44 final, Brussels: European Commission

Connolly, E. (2006), 'The Institutionalisation of Anti-Poverty Policy in the Social Partnership Process', presentation to Combat Poverty Agency research seminar series, 9 May

Cousins, M. (2005), *Explaining the Irish Welfare State,* Lewiston, NY: The Edwin Mellen Press

CORI (2007), 'Analysis and Critique of Budget 2007', Dublin: Conference of Religious of Ireland: www.cori/budget/2007/accbud07/index.htm

CSO (2005), *EU Survey on Income and Living Conditions,* Dublin: Central Statistics Office

Denny, K., Harmon, C. and O'Connell, P. (2000), *The Labour Market Impact of Human Resource Intervention Funding under the 1994–1999 Community Support Framework in Ireland,* Dublin: ESRI

DSFA (2006a), *Annual Statistical Report 2005,* Department of Social and Family Affairs, Dublin: Stationery Office

DSFA (2006b), *Proposals to Support Lone Parents,* Department of Social and Family Affairs, Dublin: Stationery Office

Duggan, C. and Loftus, C. (2006), 'A Study of Labour Market Vulnerability and Responses to It in Donegal, Sligo and North Dublin', Dublin: National Economic and Social Forum: www.nesf.ie

Dukelow, F. (2004), 'The Path Towards a More "Employment Friendly" Liberal Regime? Globalisation and the Irish Social Security System', paper presented at the Foundation for International Studies of Social Security Seminar, Stockholm, June

Duncan, S. (2003), *Mother Knows Best: Social Division and Work and Childcare*, Families, Life Course and Generational Research Centre Working Paper Series no. 31, Leeds: Leeds University

FÁS (2004), *The Irish Labour Market Review 2003: Challenges Facing the Irish Labour Market*, Dublin: FÁS

Finn, D. (2000), 'Welfare to Work: The Local Dimension', *Journal of European Social Policy*, vol. 10, no. 1, pp. 43–57

Gannon, B. and Nolan, B. (2004), *Disability and Social Inclusion in Ireland*, Dublin: ESRI

Halpin, B. and Hill, J. (2006), 'Active Labour Market Programmes and Poverty Dynamics', presentation to Combat Poverty Agency research seminar series, 23 May

Holland, J. (2005), 'Evaluation of the Extension of the New Deal for Lone Parents' Eligibility', London: Department for Work and Pensions: www.dwp.gov.uk

Indecon (2002), *Review of Active Labour Market Programmes*, Dublin: Indecon International Economic Consultants and Department of Enterprise, Trade and Employment

Indecon (2005), *Review of the National Employment Action Plan Preventative Strategy*, Dublin: Indecon

INOU (2006), 'What's in a Name?: Pre-retirement and Job Seekers Allowance', *Bulletin*, March/April, p. 1

INOU (2007), *2007–2010 Strategic Plan,* Dublin: Irish National Organisation of the Unemployed

Ireland (1987), *Programme for National Recovery*, Dublin: Stationery Office

Ireland (1997), *Sharing in Progress: National Anti-Poverty Strategy*, Dublin: Stationery Office

Ireland (2000), *Report of the P2000 Working Group on Women's Access to the Labour Market*, Dublin: Stationery Office

Ireland (2002), *Building an Inclusive Society*, Dublin: Stationery Office

Ireland (2006), *Towards 2016,* Dublin: Stationery Office

Ireland (2007), *National Action Plan for Social Inclusion 2007–2016,* Dublin: Stationery Office

Irvine, T. (2007), 'Time We Considered Work Life Balance as a Legal Right', *The Irish Times*, 2 February

Kirby, P. and Murphy, M. (forthcoming), 'Ireland as a Competition State', in Adshead, M., Kirby, P. and Millar, M. (eds.), *Contesting the Irish State*, Manchester: Manchester University Press

Levitas, R. (2001), 'Against Work: A Utopian Incursion into Social Policy', *Critical Social Policy*, vol. 21, no. 4, pp. 449–465

Lyons, M. and Lynch, K. (2005), 'States of Care, Time Poverty and the Moral Imperative to Care', paper presented to Equality, Care and Social Inclusion conference, UCD/QUB Armagh City Hotel, 24 June

McCabe, B. (2006), 'Economic Implications of Non-Standard Employment', presentation to Combat Poverty Agency research seminar series, 26 September

McCashin, A. (2004), *Social Security in Ireland,* Dublin: Gill & Macmillan

McGinnity, F., Russell, H., Williams, J. and Blackwell, S. (2005), *Time Use in Ireland 2005 Survey Report*, Dublin: ESRI

Molloy, R. (2007), in an interview with Gabrielle Monaghan, *The Irish Times*, 2 February

Murphy, M. (2003), *A Woman's Model of Social Welfare*, Dublin: National Women's Council of Ireland

Murphy, M. (2007), *Reframing the Irish Activation Debate: Accommodating Care and Safeguarding Social Rights*, Studies in Public Policy, Dublin: The Policy Institute

Nash, V. (2004), 'Wages and Poverty Risks of Atypical Workers', presentation to Combat Poverty Agency research seminar series, 28 May

NESC (2005), *The Developmental Welfare State*, Dublin: National Economic and Social Council

NESF (1994), *Ending Long-term Unemployment,* National Economic and Social Forum Report no. 4, Dublin: Stationery Office

NESF (2006), *Creating a More Inclusive Labour Market*, National Economic and Social Forum Report no. 33, Dublin: Stationery Office

Nicaise, I. (2005), 'Peer Review of Experiment in Social Activation in the NL Peer Review in the Field of Social Inclusion Practices', EC DGV Belgium: www.peer-review-social-inclusion.net

Nolan, B. and Marx, I. (2000), 'Low Pay and Household Poverty', in Gregory, M., Salverda, W. and Bacon, S. (eds.), *Labour Market Inequalities: Problems and Policies of Low Waged Employment in International Perspectives*, Oxford: Oxford University Press

O'Brien, M. (2004), *Workfare: Not Fair For Kids – A Review of Compulsory Work Policies and Their Effects on Children*, Auckland: Child Poverty Action Group

O'Connell, P. J. and McGinnity, F. (1997), *Working Schemes? Active Labour Market Policy in Ireland*, Aldershot: Ashgate

OPEN (2006), 'Submission in Relation to Government Discussion Paper: Proposals for Supporting Lone Parents', Dublin: OPEN

Rahaleen (2006), 'An Evaluation of FÁS Services to Lone Parents', unpublished document, Dublin: FÁS

Russell, H., Layte, R., Maître, B., O'Connell, P. J. and Whelan, C. T. (2004), *Work Poor Households: The Welfare Implications of Changing Household Employment Patterns*, Policy Research Series no. 52, Dublin: ESRI

Scharpf, F. and Schmidt, V. (eds.) (2000), *Work and Welfare in the Open Economy Volume 1, From Vulnerability to Competitiveness*, Oxford: Oxford University Press

Skevik, A. (2005), 'Women's Citizenship in the Time of Activation: The Case of Lone Mothers in Needs Based Welfare States', *Social Politics*, vol. 12, no. 1, pp. 42–66

Sweeney, J. and O'Donnell, R. (2003), 'The Challenge of Linking Society and Economy in Ireland's Flexible Developmental Welfare State', paper presented to the Conference of the Society for the Advancement of Social Economics, Aix en Provence, France, 26 to 28 June

Vermeylen, G. (2004), 'The Working Poor in Europe', presentation to Combat Poverty Agency research seminar series, 21 September

Whelan, C. T. (1994), 'Poverty, Unemployment and Psychological Distress', in Nolan, B. and Callan, T. (eds.), *Poverty and Policy in Ireland*, Dublin: Gill & Macmillan

Williams, F. (2004), 'Rethinking Families, Rethinking Care', keynote address to the Irish Social Policy Association's Families, Children and Social Policy: 10 Years On from the Year of the Family conference, Croke Park, Dublin, 16 to 17 September: www.ispa.ie/documents/160904fwilliams.doc

Chapter 5

Income support for older people

Anthony McCashin

Introduction

Pensions have been to the forefront in social policy
controversies, both academic and political, in many welfare
states for the last two decades or so. The approximate
source of these controversies is the challenge posed to many
developed welfare states by the combined experiences of
population ageing and low economic growth. These problems
have generated questions about the sustainability of social
protection programmes and pensions in particular, and led to
a flurry of policy change and reform (ILO, 2000).

In Ireland too pensions are changing, in the sense that
pension provisions are rapidly evolving, and debate and
analysis about future pension strategy – usually the preserve
of specialists and experts – has become politically salient,
although not yet intensely controversial. Ireland's starting
point in this debate is unusual in an international context.
Many countries are adapting their long-standing pension
systems to cope with economic and demographic burdens.
Ireland, however, is still developing its pension system and
debating what system is most compatible with its new-found

status as a successful 'developmental state' (O'Riain and O'Connell, 2000, p. 212) experiencing exceptional economic success without the so-called burden of an ageing population. Briefly, and to anticipate the discussion below, the choices for the future can be distilled into a stronger, more comprehensive state pension supplemented by occupational and private pensions, or a more modest state pension complemented by a substantial system of occupational and private pensions. At the time of writing, a government green paper on pensions is awaited, and presumably it will offer an overview of future policy options.

Against this background, the next section gives a very brief account of the development of pensions over the last two decades. This is followed by a discussion on the substantive policy issues at stake and a critical account of the failings of current provisions and policies. The last substantive section suggests a way forward for the future, given the importance of pensions to the achievement of the social policy goals enunciated in the *National Action Plan for Social Inclusion 2007–2016* (Ireland, 2007) and associated policy frameworks.

The pension system is complex and some clarifications are necessary at this point. First, the state provides a suite of old age pensions: state pensions based on the social insurance system, and the means-tested state pension.[1] Entitlement to the former is governed by social insurance contributions, and eligibility for the latter is determined by a means test. Many claimants of widow(er)'s pension are also over 65 years.

---

[1] The insurance pensions are state pension (transition) and (contributory) (formerly known as the retirement pension and the old age contributory pension); the means-tested pension is the state pension (non-contributory) (formerly the old age non-contributory pension).

Taken together, these pensions are referred to as the first tier of the pension system or the state pension system. The second tier comprises supplementary pensions such as occupational pensions paid by employers (in many cases in addition to a full or partial first-tier pension) and also pensions acquired by individuals such as the Personal Retirement Savings Account (PRSA) recommended by the Pensions Board.[2] It is the combination of these two tiers that determines the overall character of the pension system, and it is the balance between them that is the subject of contention.

Developments in pensions 1986–2006

Table 5.1 gives a thematic overview of pension policy developments since 1980. These developments cannot be concisely understood in a strict chronology as they reflect general trends and strategies at work throughout the period, at times overlapping and at other times with one development predominating.

As Table 5.1 suggests, the construction of the social insurance system was a continuing pre-occupation. In the mid-1980s the Commission on Social Welfare gave the final impetus to the evolution of social insurance, recommending that the social security system should adhere broadly to a Beveridge-type system of comprehensive social insurance. In

---

[2] These clarifications simplify matters greatly. In theory a third tier of pensioner income could be described, comprising investment income, interest on personal savings and so on, and in the future, when continued employment becomes more common among older people, their earnings will have to be added into this metaphor of tiers of income. Also, the description here ignores retired public sector workers who receive occupational pensions outside of the first-tier pension system.

Table 5.1: Summary of pension policy themes, 1980–2007

Theme	Key reports and documents	Examples of policy change or initiative
Developing comprehensive social insurance	Commission on Social Welfare, *Report*, 1986	Inclusion of self-employed and public servants in PRSI
	National Pensions Board, *Developing the National Pension System*, 1993	Broadening the range of credited contributions
		Social insurance for part-time employees
Consolidating second-tier voluntary system	*First Report of the National Pensions Board*, 1987	1990 Pensions Act establishing Pensions Board on a statutory basis
	National Pensions Board, *The Tax Treatment of Occupational Pensions*, 1989	Implementation of Pensions Board's recommendations on funding, rights of members, equality of treatment, role of trustees etc.
Increasing voluntary coverage – occupational and private	Pensions Board, *Securing Retirement Income*, 1998	Introduction of PRSAs
	Pensions Board, *National Pensions Review*, 2005	Campaigns to increase take-up of private pensions
	Pensions Board, *Special Savings for Retirement*, 2006	Consideration of compulsory second-tier pensions

Table 5.1: Summary of pension policy themes, 1980–2007 (contd)

Theme	Key reports and documents	Examples of policy change or initiative
Cross-cutting influences		
Poverty–benefit adequacy	Pensions Board, *Securing Retirement Income*, 1998	Target of 34 per cent of average earnings for state social insurance pension
	Pensions Board, *Special Savings for Retirement*, 2006	State pension at 40 per cent of average earnings in the context of a mandatory, private second-tier pension
	Commission on Social Welfare, *Report*, 1986	
	Programme for Prosperity and Fairness, 1999	Adoption of targets for benefit levels and priorities for increases
Gender	EU Equal Treatment Directive, 1979	Equalisation of dependency status of men and women
	Report of Second Commission on Status of Women, 1993	Equal rights for women in occupational pensions
		Introduction of social insurance credits for home-based care

the period to the late 1990s the implications of this policy for pensions unfolded. Part-time employees, public sector workers and the self-employed were all included in the social insurance contribution system. As a result, there was a growth over time in the proportion of the retired population in receipt of a social insurance pension, and of the working population contributing to the social insurance system.

A second theme was the consolidation of the second tier of pensions, focused on supporting, regulating and expanding occupational pensions. This series of developments emerged from the aftermath of the pension debates of the late 1970s. A green paper evaluating the rationale for a second-tier state pension was published in 1978, and this was to be followed by a white paper (Department of Social Welfare, 1977). Policy-makers and advocates of pension developments seemed to abandon the prospect of substantial improvement to the state pension in the context of the political instability and unfolding economic crisis of the early to mid-1980s. The white paper was drafted but never published, and the policy emphasis shifted to occupational pensions. This shift was facilitated by political concern over the widely publicised failure of some occupational pension schemes, and the Commission on Social Welfare's recommendation that the state pension should remain a first-tier, flat-rate benefit.

The net outcome of these developments was the establishment initially of the advisory National Pensions Board (NPB) (1986 to 1993) and the subsequent establishment of the statutory Pensions Board (which combines regulatory and advisory functions) in 1990; and the publication of specialist reports on issues such as the regulation of occupational pensions, the tax treatment of pensions, social insurance for the self-employed and equal treatment of men and women. Legislation in the early 1990s gave effect to the NPB's recommendations, resulting in a new regulatory framework for occupational pensions governing the role of trustees, funding standards, auditing procedures, the rights of pension contributors and so on. Critically, in a 1993 report, the NPB considered what the overall structure of the pension system should be. The Board was divided: a majority argued for a basic state pension combined with a voluntary, regulated second tier underpinned by tax allowances; a minority (the trade unions) expressed support for a compulsory second-tier pension either as part of the social insurance or the occupational pension system. Briefly, the design advocated by a majority of the NPB, a modest, but comprehensive, first tier supplemented by a tax-supported, regulated, voluntary second tier, has been implemented.

A third theme emerged in the mid-1990s. Notwithstanding the improved regulation of the occupational sector and the continuation of tax subsidies, coverage of private and occupational pensions remained stubbornly low – about 50 per cent of the labour force as a whole. This led to a concern about expanding the coverage of second-tier pensions. The Pensions Board invented the PRSA to increase individual private pension provision, and campaigned with the private pension industry and the financial institutions to exhort the workforce to save for retirement (Pensions Board, 1998). By mid-2005 it was clear that this new instrument would not increase coverage. In that context the option of making second-tier pensions compulsory emerged, and in its recent reports the Board (2005, 2006) analyses the rationale for that option and how it compares with other approaches.

The three broad strands of policy have interacted with other more general policies to shape current provisions, as the lower half of Table 5.1 shows. Poverty and benefit adequacy generally have featured in social policy discourse since the mid-1980s. A variety of analyses, beginning with the Commission on Social Welfare (1986), examine the link between relative income poverty and the level and structure of benefits. Over the period under review a number of poverty-related targets – some specific to pensions and some more general – have shaped both debate and policy. For example, the Commission outlined an indicative target for a minimally adequate benefit for the social security system as a whole, suggesting that social insurance pensions were then in the range of adequacy. In 1998, the Pensions Board offered a target specifically for pensions (34 per cent of average earnings for social insurance pensions) in the context of setting a first-tier pension supporting voluntary second-tier pensions that would give an income replacement (in total) of half the average earnings.

Gender was an equally important influence on policy and provisions. The proximate source of this influence was the EU's Equal Treatment Directive of 1979 and its implementation in Ireland in the 1980s and 1990s. In giving effect to the Directive, Ireland altered the level and structure of pensions and other benefits and redefined the nature of dependency in the benefit system as a whole. Aside from these formal changes, however, the equal treatment debate both reflected and reinforced concerns articulated in feminist critiques of social security about the 'male breadwinner' character of the social security system. In turn, this led to some degree of individualisation of state pensions and some recognition of caring roles in the social insurance contribution system.

The pension system in context

What type of system does Ireland now have? Table 5.2 places Ireland in a standard typology: in the terms of this typology, Ireland has a 'social insurance lite' [sic] pension regime. At first tier it offers a comprehensive system of social insurance, but the benefit level is low relative to earnings, approximately 33 per cent of gross earnings. The underlying rationale for Ireland's first-tier pension is poverty relief rather than income replacement. There are other countries that also have low pensions at the first tier, but as the typology shows, many of these have compulsory and/or very widespread second-tier provisions.

Table 5.2: Classification of pension systems, c.2001

First tier	Second pillar	
	Voluntary and limited coverage (40 to 60 per cent of the workforce)	**Compulsory and/or widespread coverage (80 to 90 per cent of the workforce)**
Non-existent	Incomplete (Taiwan)	
Low level of benefits	Social insurance lite (Canada, US) **Ireland**	Multi-tier systems (Switzerland, UK, Australia, New Zealand)
Full income replacement	Social insurance (France, Italy, Germany)	Sweden (after 1990)

Source: adapted from Bonoli and Shinkawa, 2005, p. 6

The typology distinguishes Ireland's system from other European systems on the basis of the relative levels of their state pension. France and Germany, for example, also have low coverage at the second tier, but their first tier offers a high level of income replacement. Prior to its pension reform in the 1990s Sweden was closer to the social insurance model, but it now has a funded, compulsory second tier.

The debate about pension systems in Ireland can be understood as a debate about the cell in the typology to which Ireland should move. If, for example, the government was to follow the experience of Australia and introduce the compulsory second tier in the form outlined in *Special Savings for Retirement* (Pensions Board, 2006), it would entail a move to the right in the figure into the multi-tier category. On the other hand, those who have argued for a universal state second tier (the minority view in the NPB's 1993 report) aspire to move the Irish system into the social insurance category in the lower left-hand cell. The emphasis in the Pensions Board's reports has been on the former: construct a more comprehensive, but private, second tier.

To place Ireland's current debates and choices in an international context, it is useful to note some key international trends and to observe whether they are reflected in recent Irish developments. The trends identified in the authoritative review of international pension policy conducted by the International Labour Organization (ILO, 2000) are summarised below:

- There is a discernible trend towards a reduction in social security pension benefits. These reductions are usually indirect, and phased, and include changes to the details of the pension indexation formula (UK), adjustments to the earnings base governing the initial pension benefit (Australia) and greater targeting, through tax clawbacks and means tests, of universal pensions (Finland, Sweden). This pattern does not apply in Ireland's case.

- Many countries are increasing their social security contribution rates. This is being done in some cases through outright increases in the core contribution rates (France, Canada) and in other cases through widening the income base on which contributions are levied (Japan, Norway). Contrary to this trend, Ireland's contribution rates have been stable for some time and the base remains unchanged: earned income.

- Governments are implementing measures that result, directly or indirectly, in an increase in the age at which pensions are paid. The US, for example, effectively reduced pension benefits by phasing in an increase of two years (from 65 to 67) in the normal pension age (starting for workers aged 62 years in 2002). The traditionally lower pension age for women is also being phased out: Portugal, Greece and the UK are all implementing equal pension ages by increasing the age for women. Also, in the last decade the historic trend towards lower pension ages and earlier retirement came to an end. Governments are increasingly offering (actuarially) reduced pensions at early retirement and increased pensions for deferred retirement. In Ireland, in the case of the state pension, the age of 66 years has remained unchanged since the late 1970s.

- Nearly one-third of the OECD countries reviewed in the ILO study adopted privatisation measures, broadly defined. In some cases this has entailed permission to contract out of state second-tier pensions (UK), and in others it has involved mandatory participation by employers and employees in industry-wide pension schemes (Netherlands, Switzerland). Australia introduced a private retirement income scheme based on mandatory contributions by employers, employees and the state to defined contribution funds. In Ireland, this was the model advocated by the then Minister for Social and Family Affairs Séamus Brennan and analysed in *Special Savings for Retirement* (Pensions Board, 2006).

- There is a shift towards defined contribution arrangements in the occupational pensions sector and notional defined contributions in some countries' social security pensions. In the latter case (Sweden and Italy are examples) pension benefits were historically fixed as a proportion of earnings, but these systems have been changed so that part of the contributions are notionally paid into an individual's account; the account is re-valued annually using an index such as GDP growth. An individual's pension benefits are partially determined by the fund and a conversion factor that varies according to the age at retirement. The occupational pensions sector in Ireland shows some of the same pattern – a shift away from defined benefit to defined contribution schemes and therefore a shift in the burden of risk to employees – but the first-tier pensions have remained as modest, flat-rate pensions with the level of the pensions determined annually as a political matter.

This comparative sketch suggests that the revision and retrenchment measures adopted internationally to cope with ageing and fiscal pressures have not been in evidence in Ireland. It also highlights one important feature of current and recent Irish policy. During a sustained period of economic growth, and in the context of a stable demographic structure, policy-makers in Ireland did not use the opportunity to expand the state pension system, even when it was clear that the second tier was not capable of providing a high level of income replacement for all.

Pension policy: Key issues

Poverty is clearly a key issue, and here the data tell a sombre story about the link between pensions (and benefits in general) and incomes in the economy as a whole. As Table 5.3 records, relative poverty among older people rose sharply in the 1990s and beyond, stabilised, and then declined (see Prunty, 2007). Significantly, as the gap between pension levels and the evolving poverty line widened and then narrowed again, the poverty rate rose and then fell in tandem.[3]

The data for the period to 2001 and from 2003 to 2005 are not strictly comparable and, as can be seen in the table, the reduction in poverty is due to the fact that the poverty line stabilised post-2001 allowing pensioners to 'catch up' rather than to higher increases in pensions themselves.

---

[3]   The poverty data here refer specifically to relative income poverty. This is partly to keep the discussion within manageable limits, and partly because an analysis of pensions and older people is de facto a discussion of incomes. Of course, there are data on poverty defined in terms of deprivation of specific necessities and the official Central Statistics Office data from the EU-SILC survey record levels of deprivation for the population as a whole, and for subgroups such as older people. See Chapter 2 for further information.

Table 5.3: Trends in pensioner poverty, 1994–2005

Poverty	1994	1997	1998	2000	2001	2003	2004	2005
1. Poverty line* (€ weekly)	98.60	125.54	139.45	165.66	187.84	185.28	185.51	192.74
2. % of persons poor	15.6	18.2	22.6	23.7	21.9	19.7	19.4	18.5
3. % of older** poor	5.9	24.2	32.9	38.4	44.1	36.4	27.1	20.1
4. State pension*** (€ weekly)	90.17	99.06	105.41	121.92	134.59	157.30	167.30	179.30
5. Poverty gap (€ weekly) [1–4]	–8.43	–26.48	–34.04	43.74	–53.25	–27.98	–18.21	–13.44

* The poverty line is 60 per cent of median equivalised disposable income per week for 2003 to 2005 and 60 per cent of mean income for 1994 to 2001 and the figures are not strictly comparable
** Older people refers to persons aged 65 and over
*** The state pension level refers to the contributory pension payment for one adult
Sources: Whelan *et al.*, 2003 and Central Statistics Office, 2006

Looking at older people in terms of income distribution across the lifecycle, the data for 2005, summarised in Table 5.4, show that older people are concentrated in the lower deciles. Approximately 11 per cent of the population are in the 65+ age group and 70 per cent of them are in the lowest two quintiles, with almost one-third in the lowest quintile. These data on poverty and low income show the financial vulnerability of older people relative to the population as a whole, and clearly point to the need for pension levels and the pension structure as a whole to be viewed primarily from the standpoint of adequacy rather than coverage.

Table 5.4: Percentage distribution of different age groups in the population by income quintile, 2005

Quintile*	Age 0–14		Age 15–64		Age 65+	
	%	Cumulative	%	Cumulative	%	Cumulative
1	23.4	23.4	17.3	17.3	32.2	32.2
2	19.8	43.1	17.2	34.5	37.9	70.1
3	21.1	64.2	20.3	54.7	15.7	85.8
4	20.2	84.4	21.8	76.5	8.9	94.7
5	16.5	100	23.5	100	5.7	100

* A quintile is a one-fifth share of the distribution; quintiles are ranked here from the lowest one-fifth of incomes (quintile 1) to the highest (quintile 5)
Source: Central Statistics Office, 2006

Taking a wider perspective on pensioners' incomes, the second key issue is the inequitable distribution of the benefits of second-tier pensions. This results from a combination of two well-documented patterns. On the one hand, overall coverage of these pensions, approximately 50 per cent, is low by international standards, and is skewed towards certain categories: men rather than women; public rather than private sector workers; larger rather than smaller employers; higher paid rather than lower paid employees. Pension coverage at this tier is therefore concentrated in the higher income groups. Figure 5.1 illustrates the sharp income gradient for second-tier pension coverage.

Figure 5.1: Percentage of employees with pension entitlements by income decile*, 1994

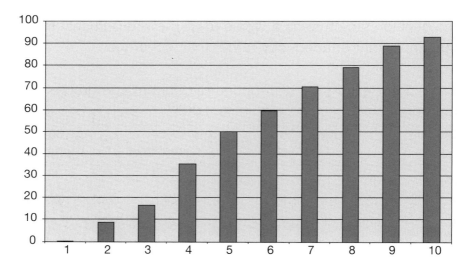

* A decile is a one-tenth share of the distribution; deciles are ranked here from the lowest one-tenth of incomes (decile 1) to the highest (decile 10)
Source: Hughes, 2001

On the other hand, substantial indirect expenditure accrues to this tier of pensions through the tax expenditures (arising from the tax exemptions for occupational and private pensions). In 2002 these expenditures were approximately €2.4 billion, significantly in excess of direct state spending on pensions. Critically, these substantial expenditures disproportionately benefit employees in the higher income groups. The scale of the tax expenditures should, of course, be considered in the light of the cost implications of improving the state pensions. In its reports the Pensions Board (1998, 2005) treats the direct expenditures on state pensions and the indirect tax expenditures as quite independent of each other. However, both sets of expenditures are a cost to the exchequer and both have significant distributional effects. This point has practical implications. Clearly, the cost of improving state pensions could be offset in part by a reduction in the tax privileges for pensions, and, equally important, future projections of pension costs should include the indirect tax costs – a practice not reflected in the Pensions Board's reports.

A third important aspect of pensions is the differential access of men and women to pensions at first and second tier. It is not possible with the available data to construct a full profile of the pension status of the retired and working populations, male and female. Tables 5.5 and 5.6 show that, notwithstanding the removal of formal gender discrimination in the workplace and the social security system, men and women have differential access to pensions. The percentage of the older male population in receipt of a state old age pension is significantly higher than the proportion for the female population; 95 per cent in contrast to 80 per cent. More than three-quarters of men receive an insurance pension whereas among women the figure is over one-half.

There are no comparable data for retired men and women about second-tier pensions, but the *National Pensions Review* data on coverage in the current workforce (Pensions Board, 2005) indicate a gender difference. The data in Table 5.6 referring to second-tier pensions give an overall coverage rate of just over 50 per cent and confirm a noticeably lower coverage rate among women. This difference is smaller than

that revealed for the state pension among the currently
retired, but with the lifetime employment profile of women still
differing to that of men, data for men and women in the
retired population are likely to reveal a significant gender gap.

Table 5.5: State pensions (including widow(er)'s pension)
among the male and female population aged 65+, 2005

	Male	Female	All
Total population (000s)	197.2	253.7	450.9
Insurance pensions (000s)	151.4	142.1	293.5
Assistance pensions (000s)	35.6	61.5	97.1
Total pensions (000s)	187.0	203.6	390.6
% of population with insurance pension	76.8	56.0	65.1
% of population with assistance pension	18.1	24.2	21.5
Total (%)	94.8	80.3	86.6

Source: Department of Social and Family Affairs, 2005

Table 5.6: Coverage rates for second-tier pensions, 1995,
2002, 2004

Employees aged 30 to 65	1995 (%)	2002 (%)	2004 (%)
Male	49	56	56
Female	40	45	47
All	46	51	52

Source: Pensions Board, 2005

Finally, the complexity of the pension system as a whole,
alluded to at the outset, raises important issues in the context
of a growing acceptance of rights-based approaches to
social policy. The effect of the pension system is such that,
as many adults approach retirement age, there is no clear
right to any form of pension guarantee. In the case of state

pensions, a higher proportion of the population is likely in the future to obtain a state insurance pension. The rules about entitlement are so complex, however, that many may judge their future entitlements incorrectly and make financial and other decisions accordingly. Over time the real value of this pension has risen, although there is no statutory indexation of pension levels, and its value relative to earnings fluctuates somewhat. In the case of the state's social assistance pension, the amount of any pension awarded is contingent on a number of variables (age, earnings, other income, spouse's income, for example). Also, the contribution rules for social insurance and the rules relating to social assistance change. This picture must be viewed alongside the uncertain returns that second-tier pensions may offer – in particular defined contribution schemes. In effect, many of the pre-retired in Ireland, and in particular women, have no clear rights in relation to retirement income and no clarity about what their income in retirement is likely to be.[4]

The lack of a firm pension guarantee in some form is significant in its own right but it has added importance in the light of prospective developments in pension policy in the near future. Policy-makers, it seems, are intent on expanding the second tier of the pension system. The Pensions Board introduced the new PRSAs to enhance the take-up of individual private pensions, and more recently policy-makers have argued the merits of mandatory private pensions. Critically, the PRSAs are defined contribution in nature, so too will be any new mandatory private pension: the value of individuals' pensions will be determined by the return on the

---

[4] This does not apply to the retired population with defined benefit occupational pensions.

funds. This will also be the case with the increasing number of defined contribution occupational pensions. There are important social and economic arguments against such arrangements, but if policy-makers wish to implement them they should first ensure that first-tier pensions are significantly enhanced and that they confer clearer and more predictable rights.

The future

The first – and very immediate – question is: what structural choices should Ireland make in the future? In other words, what cell in Table 5.2 should Ireland attempt to occupy? The options in this regard have been well documented, and the arguments for and against each option have been fully rehearsed (Commission on Social Welfare, 1986; McCashin, 2004; Stewart, 2005; NPB, 1993; Pensions Board, 2005; Department of Social Welfare, 1977). This writer argues that the core of the future pension system should be the state pension, and that this first tier should be substantially improved. An acceptance of this argument could imply a number of variants, but in the context of the specific options raised in the Pensions Board's recent reports it suggests that the state pension should be raised to 50 per cent of average earnings, with an immediate impetus towards this target, and with the budgetary costs offset by a reduction in the tax expenditures on private and occupational pensions.

What is the reasoning behind this argument, and why are the options of voluntary or mandatory second-tier pensions not appropriate in the Irish context? Briefly, reducing pensioner poverty among current pensioners requires a substantial increase in the short term in the state pension. Even if coverage could be substantially improved in the current workforce, the impact of improved coverage on pensioners' incomes would not materialise until they retire. It is also important to stress that the coverage of the state pension system, unlike that of second-tier pensions, is high and continuing to rise. When the qualified adults of state pension recipients are included, state pensions affect the incomes of over 90 per cent of the older population.[5] It should be noted too that a detailed analysis of the composition of pensioners' incomes showed that 'State social security payments were the main sources of retirement income' (Stewart, 2005, p. 35). Therefore, because of the coverage of the state pension and the relative importance of income from this source, it offers the greatest scope to improve the incomes of older people.

The argument advanced here will be contested on two related counts. In the first instance, the question of the sustainability of a more generous state pension is critical, as the Pensions Board has pointed out. Ireland's current situation is one where the share of the population has remained remarkably stable, as Table 5.7 indicates, and where the cost of state pensions as a share of national income has declined. Furthermore, there is no demographic challenge of a substantial rise in aged dependency looming in the near or medium-term future, as the Pensions Board's population projections show (Pensions Board, 2005). In fact, recent academic research is careful to point out that any projections about the size and age structure of the Irish

---

[5] Only qualified adults on contributory state pensions and over 66 years of age are included. Qualified adults of state pension (non-contributory) are mainly under 66 years.

Table 5.7: Trends in old age pensions, 1995–2005

	1995c.*	2005c.*
% of total population aged 65+	11.4	11.2
Social insurance pensioners (000s)	199.5	293.5
Social assistance pensioners (000s)	118.6	97.1
Total state pensioners (000s)	318.1	390.6
Insurance pensions as % of total	62.7	75.1
Total as % of population aged 65+	76.9	86.6
Total (including qualified adults) as % of population aged 65+	82.0	94.2
Pension expenditure as % of GNP	3.3	2.7
Contributory pension as % of poverty line**	91	93
Non-contributory pension as % of poverty line**	79	86

* The figures in each column are not all for the same year
** The poverty line for 1995 is 60 per cent of the mean equivalised income and for 2005 it is 60 per cent of median equivalised income
Sources: Department of Social, Community and Family Affairs and Central Statistics Office

population are highly contingent on assumptions about migration flows, and if the very recent trends in immigration are assumed to continue they will impart a higher total to the projected population and a lower share of older people in the population than would apply otherwise (Connell, 2005, p. 53):

On the basis of our forecasts, our overall conclusion is that Ireland's dependency ratios remain low by international standards for the next 20 years but increase thereafter. In particular, the ratio of those in the labour force to those aged 65 and over will fall only gradually in this period and will be high by international standards in 2026. Hence, the issue of the cost of medium pension payments [sic] is not as important for Ireland as for some other countries.

Another argument about the proposed improvement to the state pension is a qualitative one: that the future pension system should be less reliant on pay-as-you-go (PAYG) systems (with pensions paid out of current revenues) and should shift to funded pensions (where they are paid out of funds saved and invested prior to retirement as in the case of PRSAs or mandatory private provision). This is a complex and controversial issue. In this context, it is important to note that there is little agreement on it in the theoretical and empirical literature. The most recent academic synthesis of the arguments and evidence concludes that funding as a pension strategy is not, *a priori,* to be preferred to a PAYG system (Barr, 2001). It is more important, however, to note the empirical evidence that funding does not seem to generate improved economic performance, as is claimed by its proponents, while comprehensive PAYG systems may be more effective at poverty reduction. As recent analyses of the funding versus PAYG choices in Ireland suggest, the balance of the argument and the empirical evidence internationally would not support the adoption of funding strategies such as PRSAs and mandatory private provision (McCashin, 2004; Stewart, 2005).

Whatever the outcome of the continuing debate about the structure of the pension system, there are two specific neglected issues that arise in pensions. The analysis of pension levels in the Pensions Board's reports and in the accompanying commentary and critique of these has focused on a target for the level of the contributory pension expressed as a proportion of average earnings. This type of target (for example 34 per cent of average earnings in the 1998

Securing Retirement Income) was identified as one that is compatible with the goal of achieving a replacement rate of 50 per cent of pre-retirement earnings for retired workers when the contributory pension is supplemented with a second-tier pension; the target assumes that the state pension will be supplemented with a second-tier pension for medium to high earners. Arguably, the next phase of pension reform should focus on targets related to relative income poverty. The concentration of older persons in the lower income groups and their risk of poverty justify a target chosen on the basis of poverty-reduction goals. This approach is now possible, as the annual EU-SILC survey data allow pension levels to be benchmarked against a representative indicator of incomes in the economy. A related issue is the non-contributory pension. It is further below the poverty line than the contributory pension. While the role of this means-tested pension in the pension system is declining – 22 per cent of the older population receive it – future pension policy needs to integrate this pension into the development of targets about pension levels and poverty reduction.

The question of gender and access to pensions has been largely neglected since the introduction of the formal equality measures in social security and occupational pensions. However, the data in Tables 5.5 and 5.6 show that a gender gap in direct access to old age pensions persists. This may narrow over time as the pension system begins to reflect increasing rates of female labour force participation; furthermore, the option for spouses to receive their share of the state pension personally (administrative individualisation introduced in 2002) will also widen access to state pensions. Spouses of pensioners will also benefit from the raising of the allowance for spouses to the rate for the non-contributory state pension.[6] There is still a need, however, for the state social insurance pension to be reviewed so that more women become recipients of social insurance pensions – these pensions are at the core of the state pension regime.

Finally, while this chapter is concerned primarily with pensions, these can only be viewed in the light of wider issues affecting older people. The potential to view pensions in an appropriately broader context is very real in view of the lifecycle framework outlined in the NESC's *The Developmental Welfare State* (DWS) and incorporated in *Towards 2016*, the current national partnership agreement. The DWS model for the future of social policy in Ireland – a model supposedly compatible with achieving success in a competitive, globalised economy – would comprise the following: a range of universal services, sensitive activation measures and a participation-based income support system. Achieving this model will in turn, according to the NESC, require attention to five aspects of policy development: governance and leadership, rights and standards, integration at local level, operational effectiveness and support for people over the lifecycle (NESC, 2005). The NESC document is silent about the detail of policy, while *Towards 2016* expresses a vision of older people being enabled 'to maintain their health and well being, as well as to live active and full lives, in an independent way, in their own homes and communities for as long as possible' (Ireland, 2006, p. 60). *Towards 2016* also lists a range of very specific commitments and targets, spanning housing, healthcare, mobility, employment and so on.

---

6   The *National Action Plan for Social Inclusion 2007–2016* contains a specific commitment that this will be implemented by 2009 (Ireland, 2007).

Against this background of a move towards a more coherent approach to older people and the retired, and an approach framed in terms of active participation in society, a range of questions arise about the substance and governance of pension policy. These are too numerous to be dealt with here, but two key points illustrate the implications for policy-makers of pursuing this lifecycle approach. While pensions are clearly an important aspect of older people's welfare, it is no longer obvious that pension policy and analysis should be at one remove from wider debates about the cost of long-term care, health insurance and other issues. Pension planning – at both personal and societal levels – is technical and esoteric, and for this reason the detail of pension policy formulation requires distinct expertise and, perhaps, a separate structure such as the Pensions Board. However, there is clearly a need for deliberation on pensions to be integrated into an overall analysis of the needs of older people and for some overarching structure that delivers what the NESC terms 'governance and leadership'; it is notable, for example, that the DWS report calls for an overall national plan for older people (NESC, 2005, p. 222).

Some of the issues raised in this chapter – and others that are implicit – illustrate the need for greater policy integration in the future. Poverty is defined in this chapter in terms of relative income poverty, and therefore poverty among older people, defined in these terms, is de facto about pension policy. However, the levels of poverty are significantly different (in fact, significantly lower) if measured in terms of deprivation as recorded by the Central Statistics Office. The point here is not to argue the relative merits of income-based poverty lines and deprivation indicators in researching poverty in the general population, but to suggest that research based on the needs of older people – rather than the incomes of older people – might generate a more nuanced picture of the levels and patterns of pensioner poverty. In meeting the needs of older people, perhaps the most challenging questions for research and policy are to determine how significant low income is as a predictor of general deprivation among older people, and to identify the importance of improved pensions as opposed to enhanced health and social care services in improving the overall welfare of older people.

This all implies that future policy and research should reflect the experiences and views of older people themselves in defining what poverty and deprivation mean at this stage of the lifecycle. Furthermore, it raises questions about the utility of general poverty reduction targets of the type outlined in the *National Action Plan for Social Inclusion 2007–2016* (Ireland, 2007). This policy document also embraces a lifecycle approach. However, it expresses its poverty-related goals in terms of a reduction in consistent poverty for the population as a whole to a figure in the 2 to 4 per cent range by 2012 and to zero by 2016. In parallel, the plan offers a commitment to maintain the lowest state pension at its real 2007 value, and also expresses very general aspirations about the wider policy goals for this stage of the lifecycle. A lifecycle approach will require a more careful integration of generic poverty targets with policy challenges affecting the older population specifically.

Finally, the lifecycle model in DWS has advanced to the point where *Towards 2016* expresses support for specific policy changes about retirement that have potentially important implications for pensions. *Towards 2016* calls for a range of measures that will facilitate and encourage older persons to be socially involved, and to remain in the labour market 'to meet the challenge of an ageing society' (Ireland, 2006, p. 64). It also alludes to phasing-out the pre-retirement allowance for those aged 55 to 64 years and to the need for enhancing the skills of older/low-skilled workers to improve their employability. These prospective changes – and the context in which they are proposed – again illustrate sharply the need for coherent policy formulation. The active ageing agenda presumes an increasing element of choice on the part of older people; the choice to be socially active after retirement requires an adequate income and, perhaps, a choice of retirement age. Remarkably, the pension age for the state pensions has remained unchanged since the late 1970s. None of the growth in the economy in the last decade has materialised in the form of lower retirement ages for workers dependent on the state pension or any flexibility about retirement below the 'pension age'. Nor has there been any serious discussion about the topic – it is not mentioned, for instance, in the relevant chapter in the *National Action Plan for Social Inclusion*.

The point at issue here is that discussion of retirement policy should be framed, to begin with, in terms of pension provisions, and the next practical step to realising the vision of the *National Action Plan for Social Inclusion* and *Towards 2016* of an active, participating older population would be a commitment to reviewing the pension age within a broad lifecycle perspective. This is not to suggest that older workers should not be encouraged to remain in employment: in fact, once population ageing gets underway and pension costs begin to rise, increasing the size of the workforce by raising the average age of retirement would be a rational policy response. However, the danger inherent in the *Towards 2016* perspective is that low-income workers in the boom economy may retire into a regime where an even higher pension age might apply. An activation ethos focused on maximising work participation has permeated social policy generally in the last decade (see Chapter 4). Whatever about the rationale and impact of this activation strategy on the labour market in general, there are no grounds for supposing that it should be applied on a general basis to older, low-income workers. This would represent a triumph – and an unnecessary one – of economic calculation over wider social objectives.

References

Barr, N. (2001), *The Welfare State as Piggy Bank. Information, Risk, Uncertainty and the Role of the State*, Oxford: Oxford University Press

Bonoli, G. and Shinkawa, T. (2005), 'Population Ageing and the Logics of Pension Reform in Western Europe, East Asia, and North America', in Bonoli, G. and Shinkawa, T. (eds.), *Ageing and Pension Reform Around the World. Evidence from Eleven Countries*, Cheltenham: Edward Elgar

Central Statistics Office (2006), 'EU-SILC 2005': www.cso.ie/eusilc (accessed 16 November 2006)

Commission on Social Welfare (1986), *Report*, Dublin: Government Publications

Connell, P. (2005), 'Demographic Projections. Diffusing the Time Bomb', in Stewart, J. (ed.), *For Richer, For Poorer. An Investigation of the Irish Pension System*, Dublin: New Island

Department of Social and Family Affairs (2005), *Statistical Information on Social Welfare Services 2005*, Dublin: DSFA

Department of Social Welfare (1977), *A National Income-Related Pension Scheme*, Dublin: Government Publications

Hughes, G. (2001), 'The Cost and Distribution of Tax Expenditure in the Republic of Ireland', in Feldstein, M. (ed.), *Thirty-First Geary Lecture*, Dublin: ESRI

ILO (2000), *Social Security Pensions: Development and Reform*, Geneva: International Labour Organization

Ireland (1999), *Programme for Prosperity and Fairness*, Dublin: Stationery Office

Ireland (2006), *Towards 2016. Ten-Year Framework Social Partnership Agreement 2006–2015*, Dublin: Government Publications

Ireland (2007), *National Action Plan for Social Inclusion 2007–2016*, Dublin: Government Publications

McCashin, A. (2004), *Social Security in Ireland*, Dublin: Gill & Macmillan

National Pensions Board (1987), *First Report of the National Pensions Board*, Dublin: Government Publications

National Pensions Board (1989), *The Tax Treatment of Occupational Pensions*, Dublin: Government Publications

National Pensions Board (1993), *Developing the National Pension System*, Dublin: Government Publications

NESC (2005), *The Developmental Welfare State*, Dublin: National Economic and Social Council

O'Riain, S. and O'Connell, P. J. (2000), 'The Role of the State in Growth and Welfare', in Nolan, B., O'Connell, P. J. and Whelan, C. T. (eds.), *Bust to Boom? The Irish Experience of Growth and Inequality*, Dublin: Institute of Public Administration

Pensions Board (1998), *Securing Retirement Income*, Dublin: Pensions Board

Pensions Board (2005), *National Pensions Review*, Dublin: Pensions Board

Pensions Board (2006), *Special Savings for Retirement*, Dublin: Pensions Board

Prunty, M. (2007), *Older People in Poverty in Ireland: An Analysis of EU-SILC 2004*, Dublin: Combat Poverty Agency

Second Commission on the Status of Women (1993), *Report to Government*, Dublin: Stationery Office

Stewart, J. (2005), 'Incomes of Retired Persons in Ireland', in Stewart, J. (ed.), *For Richer, For Poorer: An Investigation of the Irish Pension System*, Dublin: New Island

Whelan, C. T., Layte, R., Maître, B., Gannon, B., Nolan, B., Watson, D. and Williams, J. (2003), *Monitoring Poverty Trends in the Republic of Ireland: Results from the 2001 Living in Ireland Survey*, Dublin: ESRI

Chapter 6

Education and poverty

Roland Tormey[1]

> Education is central to development. It is the primary vehicle by which economically and socially marginalized adults and children can lift themselves out of poverty, better understand and improve their health, create sustainable livelihoods and obtain the means to participate more fully in their communities.
>
> (Ireland, 2006, p. 43)

Introduction

Although written with overseas development aid in mind, the above quote effectively summarises the way in which many people in Ireland have come to view the role of education in tackling poverty. The recognition that education can confer knowledge, skills, cultural and social capital and qualifications that can enable people to access better-paid employment and to improve their life chances has often been central to the belief that one of the key ways in which anti-poverty work can be done is through improving educational outcomes. It is

---

[1] My thanks to Jim Gleeson, Claire W. Lyons and David Millar for their assistance in the development of this chapter.

no surprise then that the *National Anti-Poverty Strategy* explicitly identified that, along with social welfare and tax systems, 'the education system has a key role to play in providing a route out of poverty' (Ireland, 1997, p. 6).

Research in Ireland and internationally has long identified an association between low levels of educational qualifications and unemployment, as well as between educational attainment and rates of pay (McCoy and Williams, 2000; Gorby *et al.*, 2005). Research has also found that in times of economic decline those without formal educational qualifications are most likely to suffer job loss (figures quoted in Boldt and Devine, 1998), and that the gap in income and job security between those with educational qualifications and those without widens over time (NESF, 1997). In fact, this linkage between education and future life chances may even be stronger in Ireland than is the case in many other industrialised countries (OECD, 1997). In such a context, it is little surprise that so many people would place such an emphasis on the role of education in enabling people to lift themselves out of poverty.

The difficulty, however, is that it is precisely those from poor and working-class backgrounds who fare worst within our education system and, despite forty years of governmental attempts to address this relationship, a strong association between poverty and low educational attainment persists. Young people in schools in areas designated as disadvantaged have a greater risk of having significant reading difficulties when compared with the population as a whole (McDonald, 1998). Studies of school attendance highlight that absenteeism is notably higher in schools in areas identified as having high levels of disadvantage than is the case in schools in areas with the lowest levels of disadvantage (Ó Briain, 2006). Following on from this, young people from poverty backgrounds tend to leave school earlier and with fewer qualifications when compared with those from non-poor backgrounds (Gorby et al., 2005). Even where young people finish school, there is evidence that students from working-class backgrounds take fewer honours subjects at Leaving Certificate and achieve fewer points than those from middle-class backgrounds (Power and Tormey, 2000; Gorby et al., 2005).

Worryingly, Archer and Weir (2004) conclude that although Irish intervention schemes to address educational disadvantage tend to be in line with international models of good practice and tend to be evidence-based in their formulation, they show little evidence of actually having an impact upon the educational attainment of the targeted populations. This, they note (with some degree of understatement), 'may be regarded as disappointing' (p. 31).

This issue is not one which has only recently emerged in Irish policy debates. Writing in the 1960s, the *Investment in Education* team noted, 'There are … inequalities in the participation in post-primary education of children at all levels, based on social group and geographical location. There is, clearly, a need for public policy to concern itself with these anomalies' (OECD, 1965, p. 389). More than twenty-five years later, the Conference of Major Religious Superiors argued, 'the continued existence of a link between education and poverty represents the greatest single challenge facing our education system' (CMRS, 1992, p. 99). Fifteen years on from this second pronouncement, and more than forty years on from the first, it is arguable that the association between poverty or social class and educational outcomes remains as much a feature of the Irish educational landscape as ever.

This is not to suggest that we are exactly where we were in the 1960s or, indeed, in the early 1990s. It is clear that during the last forty years the attainment levels and participation rates of working-class and poor young people in education have improved significantly. The proportion of school-leavers from backgrounds of unemployment who went on to further study rose from 12 per cent in 1999 to 26 per cent in 2004, for example. Yet, as the learning attainment of working-class and poor young people improved since the 1960s so did that of those from middle-class backgrounds, ensuring that whatever learning gains young people from poor backgrounds made, they continued to be outpaced by their more advantaged counterparts. So, while the educational gains made by those from unemployed backgrounds between 1999 and 2004 are clearly impressive, they remain far behind the participation levels of those from professional backgrounds (69 per cent of whom go on to further study), those from managerial/employer backgrounds (for whom the figure is 63 per cent) and those from farming backgrounds (over 50 per cent) (Gorby et al., 2005; see also O'Connell et al., 2006). And here we come to the crux of the problem: disadvantage itself can be seen as a function of advantage. As long as there are those who can mobilise their resources to do better than others, there must, by definition, be those others who do worse than them. And, as long as the educational attainment of poor or working-class pupils improves, the advantaged either raise the bar or seek to find alternative routes of ensuring their advantage (Layte and Whelan, 2000). As Derman-Sparks has put it, 'The meaning of advantage is the ghost that lurks within the meaning of disadvantage' (2002, p. 59). In other words, it is precisely because education can play such a clear role in conferring competitive advantage upon learners that it is so hard to address the glaring inequalities in educational outcomes that characterise the system.

In this chapter I explore this conundrum in the Irish context. Beginning by exploring the different ways in which the relationship between poverty and educational outcomes (or 'educational disadvantage' as this phenomenon tends to be called) is defined and conceptualised in Ireland, I highlight the ideological battle that is played out, often unnoticed, in attempts to address this phenomenon. I then explore *one* of the ways in which the relationship between education and life chances has been understood in the international community, before using this as a lens to reflect back on what these international debates can tell us about what we have previously missed in policy discussions in the Irish context. Ultimately, I argue that the quote at the beginning of this chapter may be misleading and that, rather than seeing poverty as a function of educational disadvantage, we need to begin to recognise fully the ways in which educational disadvantage is a function of the relationship between education and the economy and, consequently, of economic inequality.

The non-debate about educational disadvantage

When writers start to 'define their terms', readers often start to skim through the pages. Definitional debates can appear to be a fairly academic exercise in the worst sense of that term: sterile debates about words that have little impact on or relevance for real lives. This is far from being the case with regard to the relationship between education and poverty. Definitional debates in this area are ideological debates which impact upon how targets are set and interventions are framed and, consequently, have a major impact upon people's lives.

'Educational disadvantage' is the term that is commonly used to designate the fact that there exists a relationship between the background of learners and their educational attainment and participation. On the one hand, it is arguable that the meaning of this term should be relatively uncontested given that it is defined in law. Section 32, paragraph 9 of the Education Act 1998 identifies that the term educational disadvantage means 'the impediments to education arising from social or economic disadvantage which prevent students from deriving appropriate benefit from education in schools'. On the other hand, however, O'Sullivan has noted that there are many different processes implied by different people in the use of this common term, and that its widespread usage must be thought of as representing a 'phoney consensus' or an exercise in avoidance (1999, p. 18). He argues further that the use of this common term in the policy process by people who mean different things by it represents a process of 'pastiche'-making, through which traces of different understandings become merged and mixed in a manner which ignores or hides the dynamic contestation between different positions and, as such, denies the possibility to think critically about these different positions (2005, p. 319).

O'Sullivan is not the first to draw attention to different positions relating to educational disadvantage. There are numerous accounts within the Irish literature alone which use the deficit/difference categorisation to identify different approaches to educational disadvantage (for example CMRS, 1992; Drudy and Lynch, 1993; Kellaghan et al., 1993; INTO, 1994). This two-fold categorisation is based on identifying what is seen as being the 'cause' of educational disadvantage. The 'deficit' perspective focuses on a presumed deficit in the family or community of the disadvantaged person such as particular patterns of parent–child interaction, neglect or abuse, a culture of poverty or an urban ghetto. The 'difference' perspective identifies cultural difference or dissonance as being the primary cause for educational disadvantage. The focus here is on the cultural capital that is valued by the school (Bourdieu and Passeron, 1977) including the language choices the school makes (for example Tizard and Hughes, 1984) or on the style of teaching and thinking that the school chooses to value.

Although this two-fold division is the standard analytical framework that is applied to educational disadvantage in the literature – both in Ireland and internationally – it remains quite limited in its utility. Any attempt to categorise does, of course, do some degree of violence to the different positions that are categorised together, but the task must be to produce a system of categorisation that can capture a diversity of positions without leaving the area so complex as to render the approach useless. The deficit/difference model tends to render problematic any attempt to make sense of the relationships between and within what are referred to as common positions. By reducing a number of diverse positions to just two, the deficit/difference model avoids pastiche but becomes something of a parody. O'Sullivan (1999, 2005) presents a more complex model, with six different positions which are covered by the term 'educational disadvantage'. These are:

- A sense of the *constitutional limitations* of the person, that is identifying that people who are educationally disadvantaged have a low intellectual capacity

- A sense that the socialisation of pre-school children makes them unable to benefit fully from the education offered by school and as such leaves them with a *personal deficit*

- A sense that the cultural environment of some children is deficient and that this *cultural deficit* leads to them developing anti-school and antisocial attitudes and values

- A sense that schooling practices can be derived from a middle-class culture and, as a consequence, can be *culturally irrelevant* to working-class pupils or at least discontinuous with their home culture in a way that is not true for middle-class pupils

- A sense that the *material condition*, the wealth or poverty, of the pupil's community impacts upon their housing, their healthcare and, consequently, on their school conditions

- A sense that inequality is a function of the *political economy* of our society, and that disadvantage exists because some parents are in a position to give their children an advantage in society (through education) thereby placing others at a disadvantage.

For O'Sullivan, the purpose of exploring these diverse positions as diverse positions is precisely that the interplay between them generates critical thinking about them. One way into this massive task is to look at the way in which debates concerning the measuring of educational disadvantage have played out, a task I have explored elsewhere (Tormey, forthcoming) and which I will summarise here. Although this has the disadvantage of returning to a binary model of thinking about the issues, it does at least allow one part of the web of oppositions implicit in O'Sullivan's typology to be explored in greater depth.

Throughout the 1990s the measurement of educational disadvantage became a key issue as governments sought to quantify the problem in order that progress or a lack of progress in addressing the problem could be clearly identified (for example Kellaghan *et al.*, 1995; NESF, 1997; the range of attempts are summarised by Boldt and Devine, 1998). Power and Tormey (2000) identify that, broadly speaking, two different sorts of measurement models were used: an *outputs model* which focused on setting minimum standards of attainment deemed appropriate and then identifying as disadvantaged those whose attainment fell below these levels; and a *comparative model* which sought to identify systematic differences between social groups in participation or attainment across the educational system. Those using an outputs model may, for example, identify that those who fall below a certain standard on a reading test or those who leave school without five passes in the Leaving Certificate are educationally disadvantaged (for example Crooks and Stokes, 1987). A more complex variant of the same approach is to identify those whose educational attainment falls below a certain level and who are also poor as being educationally disadvantaged (for example Kellaghan *et al.*, 1995). Those using a comparative model on the other hand will tend to look for systematic differences between social groups, such as by exploring how the attainment or participation rates of pupils of working-class or unemployed parents compares with those of pupils of middle-class or professional backgrounds (for example Clancy, 1995; Clancy and Wall, 2000; Power and Tormey, 2000; Gorby *et al.*, 2005; O'Connell *et al.*, 2006).

The outputs approach tends to focus on low levels of educational attainment by poor pupils, and, in line with the maxim 'that which gets measured gets addressed', those who use this approach tend to look for interventions that are aimed at raising the level of educational attainment by these pupils. As discussed in the introduction, this tends to ignore the capacity for pupils from middle-class or professional backgrounds to raise their own levels of attainment and participation as necessary in order to protect their competitive advantage or to find alternative routes of conferring advantage upon themselves, such as the use of social networks. In this respect, the outputs approach to measurement is associated with a conservative political position that seeks to work upon the 'disadvantaged' while ignoring the role that the 'advantaged' play in the creation and perpetuation of inequality in educational attainment and life chances. The comparative approach on the other hand is associated with a more liberal and egalitarian political model that draws attention to both the role of advantage and disadvantage and the relationship between the two.[2]

The tendency to see such measurement positions as a technical debate, only of concern to those with an interest in educational statistics, allows the truly political nature of the decisions about measurement to be obscured (Tormey, forthcoming). In this context it is notable that, while the state has often used a language which draws on liberal conceptions of equality, the targets that have been set in relation to educational disadvantage have been politically conservative output measures (see Ireland, 1997, 2002). Indeed, this process continues to be evident today, with at least some of the targets set for the *National Action Plan for*

---

[2] See Lynch (1999, p. 55ff) for a critical account of this liberal political approach to the measurement of educational inequality.

Social Inclusion 2007–2016 being little more than re-heated versions of previous output measures (Ireland, 2007). While the 1997 *National Anti-Poverty Strategy* set a target of 90 per cent of students completing senior cycle by 2000, and 98 per cent by 2007, this was later revised downwards to 85 per cent school completion by 2003 and 90 per cent by 2006 (Ireland, 1997, 2002). These targets, which have been repeatedly missed, have now once more been presented in the *National Action Plan for Social Inclusion 2007–2016*, which has set as one of its goals that it will 'Work to ensure that the proportion of the population aged 20–24 completing upper second-level education or equivalent will exceed 90 per cent by 2013' (Ireland, 2007, p. 33).

There is then, as O'Sullivan (1999) suggests, a need to get beyond the phoney consensus on educational disadvantage and make sense of the different positions that are hidden behind the term. These different positions do not just reflect an academic debate but also demonstrate widely divergent political perspectives on how educational disadvantage is caused, on the nature of the problems to which it gives rise, on how it is to be measured and on how it is to be addressed. These issues should not be treated as technical questions to be addressed by experts but should be recognised as being deeply political and having a real impact upon how the state comes to intervene to address educational disadvantage. In this context, the tendency towards pastiche that O'Sullivan describes has real political effects.

The international perspective(s)

There have been a number of attempts to identify how we in Ireland can learn from the international experience of educational disadvantage. As such there is a body of Irish literature that looks at the international experience of interventions to address low attainment by poor or disadvantaged pupils (see Kellaghan *et al.*, 1995; Archer and Weir, 2004). It is therefore instructive to choose a perspective that has not been used as a lens through which to think about educational policy in Ireland. In this section I will look at the international debates on the role of educational markets in the perpetuation of inequality, particularly within the context of neo-liberal or 'new-right' educational policy reforms in many English-speaking countries.

While there is no single new-right reform package in education, the reforms that happened in the UK, US, Australia and New Zealand since the 1980s tended to draw from a similar menu. At the core of the neo-liberal educational reforms internationally is the generation of markets in education through creating a 'choice' for parents (or 'clients') as to where to have their children educated. In contexts in which the state had played a strong role in overseeing and managing schools, management was handed back to schools and they became 'self-managing'. Alongside this, parents were encouraged to make choices as to where to send their children to school. In order to facilitate this choice, a number of countries moved to produce comparisons between schools ('league tables') that would provide parents with information upon which to base their decision. While many countries had seen 'school zoning' in the 1960s in order to ensure a social mix within schools and to combat segregation in education, neo-liberals now promoted the removal of such zoning in order (they said) to enable those in disadvantaged areas (often city-centre areas) to move into more successful (middle-class, suburban) schools (Coleman, 1990). The implications of these policies are hardly surprising in the context of the operation of markets: those schools that score well on the league table are expected to attract pupils and the resources which go with them. Those that score poorly are expected to attract fewer pupils and consequently fewer resources. This, it was envisaged, would ensure that 'excellent' schools grow, while 'failing' schools are motivated to improve or will, eventually, be shut down and removed from the market.

It is worth remembering that this new-right reform movement for education did not develop in a vacuum, but as a response to existing educational ideas. As Brown (1990) observes, the discourse of educational reform since the end of World War II tended to focus on ideas of equality and meritocracy in education. In Britain, this meant increased investment in education and, in the 1960s, a move towards comprehensive education in order that working-class pupils and middle-class pupils would be educated side by side rather than in separate schools. The US in the same period, and following on from the Brown *v.* the Board of Education of Topeka (1954) Supreme Court ruling, also saw an end to segregated schooling. In New Zealand in the 1950s a school zoning policy was introduced in order to promote equality of educational opportunity (Olssen *et al.*, 2004). As Brown (1990) argues, the end result of this series of policies, in the UK at least, was an improvement in educational standards and a reduction in gender-based and social-class-based inequalities in education.

Brown goes on to argue that, in this context, neo-liberal reforms should be seen as undermining the principles of equality of educational opportunity. His position is vigorously supported by a number of authors who argue that school choice simply facilitates middle-class parents, who have greater freedom of movement due to better transportation (Apple, 2000), as well as a discourse of choice more suited to gaining advantage in the educational market (Ball *et al.*, 1995; Gewirtz *et al.*, 1995). Edwards and Tomlinson (2002, cited in Olssen *et al.*, 2004) have also argued that when 'desirable' schools become over-subscribed the processes of 'choice' become reversed and schools are able to select pupils rather than the other way around. These authors argue that the process of choice is far more complex than the sort of 'rational choice' model implied by neo-liberal proponents of markets in education and that the increase in choice has led to greater segregation of schools and greater inequality.

While Gorard *et al.* (2003) find that segregation in schools actually fell a little after the market-based reforms in England and Wales, they also identify that, from the mid-1990s, segregation increased again in England, but not in Wales. As such, they argue that parental choice may have had some impact on lessening segregation by allowing poorer parents to opt out of weak local schools. Ultimately, however, this impact was limited and short-lived (Gorard and Fitz, 2006).

In English-speaking countries other than Ireland, policy debates in relation to poverty-based and social-class-based inequalities in education have been dominated for the last few decades by the politics of markets and of choice. For some, such policies are seen as an assault on the egalitarian ideas associated with an earlier period of educational reform. For others, they are a means to overcome bureaucratic and inefficient modes of school governance and, consequently, to reduce restrictions on poorer parents, which may in turn contribute to inequality. While there is sometimes bitter disagreement between these two positions, it is broadly accepted by all that social segregation in schools is undesirable and, ultimately, that the data do not show market systems significantly lessening social segregation, but instead that they can facilitate practices of segregation. If this is the lens through which equality issues in education have been viewed internationally since the 1980s, how can this lens help us make sense of the Irish context?

Markets and choice in education in Ireland

It is a widely held belief that Ireland has successfully resisted the new-right educational reform movement since the 1980s. *Education for a Changing World: Green Paper on Education* (Ireland, 1992) represented a clear movement towards new-right thinking in relation to education (Halton, 2003) and was heavily criticised for its right-wing assumptions by almost the entire educational community (for example Drudy and Lynch, 1993). A subsequent change in government (with the replacement of a very pro-enterprise government with a Labour–Fianna Fáil government, and the appointment of a Labour Party Minister for Education) led to a movement to re-appraise the foundations of the green paper, through the calling of a National Education Convention (1994). This Convention, which drew together the major players in Irish education, re-emphasised the existing values base of the education system and the shift to the right seemed to be halted.

Hogan (2000) suggests that the employment of this distinctive partnership model led to Ireland taking a different path to that of other English-speaking countries at the time. And, while there has undoubtedly been a growth in the tendency to refer to the education system in terms of its 'clients' and 'customers' (such as in the Department of Education and Science's 'Customer Service Charter' and successive strategy statements), and in pressure from media sources either to publish league tables or to release data which would enable them to produce their own crude league tables, Hogan argues that the Education Act 1998 and the Teaching Council Bill (which became the Teaching Council Act 2001) reflect Ireland's decision not to follow the neo-liberal road. The ongoing opposition to the demands for information that might allow crude league tables to be constructed only reinforces this perception. There is a sense that Ireland has largely escaped the new-right educational reforms found in the rest of the English-speaking world, that we have, as Hogan puts it (following Robert Frost), taken the road 'less travelled by, / And that has made all the difference' (2000, p. 19).

Yet the educational reforms found in Ireland, like others elsewhere, must be seen in their particular and historical context. While in other countries the new right was a response to the liberal or left-leaning educational policies enacted since the end of World War II, it can be argued that in Ireland there had been few such left-leaning policies. While other countries had seen substantial movement towards comprehensive or de-segregated education, Ireland had seen little that was comparable. Although there had certainly been a growth in educational provision at post-primary level since the late 1960s, this was not matched by structural reform such as a move towards comprehensive education that might lessen the extent to which the school system was segregated. Indeed, while there were some attempts to introduce first comprehensive, then community, schools in Ireland in the 1960s and early 1970s, this was something which was always weakly promoted and conceptualised (O'Sullivan, 2005) and did not materialise to anything like the extent envisaged by various government ministers. While this period did see greater access to schools for young people from poor or working-class families, this access was not followed up with the economic resources (see Lee, 1989) or the cultural change in schools that might have signalled a serious attempt to generate greater equality. As a result, Ireland continued to have a system that allowed for significant segregation between secondary/academic and vocational streams (Barber, 1989, p. 84).

Indeed, while the 1980s were marked in other countries by policies aimed at increasing local management of schools and the generation of a market in education, Ireland already had locally managed schools and a fully functioning market. Local management of schools has historically been central to the Irish system of educational management (Coolahan, 1981) and, as O'Sullivan has pointed out, in Ireland, 'parents have always been free to seek a place in the school of their choice for their children' (2005, p. 168). In urban areas, he notes, the practice of sending children to schools other than the local one is common and widespread and, even in rural areas, he cites evidence of such practices since the 1960s. It has been estimated, he says, that one-half of all second-level students do not attend their nearest school. There is also anecdotal evidence that some schools that welcome children from the Traveller community experience a decline in enrolments as parents avail of the market and 'choose' to segregate the school system. Indeed, the suspicion that schools are engaging in informal exclusionary practices recently led the Minister for Education Mary Hanafin to moot the idea of an audit of school enrolments to identify if some schools show comparatively low levels of children from minority ethnic groups (*Irish Examiner*, 29 August 2006), and to identify that this audit is showing some informal exclusionary practices (*Irish Examiner*, 10 October 2006). Smyth's research, based on over one hundred schools and 10,000 pupils, has shown the educational impact of such segregation (1999, p. 49, p. 70):

> The social class mix (average social class) within a school has a significant impact upon pupil performance [at Junior Certificate level] ... Pupils in predominantly middle class schools tend to have higher exam scores than those in predominantly working class schools, even when their own social background is taken into account ... The social class mix of a school has a significant impact upon Leaving Cert grades. Those in predominantly working class schools tend to make less progress over Senior Cycle, relative to their performance at Junior Cert level.

So, while Halton (2003) argues that the new-right tendencies in Ireland in the early 1990s were associated with the influence of the OECD, O'Sullivan (2005) points out that Ireland needed little impetus from any external forces to operate the education system upon right-wing lines. Put simply, Ireland did not need new-right educational reforms when the educational system already operated on the basis of old-right principles. Yet, while inequality debates throughout the English-speaking world have focused on such practices for the last few decades, this topic has been remarkably absent from such debates in Ireland. This begs the question, if these practices are not the subject of the discussions on the relationship between education and poverty, what is?

Understanding disadvantage and intervening

In Ireland, interventions to address educational disadvantage are characterised by two apparently contradictory principles. First, they tend to be scattered. Second, they tend to be targeted. I will look at these issues in turn.

The major interventions to address educational disadvantage in Ireland have included (see boxed text for further details):

- Designation of schools as being in areas of disadvantage
- Home–School–Community Liaison scheme
- 8–15 Early School-Leavers Initiative (followed by the 'Stay in School' Retention Initiative)
- Early Start
- Support Teacher Project (Teacher/Counsellor Project)
- Breaking the Cycle
- Giving Children an Even Break
- Educational Disadvantage Committee
- Education and Welfare Board
- DEIS (Delivering Equality of Opportunity in Schools).

In addition to these might be added the additional supports provided through resource teachers, visiting teachers for Travellers and so on. A review of the evaluations of many of these initiatives has been undertaken by Archer and Weir (2004; see also Weir and Archer, 2004). They note that some of these schemes show evidence of some successes (particularly when measured in terms of principals' and teachers' views of the schemes), and that many of these schemes are in keeping with some aspects of international models of best practice, particularly with respect to parental

Major schemes to address educational disadvantage

The school-based schemes aimed at addressing educational disadvantage in Ireland have been described and reviewed in detail by Archer and Weir (2004). A brief description of the major schemes is included here.

- The designation of schools as being in areas of disadvantage (DAS) scheme began initially in 1984 but was formalised in 1990. This scheme provides for concessionary teaching posts and additional grants to primary and post-primary schools, which are selected on the basis of a number of social, educational and economic indicators. It is broadly felt that this scheme does little more than bring income and resources of schools in designated disadvantaged areas to a level comparable to schools in more advantaged areas (Kellaghan *et al.*, 1995).

- The Home–School–Community Liaison (HSCL) scheme also began in 1990, with an initial fifty-five primary schools. It was subsequently rolled out to other designated disadvantaged primary schools and to post-primary schools. The scheme allows a teacher to be appointed full time to the task of developing a stronger relationship between parents and schools and between the school and its community. Weir and Archer (2004) note that the scheme has been evaluated positively by a number of researchers, particularly in relation to its impact upon parental involvement and on teachers' attitudes to parents.

- The Early Start initiative sought to provide early childhood education in a targeted way to some schools in designated disadvantaged areas. Three-year-old children were provided with 2.5 hours of pre-school education either in the morning or afternoon throughout the school year. It was envisaged that this would contribute to the development of the child and make them more 'ready' for school. Practices in Early Start have evolved significantly since the programme was introduced, in part due to issues raised in evaluations of the scheme.

- Like the HSCL scheme, the School Completion programme sought to identify the need for engagement from the wider community in addressing educational disadvantage. It targeted post-primary schools and their feeder primary schools and provided resources which allow them to develop interventions to support those most vulnerable to dropping out of school. The programme explicitly highlights the need for a multifaceted response to early school-leaving and identifies the need for collaboration between the school and community, youth and sporting organisations as well as with institutional representatives such as community gardaí, social workers, health board personnel and so on.

- The Teacher/Counsellor Project was set up in 1996 to assist in the management of disruptive or introverted pupils. It was envisaged that the designated teacher would play a role in supporting whole school work on behaviour, bullying etc., as well as assisting individual teachers and pupils through withdrawal of particular pupils. The scheme received positive evaluations that highlight its impact upon individual pupils and on the whole school.

- Breaking the Cycle was introduced in 1995, following the review of the DAS (Kellaghan et al., 1995). The 1995 review highlighted that the criteria used to designate schools tended to discriminate against rural schools. It also highlighted that rural educational disadvantage was a significant issue. In response, the Breaking the Cycle scheme allowed for different criteria to be used in selecting urban schools and clusters of rural schools. The scheme provided extra resources to schools and allowed for the reduction of sizes in junior classes to about fifteen pupils per teacher. As with some other schemes, the views of principals and teachers tended to be more positive than the objective and measurable data seemed to support. There is some evidence that those students selected for inclusion in rural areas did not include the most disadvantaged, leading Weir and Archer (2004, pp. 17–18) to conclude that it 'may be the case also that disadvantaged pupils in rural areas are dispersed across schools rather than concentrated in a small number of schools and, therefore, using the school as the level of intervention may be inappropriate in rural areas'.

- The 1995 review of the DAS also made it clear that targeting resources at those schools that had the highest concentrations of disadvantaged pupils in effect meant that the majority of disadvantaged pupils (who were not in such concentrated settings) were not being addressed at all. The Giving Children an Even Break scheme sought to disperse funding more widely in order to reach these students. Almost all schools that made returns under the scheme received some additional funding and a smaller group were allocated additional staff. In rural areas, as with Breaking the Cycle, clusters of schools were addressed.

- In 2003, the plethora of schemes available meant that there was a patchwork of provision rather than an integrated approach to supporting those at risk throughout their educational life. As a result, while some schools hosted almost all of the available initiatives, others hosted only one or two. In response the DEIS initiative (Delivering Equality of Opportunity in Schools) was developed in order to provide a more integrated approach to targeting support at those schools which have the greatest concentration of educational disadvantage. It is envisaged that over a period of five years, Early Start, Giving Children an Even Break, the HSCL scheme, the School Completion programme and the DAS will all be integrated into a comprehensive school support programme, under DEIS.

and community involvement, class size reductions and additional financial support. However, they also note that the schemes do not fare particularly well when measured in terms of objective measures of educational attainment. In the context of this mixed assessment they note: 'In view of this progress, the fact that so few of the evaluations of existing schemes found evidence of gains in measured achievement … may be regarded as disappointing. The fact that the performance of pupils in designated schools continues to fall so far below the performance of other pupils … will also be seen as disappointing' (p. 31).

The diversity of programmes to address educational disadvantage led then Minister for Education Noel Dempsey to describe this list as a 'menu of programmes from preschool to lifelong learning' (Educational Disadvantage Committee, 2003, p. 5). O'Sullivan (2005) argues, instead, that the concept of pastiche is once more relevant here; as with the conceptualisation of disadvantage, these interventions are something of a tangle of ideas drawn from different sources and placed alongside each other without allowing them to problematise each other or to contribute to a more adequate conceptualisation of the issues. It contributes to the impression that a lot is being done to address the problem, while at the same time obscuring the question as to why we have this problem in the first place.

The second characteristic of Irish responses to educational disadvantage is that most are targeted, based on the idea that we should identify the disadvantaged and address their specific needs. As I have noted elsewhere (NESF, 2003), one of the effects of such targeted responses is to focus attention on the groups or individuals who are regarded as 'failing' within the system rather than focusing on the system itself. It should be remembered that the debate as to whether targeting is even a useful response in the case of educational disadvantage remains an open one. Although educational disadvantage is often associated in people's minds with urban areas and high-rise flat complexes, evidence from Kellaghan *et al*. (1995) notes that over 60 per cent of pupils identified as disadvantaged lived in small towns or the open countryside. Therefore, it is worth taking note of Pringle's assertion that 'the concept of targeting is probably almost meaningless in a rural context' (1999, p. 271); this view is supported by the comments of Weir and Archer (2004) in relation to the Breaking the Cycle scheme, cited above.

While targeting may enable us to reach those schools or areas with the greatest concentration of disadvantaged young people, it will probably miss most of the disadvantaged. In such a context, interventions which aim to change the education system itself are perhaps more appropriate. Even if targeting was to be defended as an appropriate means of using scarce resources (Kellaghan *et al.*, 1995), its role in deflecting attention from systemic responses remains.

What might such systemic responses look like? For a start they might begin by seeking to address those aspects of the educational system that may be contributing to inequalities. This would probably involve some move towards a centralised or regional applications and allocations system for primary and secondary education, which might work to counter market forces and effectively to de-segregate the school system. Such a centralised applications system has already been put in place in Limerick where a number of students were refused entry by schools in the city (although the focus of this system is not de-segregation as such). The regional education boards proposed under a Labour Party

Minister for Education (Ireland, 1995) might well have been an appropriate regional vehicle for addressing this issue countrywide, had they not been scrapped by the return to power of a Fianna Fáil–Progressive Democrats coalition. While parents would still be free to 'buy' themselves out of such a public education system, it would at least mean that the public purse was not actually facilitating and funding the promotion of inequalities.

A systemic approach would also see other issues, such as school practices associated with inequality (like streaming or banding), being addressed. In-career teacher development to promote more appropriate pedagogic models might also be a priority. Again, the education boards might well have played a role in this since they were envisaged as having a focus on promoting equality of access, participation and benefit from education, and specifically held a brief in relation to curricular provision, provision of support services to schools and resolving disputes concerning enrolment.

It is notable that, of late, there is some evidence that systemic and structural issues are starting to be addressed in policy debates. The National Council for Curriculum and Assessment's proposals in relation to the reform of Senior Cycle education are aimed at improving equality of outcomes through the creation of greater flexibility in pathways and accreditation and a change in school culture which might be more conducive to retention and attainment by those students who currently do poorly (NCCA, 2005). Recent work by Archer and Weir (2004) for the Educational Disadvantage Committee also reflects a move in the policy debate, in that their review of research into possible interventions to tackle educational disadvantage addresses school-based factors such as teachers' expectations of pupils and also highlights issues of teacher in-career development. Perhaps we are beginning to see a change in the content of the debates around education and poverty in Ireland. Whether this change in content will factor into a meaningful change in approach, however, remains to be seen.

Conclusions

At the outset I suggested that education is often promoted as a key means to remove people from poverty. The reality however is more complex, and it may be that it is precisely the capacity of education to enable people to access wealth and resources in later life that ensures that those who have an advantage will use the resources at their disposal to ensure their advantage is continued. This recognition – that the education system will tend to reflect the broader inequalities in society – is what is often missed (or hidden) by approaches that focus on the need to raise the educational attainment levels of poor or working-class young people.

This is not to say that attempts to improve the education of poor or working-class young people are misguided – such interventions are necessary and even the minimum goals set by the government in social inclusion policies from the 1997 *National Anti-Poverty Strategy* to the *National Action Plan for Social Inclusion 2007–2016* would be welcome were they to be met. At the same time, these must be recognised as minimum standards and should not be thought of as interventions that are aimed at greater levels of equality. Educational reforms can play a part, though the distribution of the disadvantaged throughout the country and the extent to which the current market-based structure of education is likely to be contributing to the problem suggests that those responses should be focused on the education system rather than just targeted at individuals. At the same time, educational disadvantage is tied to social and economic power and it cannot be addressed in isolation from these factors. Ultimately, we will need to confront the reality that educational disadvantage is not just related to future poverty but is also an outcome of an unequal society.

This issue has long been identified in research by the ESRI and by Lynch (1999), but has long been ignored in policy work on educational disadvantage. Following on in that ESRI tradition, Smyth and Hannan (2000, p. 113) suggest that:

> If social groups continue to differ in their financial and cultural resources, then differences in educational participation are likely to persist ... Only in Sweden (and to a lesser extent, the Netherlands) has there been any significant reduction in inequality of educational opportunity over time, a process that is attributable not only to educational reform but also to diminishing social class differences in income and living conditions.

Put simply, in order to enable education to help lift people out of poverty, we may also need first to address our problem of poverty.

References

Apple, M. (2000), *Educating the Right Way: Markets, Standards, God and Inequality*, London: RoutledgeFalmer

Archer, P. and Weir, S. (2004), *Addressing Disadvantage, A Review of International Literature and of Strategy in Ireland*, Dublin: Educational Disadvantage Committee

Ball, S., Bowe, R. and Gewirtz, S. (1995), 'Circuits of Schooling: A Sociological Exploration of Parental Choice of School in Social-Class Contexts', *The Sociological Review*, vol. 43, pp. 52–78

Barber, N. (1989), *Comprehensive Schooling in Ireland*, Broadsheet Series Paper no. 25, Dublin: Economic and Social Research Institute

Boldt, S. and Devine, B. (1998), 'Educational Disadvantage in Ireland: Literature Review and Summary Report', in Doyle, P. (ed.), *Educational Disadvantage and Early School Leaving*, Dublin: Combat Poverty Agency

Bourdieu, P. and Passeron, J.-C. (1977), *Reproduction in Education, Culture and Society*, London: Sage

Brown, P. (1990), 'The 'Third Wave': Education and the Ideology of Parentocracy', *British Journal of Sociology of Education*, vol. 11, pp. 65–85

Clancy, P. (1995), *Access to College: Patterns of Continuity and Change*, Dublin: Higher Education Authority

Clancy, P. and Wall, J. (2000), *Social Background of Higher Education Entrants*, Dublin: Higher Education Authority

CMRS (1992), *Education and Poverty: Eliminating Disadvantage in the Primary School Years*, Dublin: Conference of Major Religious Superiors

Coleman, J. (1990), *Achievement and Equality in Education*, Boulder: Westview Press

Coolahan, J. (1981), *Irish Education, History and Structure*, Dublin: Institute of Public Administration

Crooks, T. and Stokes, D. (eds.) (1987), *Disadvantage, Learning and Young People: The Implications for Education and Training*, Dublin: CDVEC, CDU and TCD

Derman-Sparks, L. (2002), 'Disadvantage and Diversity: Untangling Their Roles in Children's Development and in Education', in St Patrick's College, *Primary Education; Ending Disadvantage. Proceedings and Action Plan of the National Forum*, Dublin: St Patrick's College, Drumcondra

Drudy, S. and Lynch, K. (1993), *Schools and Society in Ireland*, Dublin: Gill & Macmillan

Educational Disadvantage Committee (2003), *Educational Disadvantage Forum, Report of the Inaugural Meeting*, Dublin: Educational Disadvantage Committee

Gewirtz, S., Ball, S. and Bowe, R. (1995), *Markets, Choice and Equity in Education*, Buckingham: Open University Press

Gorard, S. and Fitz, J. (2006), 'What Counts as Evidence in the School Choice Debate', *British Educational Research Journal*, vol. 32, pp. 797–816

Gorard, S., Taylor, C. and Fitz, J. (2003), *Schools, Markets and Choice Policies*, London: RoutledgeFalmer

Gorby, S., McCoy, S. and Watson, D. (2005), *2004 Annual School Leaver's Survey of 2002/2003 Leavers*, Dublin: ESRI

Halton, M. (2003), 'Benchmarking: Another Attempt to Introduce Market-Oriented Policies into Irish Second-Level Education?', *Pedagogy, Culture and Society*, vol. 11, pp. 331–351

Hogan, P. (2000), 'The Road Not Taken and the One with Better Claim', *Issues in Education*, vol. 5, pp. 13–20

INTO (1994), *Poverty and Educational Disadvantage, Breaking the Cycle*, Dublin: Irish National Teachers Organisation

Ireland (1992), *Education for a Changing World: Green Paper on Education*, Dublin: Stationery Office

Ireland (1995), *Charting Our Educational Future: White Paper on Education*, Dublin: Stationery Office

Ireland (1997), *National Anti-Poverty Strategy*, Dublin: Stationery Office

Ireland (2002), *Building an Inclusive Society*, Dublin: Stationery Office: www.welfare.ie/publications/naps/bais.pdf

Ireland (2006), *White Paper on Irish Aid*, Dublin: Stationery Office

Ireland (2007), *National Action Plan for Social Inclusion 2007–2016*, Dublin: Stationery Office

Irish Examiner (2006a), 'Hanafin Audit To Tackle School "Racism"', 29 August

Irish Examiner (2006b), 'Audit May Force Schools To Take Minority Students', 10 October

Kellaghan, T., Sloane, K., Alvarez, B. and Bloom, B. S. (1993), *The Home Environment and School Learning: Promoting Parental Involvement in the Education of Children*, San Francisco: Jossey-Bass

Kellaghan, T., Weir, S., Ó hUallacháin, S. and Morgan, M. (1995), *Educational Disadvantage in Ireland*, Dublin: Education Research Centre, Combat Poverty Agency and Department of Education

Layte, R. and Whelan, C. T. (2000), 'The Rising Tide of Equality of Opportunity: The Changing Class Structure', in Nolan, B., O'Connell, P. J. and Whelan, C. T. (eds.), *Bust to Boom? The Irish Experience of Growth and Inequality*, Dublin: Institute of Public Administration

Lee, J. (1989), *Ireland 1912–1985, Politics and Society*, Cambridge: Cambridge University Press

Lynch, K. (1999), *Equality in Education*, Dublin: Gill & Macmillan

McCoy, S. and Williams, J. (2000), *1999 Annual School-Leavers Survey of 1997/1998 Leavers*, Dublin: ESRI

McDonald, E. (1998), 'Reading Achievement and Educational Disadvantage', *Irish Educational Studies*, vol. 17, pp. 208–221

National Education Convention (1994), *Report on the National Education Convention*, Dublin: National Education Convention Secretariat

NCCA (2005), 'Proposals for the Future Development of Senior Cycle Education in Ireland', Dublin: National Council for Curriculum and Assessment

NESF (1997), *Early School-Leavers and Youth Unemployment*, Forum Report no. 11, Dublin: National Economic and Social Forum

NESF (2003), *NAPS Social Inclusion Forum, 30 January 2003, Report*, Dublin: National Economic and Social Forum

Ó Briain, E. (2006), *Analysis of School Attendance Data at Primary and Post-Primary Levels for 2004/2005*, Dublin: National Education and Welfare Board and MORI

O'Connell, P., Clancy, D. and McCoy, S. (2006), *Who Went to College in 2004?*, Dublin: Higher Education Authority

OECD (1965), *Investment in Education, Ireland. Report of the Survey Team Appointed by the Irish Minister for Education*, Dublin: Government Publications

OECD (1997), *Literacy Skills for the Knowledge Society, Further Results from the OECD International Literacy Survey*, Paris: Organisation for Economic Co-operation and Development

Olssen, M., Codd, J. and O'Neill, A. M. (2004), *Education Policy, Globalisation, Citizenship and Democracy*, London: Sage

O'Sullivan, D. (1999), 'Educational Disadvantage: Excavating Theoretical Frameworks', in Fahy, K. (ed.), *Strategies to Address Educational Disadvantage*, Galway: Community Workers Co-operative

O'Sullivan, D. (2005), *Cultural Politics and Irish Education since the 1950s*, Dublin: Institute of Public Administration

Power, C. and Tormey, R. (2000), 'Refocusing the Debate: An Examination of the Interplay between Measurement and Intervention in Educational Disadvantage', *CEDR Occasional Paper No. 2*, Limerick: Centre for Educational Disadvantage Research

Pringle, D. (1999), 'Something Old, Something New: Lessons to Be Learnt from Previous Strategies of Positive Territorial Discrimination', in Pringle, D., Walsh, J. and Hennessy, M. (eds.), *Poor People, Poor Places: A Geography of Poverty and Deprivation in Ireland*, Dublin: Oak Tree Press

Smyth, E. (1999), *Do Schools Differ? Academic and Personal Development among Pupils in the Second-level Sector*, Dublin: Oak Tree Press

Smyth, E. and Hannan, D. (2000) 'Education and Inequality', in Nolan, B., O'Connell, P. J. and Whelan, C. T. (eds.), *Bust to Boom? The Irish Experience of Growth and Inequality*, Dublin: Institute of Public Administration

Tizard, B. and Hughes, H. (1984), *Young Children Learning, Talking and Thinking at Home and at School*, London: Fontana Press

Tormey, R. (forthcoming), 'The Silent Politics of Measurement: Contesting the Measuring of Educational Disadvantage', in Conway, P., FitzPatrick, S., Boland, J. and Hammond, J. (eds.), *Curriculum Contestation*, Dublin: Educational Studies Association of Ireland and National Council for Curriculum and Assessment

Weir, S. and Archer, P. (2004), *A Review of School-Based Measures Aimed at Addressing Educational Disadvantage in Ireland; A Report to the Educational Disadvantage Committee*, Dublin: Educational Research Centre

Chapter 7

Health and modern Irish society: The mother and father of a dilemma

Cecily Kelleher

Introduction

The health profile of the Irish population has been relatively poor for decades, both within Ireland itself and amongst migrants from Ireland across the so-called Irish diaspora. Contemporary health statistics across the EU show relatively poor life expectancy for both men and women and higher than average rates of cardiovascular diseases and some cancers in Ireland. Recent data confirm what is seen widely in other industrialised countries, that health inequalities exist across social classes in Ireland and, as the country becomes more urbanised, pockets of severe disadvantage are apparent at area level. While health indicators are improving and the country is experiencing unprecedented economic growth, the gap between richest and poorest is widening and this must be addressed.

The international literature confirms that health disadvantage begins at the earliest stage of life and may follow a trajectory, cumulative or critical period pattern. A recent report on perinatal statistics confirms the social patterning of pregnancy-related outcomes and new cohort data support also this evidence that long-term health into adult life may be influenced by childhood circumstances. This suggests the critical importance of maternal and child health policies as an investment for the future. Research into the influence of area or location on health suggests that both community development strategies that foster social capital and community empowerment but also top-down policy strategies across the relevant sectors of health, education, social welfare, transport and housing are required to produce concerted public policies that target ghettoisation and material disadvantage. Because health status is determined across sectors, all public policy requires health proofing and, where relevant, a health impact assessment.

The health services are undergoing significant administrative and organisational reform and are receiving considerable media attention, though this focuses mainly on acute hospital services, particularly the emergency services. There is insufficient focus on the fact that concerted primary care services are required and the recommendations of the primary care strategy (DOHC, 2001a) are not yet being met. The manpower reforms in the hospital sector suggest that equity of access and consultant-delivered services, with adequate primary care and step-down facilities, should be implemented. The longstanding two-tier healthcare system needs review to provide universal equity of access, in both primary and hospital care settings. Any strategy to expand the private hospital infrastructure should address the reality that most people in Ireland today are not entitled to comprehensive healthcare, and the one-half of the population that holds private insurance currently receives hospital care predominantly in the public setting.

Irish society has transformed beyond recognition in the last decade, ensuring that the future of emerging generations is likely to be very different from the past (CSO, 2007). How this future is shaped will be highly determined by public policy, which is nowhere more controversial than in the health arena. The promotion of health and provision of healthcare are two basic values that on the face of it should be inherent to modern society, yet considerable variations in health expectancy exist between Ireland and other countries, and within Ireland according to both the location and social position of its people.

The commonly held assumption that treatment services are the main health-determining factor is only true in part. In reality, population health reflects wider social and economic conditions as well as healthcare provision and this needs to be understood when putting in place appropriate public policies. To understand the Irish health sector requires a particular comprehension of both its history and geography. This chapter examines the health status and health determinants of the Irish population, the provision of appropriate services, both within the health sector itself and as part of wider public policy, and some of the paradoxes and dilemmas posed by modern healthcare provision.

Lessons of the past

Ireland traditionally has had a very poor health profile indeed. The Irish famines of the mid-1840s defined a pattern that was to be sustained for the century to follow, not alone in Ireland but across the migrant diaspora that emerged as a consequence of emigration (Kelleher *et al.*,

2004). As is well chronicled, the rapidly expanding population in the late seventeenth and early eighteenth centuries was based on subsistence farming but a bumper high carbohydrate food supply, chiefly from potato crops, was decimated by crop failures, generating a pattern of starvation and rampant disease and, for the survivors, of mass emigration. The migrant profile of Irish people to the US and the UK was habitually poor. It was understandable that extremely disadvantaged and debilitated individuals forced into hard labour occupations might experience poor health initially. Remarkably, however, that profile of ill health persisted across generations of assimilation into the host countries, making this a more complex phenomenon to understand and interpret. In the US, for instance, the newer migrants from central, southern and eastern Europe moved up the education trajectory relatively more swiftly than the Irish, who remained in traditional blue collar communities characterised by high degrees of bonding and religiosity (Perlmann, 1988). Their lifestyle came under heavy criticism in their adopted countries. Propensity for alcohol consumption became more than something of a caricature and undoubtedly racial discrimination was a feature of their experience. Additionally, a sociological treatise of the Irish migrant male as a miserable, depressive and isolated person emerges. What is notable is that the Irish in Britain today continue to have relatively poorer health than the rest of the population, long after this period of migration has passed.

At home in Ireland severe economic restraints promoted a society of serious urban deprivation and disadvantage and of rural subsistence, which perpetuated a cycle of poverty and migration. In Ireland in the 1930s and 1940s severe material poverty was pervasive. The psychosocial as well as the material aspects of this disadvantage are well studied, though arguably strong features of so-called social capital persisted among the Irish also, including networks and family supports. The role of religion presents complex ambiguity. On one level it was a solace in situations of deprivation and was strongly associated with political resistance and identity. On the other it represented personal and social repression of identity and could be a punishing experience for the Irish poor.

The Irish healthcare system grew out of this political history (Barrington, 1987) and its legacy is discernible in public policy today, as will be discussed further in this chapter. The Poor Laws of the Famine period saw the introduction of institutional care for the disadvantaged and many of these hospitals are still sites today of modern facilities. The opportunity in 1911 to introduce comprehensive social insurance was vigorously opposed by the emerging middle classes and the dispensary system that evolved, providing care on a ticketed basis by general medical practitioners, introduced a two-tier primary care model that in 1970 became the general medical services eligibility scheme, which is still the main means-tested source of public hospital and health services eligibility today. Rather than introducing a comprehensive system of care, the notion of means testing and the partial subsidy of health insurance for the more affluent taxpayer became the norm. The Mother and Child controversy of the Fine Gael-led coalition in the 1940s, which made Dr Noel Browne a household name, set a principle of non-state interference in family healthcare which remains at the heart of public policy debate today.

Measures of health status

By comparison with international neighbours, Ireland's contemporary health status is still poor. Life expectancy at birth in 2002 was estimated at 75.1 years for men and 80.3 years for women, both below the old EU-15 average. Ireland straddles the gap between the newer accession states in the expanded EU-25 and the older EU countries. Expectancy from the age of 65 is also lower than average and the health gain in this age group has been negligible in recent years (CSO, 2004). This poor expectancy pattern is partly explained by the mortality from cardiovascular diseases, which is high, particularly for coronary heart disease. Rates of some of the common cancers, particularly colon and bowel in both sexes and for breast cancer in women, are also high. The report on *Women and Cancer in Ireland 1994–2001* (WHC and NCR, 2006) notes for instance that all cancer incidence in women in Ireland is the third highest in Europe and all cancer mortality the second highest. There is evidence of a class gradient to these patterns also.

The Institute of Public Health in Ireland (2001) illustrates clearly that the mortality difference between the highest and lowest occupational classes is appreciable, with a 300 per cent difference for circulatory diseases and a 600 per cent difference for injuries, poisonings and respiratory diseases. There is evidence of a decline in coronary heart disease from about the mid-1990s onwards in both men and women, but both the north and south of Ireland still rank amongst the highest in Europe.

It is not immediately clear why Ireland should have a poor international profile or such adverse within-country gradients. Three main possibilities exist: that treatment and care services are inadequate, that predisposing risk factor profiles are worse than elsewhere or that there are inherent genetic or constitutional differences among the Irish population. One difficulty in assessing the relative influence of these three factors has been the paucity of adequate population surveillance information. To take one example of our commonest health problem, coronary heart disease, the traditional lifestyle risk factors associated with that condition – smoking status and dietary influences leading to hypertension (high blood pressure) and atheroma (the process of artery thickening that leads to heart disease) – have not been systematically recorded in the Irish population and the social distribution of such risk factors still less so.

Data from the Kilkenny Health Project (Shelley et al., 1995) – a community intervention programme in the period from 1985 to 1992 to promote healthy lifestyles – do show the beginnings of secular (or generational) declines in risk factors during that period and later information from the SLÁN surveys of lifestyle, attitudes and nutrition in 1998/1999 and 2002/2003 show small declines in smoking rates and improvements in diet between those years (Kelleher et al., 2003a, 2003b) in keeping with downwards secular trends in heart disease. Nonetheless, smoking status shows a clear age and social class gradient in both adults and schoolchildren. As do dietary patterns. Affordability is a key influence on diet in both relative and absolute terms. For instance a two parent and two child family on the lowest income spends 40 per cent on food, compared to a similar family in the highest group which spends just 17 per cent (Friel et al., 2004). The National Taskforce on Obesity (DOHC, 2005) has highlighted the rapid growth in the problem of overweight and obesity across Irish society and the emerging social gradient, consequent on less affluent families being dependent on cheaper but energy-dense high calorie foods.

Kabir *et al.* (2007) estimate that if recent trends in major cardiovascular risk factors simply continued to 2010, targets to reduce rates in Ireland are unlikely to be achieved, but if the tobacco control measures such as the 2004 ban on indoors smoking yield significant falls in smoking prevalence there will be an improvement that could halve mortality. Such an improvement is not a given however. Latest evidence suggests a halt in the downwards trends in overall smoking rates (Boilson *et al.*, 2007) and time trend data in other countries, whilst showing falls in average population blood pressure and total serum cholesterol, imply counterbalancing upwards trends in blood sugar and body mass index associated with the obesity epidemic (Ulmer *et al.*, 2007; Kelleher *et al.*, 2006).

The Health Promotion Policy Unit of the Department of Health and Children has had responsibility for over two decades for the promotion of healthy lifestyles. Its numerous policy documents have explicitly acknowledged that healthy choices are not always easy to make without the right context and supportive environment and that social inequalities must be addressed (see www.healthpromotion.ie/publications/). The challenge for health education and promotion is to ensure that lifestyle messages can be acted upon equitably across society so that those least able to afford change do not continue to be disadvantaged, in effect widening an existing class gradient as the more affluent are empowered to make changes.

Self-rated health (SRH) serves as a good proxy for health status generally and has been shown to predict a wide variety of health outcomes at population level. In several recent analyses, SRH has been associated not just with adverse lifestyle but also with socio-economic circumstances. Those rating their health as fair to poor were more likely to report a poor quality of life, to have none or primary education only, or to have means-tested general medical services (GMS) eligibility (Kelleher *et al.*, 2002). In a multivariate model, lower education status and smoking status each independently predicted the health of men, and in women lower education and GMS eligibility were predictive (Kelleher *et al.*, 2003a). An analysis of rural communities showed that low levels of financial security and dissatisfaction with work are also predictive of poor SRH (Tay *et al.*, 2004).

Notably in Ireland, area-level analyses do not show the same variability as is seen in more industrialised countries. Only in the larger conurbations where areas of real disadvantage in social and material terms exist do we find the kind of differences in the standardised mortality ratio commonly found in the UK and the US. What this implies is that as Ireland changed in the last decades, we moved from more mixed communities where advantaged and disadvantaged people lived side by side to a situation, common in other countries, where people of similar means and occupation are clustered together in urbanised communities. This adds a contextual dimension to understanding the health profile of a community. In effect it means that individuals carry the risk of their own social status but also the added advantage or disadvantage of the area in which they live. Particularly in the last decade of unprecedented economic growth, pressure on housing and accommodation and net immigration, we are seeing a shift to the kind of public policy dilemmas facing other developed countries.

Social determinants of health

Life-course epidemiological or public health perspectives in recent years suggest a comprehensive life-course approach is appropriate to the study of health and social position (Ben-Shlomo and Kuh, 2002). Thinking has shifted profoundly in the sense that we now know that in addition to proximal influences of, for instance, maternal nutrition or smoking on intra-uterine and infant growth, which we clearly expect (Gambling and McArdle, 2004; Institute of Public Health in Ireland, 2007), patterns of cardiovascular development and long-term susceptibility to adult disease may be set in train from this critical period onwards. The Barker hypothesis postulates that biological growth patterns are influenced in this first life period (Barker, 2003) and accumulating evidence suggests that the phenomenon of tracking of growth patterns may be set from an early age (Eriksson et al., 2003; Eriksson, 2005). The implications of this for, for instance, childhood overweight and obesity are very important. A child with a propensity to overweight will tend to stay at that level as she or he grows older and may well be more susceptible to adult obesity and diabetes, particularly if exposed to an unbalanced diet of high-energy foods.

The implications for social position are even more profound. Investigators such as Davey Smith et al. (1998) show that parental social position, including occupation and education, may independently predict, to a greater or lesser degree, adult health status. Those with a manual worker father have relatively higher odds of heart disease, stroke, cancer and respiratory disease in middle age, independent of their own manual or non-manual occupation in adult life. Some patterns are mitigated strongly by adult lifestyle behaviour, such as smoking status. Thus, adult lung cancer is predominantly influenced by own smoking habit but conditions such as stomach cancer, now understood to be associated with the infectious organism *helicobacter pylori*, whose transmission is facilitated by overcrowded childhood conditions, are strongly associated with childhood socio-economic position.

The search for mechanisms to explain adult risk has been advanced by those such as Ben-Shlomo and Kuh (2002), who point out that this may be mediated by a variety of processes, some predominantly social or psychosocial, some behavioural and some biological. Data show that critical period, cumulative and trajectory influences are all important for long-term development. For instance, an infant born into poor circumstances, with inadequate childhood nutrition, may also receive inadequate early education, including parenting and school exposure. This sets in place a trajectory pattern of poor employment prospects, with inadequate income perhaps leading to poor health behaviours. Conversely, a child born in similarly poor childhood standards receiving a good education will have a better outcome but may have some critical period risks in the long term. Others may experience cumulative disadvantage across the life course at every time point. The significant policy point from this type of research is that investment in maternal and child health may pay dividends long into the future of that child.

Another significant debate in recent years in the health inequalities literature is the extent to which social position may mediate its health influence through material or psychosocial conditions. Marmot and Wilkinson (2001), for instance, point out that most health indicators show a social gradient across all classes, rather than a threshold pattern where a cut-off is experienced only by the most disadvantaged. This graduated pattern applies not just to health behaviours like smoking or diet, but also to intermediate biological risk factors like total serum cholesterol or health utilisation indicators. The importance of this graduated pattern, rather than a dichotomous or threshold one where a clear differentiation can be made between rich and poor, is that it suggests social relationships may be important, not alone in driving these patterns of lifestyle and health behaviours across social groups in society, but also as a reflection of social organisation. Perception of disadvantage may exert an independent influence in itself. Wilkinson (1996), a strong proponent of the psychosocial consequences of disadvantage, indicates that the hierarchical post-industrial society not alone creates inequality in terms of means and control of resources, as in a classical Marxian economic interpretation, but that it also affects sense of dignity and self-worth in a corrosive way. He cites, for instance, prisoners, who are a highly materially disadvantaged group but understand their position in the incarcerated pecking order and express their resentment at infringements on their dignity. As he points out, social variations in health expectancy teach us as much about society as they do about health.

Other studies show that chronic stress, associated, for instance, with impending loss of work or unemployment, may manifest not just in psychological distress as objectively measured by appropriate psychometric scales but also at a patho-physiological level as measured by the stress hormone cortisol secretion patterns. The extension of the social support literature, showing essentially that major life events and significant others may exacerbate or ameliorate major health outcomes like heart disease, to a psychosocial paradigm has been much investigated and debated in recent years (Stansfield and Marmot, 2002).

Social capital and community development

The concept of social capital derives from several sources but received major impetus in recent years by Putnam, who highlights in his book *Bowling Alone* (2000) the change in US society from a more caring and socially supportive voluntarist society to one characterised by individualism and intense social division. He extends this argument to imply that such polarised societies promote inequality by the loss of this protective social fabric. The social epidemiology research group at Harvard has shown empirically that states in the US with high levels of income inequality exhibit both poor social capital as measured by indicators of trust and reciprocity but also more adverse health (Kim and Kawachi, 2007). This literature is controversial but is highly relevant to Ireland, a society in major economic transition, characterised recently by the disappearance of more traditional indicators of social capital and support (Taskforce on Active Citizenship, 2007) and ever-increasing income inequality. The National Economic and Social Forum has explicitly examined social capital and networks in the context of social inclusion (NESF, 2003). The argument that community development supports otherwise disadvantaged communities by processes of empowerment, advocacy and bridge building is intuitively strong.

Communities with state-supported resources and amenities create a public good common to all, irrespective of individual means and resources. At one level a bottom-up strategy is inclusive, involves community agendas and concerns and maximises participation. There are compelling social marketing arguments of change. The essential argument, as made in the book *The Tipping Point* (Gladwell, 2000), is that there comes a point of critical change in a social community that leads to a new norm of behaviour. In the Rogers

Innovation Diffusion Theory (Rogers, 1995), early adopters lead the way with a new trend, trickling down through society until a critical climate of public opinion is reached by an early majority of the population. Social forces as diverse as environmental controls on plastic bag purchase and the indoors smoking ban are prosaic if powerful examples. Can the same processes shift inequality patterns in health?

The converse or neo-material view is that such interpretations place undue responsibility on the individual to initiate change, particularly when that person is disadvantaged and has not the appropriate amenities and resources in place (Muntaner *et al.*, 2002). Critics point out that when a material threshold of income is reached within a country, the so-called epidemiological transition, it is true that pure material deprivation no longer explains morbidity and mortality. Nonetheless a less stark social gradient remains and health inequality persists within societies that are clearly means related. In such scenarios corrective actions may relate to robust income re-distribution at policy or taxation level, because the most unequal societies tend to have the most ill health. The provision of adequate income and of material amenities remain the primary issues to be addressed.

Public policy implications

The pragmatic position is that both top-down and bottom-up strategies are required in policy terms. Strategies based around community development and local resources may arguably empower change but if the onus is placed excessively on voluntarism and community action, the responsibility of the state, and by extension the taxpayer, is reduced. Such a model is consistent with low taxation, minimalist state intervention and support. The alternative neo-material position stresses robust public spending on amenities such as health and education, adequate thresholds of social welfare and reduction in income disparity. This implies also a level of stateism that can be equated with nanny interventions to promote, for instance, issues as diverse as smoking restriction in shared public or working environments, subsidies on foods and food supply, interference with commercial practice in fast food restaurants and, generally speaking, the movement of the old left to a more moderate lifestyle-associated territory.

Lee (2006) discusses the current issues and challenges for community development in a paper for the Combat Poverty Agency. While she argues that the development of the voice of people who experience exclusion is key to effective social change, the factors that give rise to poverty are generally neither created nor solved at local level. Community development strategies rooted in liberal, humanistic values, with an emphasis on the capacity and worth of individuals, may undermine more radical collective strategies. Empowered communities are not necessarily in positions of power. Two practical means of influencing decision-making are the mainstreaming of social inclusion in public policy (see O'Kelly, 2006) and the development of health impact assessment tools for proofing of cross-sectoral public policy. Whilst attractive in principle, in practice working tools are required to avoid a cumbersome and overly bureaucratic situation and considerably more dialogue and debate is required between sectoral actors to bring this about.

Another clear policy issue is whether we should be moving to combat poverty, which clearly implies a marginalised group who need to be shifted towards a threshold norm, or whether we should be aiming to reduce inequality, which might have the possibly unintended effect of lowering the health expectations of some. Again there are cases to be made for both positions, depending on circumstances. Measurement of poverty usually entails one of three indicators: relative income, defined as having an income at 60 per cent of the national median income; deprivation of at least two of a number of key material indicators; and consistent poverty, which is the combination of these two (CPA, 2006). At 20 per cent, Ireland's rate of income poverty ranks as one of the highest across the EU, which averages 16 per cent (see Chapter 2). Notably, lone parents, households headed by a person with a disability and households with children are inordinately likely to be poor. The Women's Health Council has produced a number of papers indicating the importance of maternal and child health, the relative importance of women as caregivers in society and the inordinate burden women experience of disadvantage as well as explicitly linking such circumstances to health outcomes (see www.whc.ie/publications/factsheets.html). The recognition that marginalised groups such as Travellers require appropriate and culturally sensitive investments is also clear. The gap in health expectancy between Travellers and others is at least sixteen years for women (CSO, 2007) and in 2007 a major Traveller health status census survey is planned.

However, wider strategies to reduce health inequities across society merit consideration also. If the evidence points to the fact that more rapidly developed industrialised societies create vast conurbations of essentially ghettoised people, then infrastructural policy must address this issue. Strategies to date in Ireland around decentralisation, urban and rural development and the creation of hub areas are all arguably both somewhat half-hearted and provisional and none are driven by a clear and explicit health policy agenda. Social variations in health expectancy across society are driven by divisions not alone between the richest and poorest but across the social spectrum. This presents a policy challenge also in that it means sectors outside the traditional health brief must have in place a means of undertaking meaningful health proofing of policies and health impact assessments. As Tussing and Wren (2006) point out, the twenty years of social partnership, afforded by an historic agreement to moderate wage claims and a consequent opportunity to cut taxes, laid the foundations for economic success. The consequence is that public investment in amenities and public services to the benefit of all is appropriate. All the evidence is of widening income inequality and of major challenges to be addressed now in public spending to improve the overall public health still further and to narrow the gap in health status.

Healthcare delivery

The outstanding issue for discussion remains the state of the Irish health services. The health strategy *Quality and Fairness: A Health System for You* was published in 2001, notably from a cross-sectoral perspective with a foreword by Taoiseach Bertie Ahern, as well as then Minister for Health and Children Mícheál Martin and Michael Kelly, then Secretary General of the Department of Health and Children, who had been associated with visionary policy documents dating back to *Health, the Wider Dimensions* in 1986. Between 2001 and 2006, a number of implementation milestones were documented on the Department of Health and Children's website (www.healthreform.ie/news/milestones.html). These predominantly refer to the processes of establishing the

Health Service Executive (HSE) and the Health Information and Quality Authority and apparently represent a more limited version of what was originally envisaged.

The vision espoused in the 2001 strategy was for a health system that supports and empowers the individual, the family and the community to their full health potential. It stressed four core principles of equity, people-centeredness, quality and accountability. The four goals were based on better health for everyone, fair access, responsive and appropriate delivery and high performance. A wide range of service objectives were summarised, many of which were in train at the time.

The adequacy of the services has since been critiqued widely (see, for instance, Tussing and Wren, 2006) and numerous reports have been produced on the viability of the system and aspects of potential reform. The ageing population and the development of effective treatments for major chronic diseases such as cancers and heart disease mean that the services must be adequate. As Tussing and Wren assert, many of the stakeholders in this reform process, particularly around the primary care strategy, believe little has been implemented to date.

Many models of healthcare delivery abound and, as measured by efficiency and equity of access, Ireland's system does not fare well. The stringent cutbacks of the mid-1980s were driven by an historical over-reliance on acute hospital beds. Nonetheless cutting back those resources, crucially without the creation of step-down services or adequate community-based care, made inevitable a perception of inadequacy about the health service as a whole. The general practitioner, at the core of primary care delivery, was often single handed without administrative, nursing or paramedical support, inevitably leading to inadequate out-of-hours cover and the practical recognition that for any service to flow the acute hospital had to be the first route into the system for many acutely ill patients.

The consequent focus on the accident and emergency crisis is without question a high-profile media issue but it may be neither as universally bad as painted for most of the people most of the time, as judged by consumer satisfaction surveys (HSE, 2007), nor necessarily the solution to tackle this issue in isolation. It is without doubt a fundamental measure of a compassionate society that the sick and vulnerable should not be left for prolonged periods on makeshift trolley beds in hospital corridors, particularly as taxpaying citizens over decades who are now in the latter part of their lives, but it is not necessarily the barometer of well-met health need it implies and diverts strategic public debate from the real unmet need. While perhaps some hundreds of people a day in mid-winter experience the inefficiency and ineffectiveness of emergency services in thirty-five acute hospitals (and recent evidence suggests in fact 76 per cent of people were satisfied with those services), thousands more are unknowingly going without adequate first line services.

The real crisis in Irish healthcare is not the acute sector but the slumbering iceberg of primary, continuing and community care that could, if configured properly (DOHC, 2001a), deliver on much-needed health service requirements. We require a system that keeps the maximum number of people from hospitalisation in the first place and minimises the amount of time anyone has to spend in hospital. Hospitals should be high-level specialist investigation units, acute crisis and respite centres at critical points in care, not facilities where people languish for prolonged periods awaiting investigation and results. Institutionalisation is expensive and inefficient. The long-awaited primary care strategy rollout is moving beyond pilot to early implementation stage with 215 primary care teams planned to be in place by the end of 2007, but it is clearly nowhere near its stated aims and objectives (DOHC, 2001a).

The low population density compounds the controversy about access across large parts of the country and the over-reliance on the county hospital model of care, in place since Famine times, which seeks to duplicate resources more appropriate to regional centres. The reality is that comprehensive low technology interdisciplinary services at primary care level, with an adequate first line accident and emergency service at county level, should deliver the most cost-effective health outcome. However, the widespread public perception of being short-changed by such a model is difficult to unsettle and is not helped by instances of apparently appalling individual case management, which receive high-profile media attention but are as likely to reflect bureaucratic communication failures as malpractice.

In 2003 the Hanly Report of the National Task Force on Medical Staffing was launched and this contained a groundbreaking suggestion (DOHC, 2003). In meeting the overtime ceilings for non-consultant hospital doctors (NCHDs) set in the EU Directive on Working Time, it proposed four possible strategies: first to do nothing, second to recruit more NCHDs, third to create a new permanent career NCHD grade and fourth was to move to a consultant-provided rather than a consultant-led service, in effect doubling the consultant expertise and radicalising the hospital delivery system. In the new model the consultant would provide more direct patient contact on a daily basis, rather than supervising junior staff. A drawback of this report and of the Fottrell Report of the Working Group on Undergraduate Medical Education and Training (DOHC, 2006a) and the Buttimer Report of the Postgraduate Medical Education and Training Group (DOHC, 2006b) was that the consequences for primary care were not quantified because of their terms of reference.

The provision of consultant-delivered rather than consultant-led services would ensure, in theory, more effective and efficient treatment but in itself, without adequate primary and step-down care, would not meet long-term need. A health system that created universal access through primary care, because it was no longer means-tested or subsidised by private insurance, and that removed the two-tier access route in both primary and acute hospital care would undoubtedly shift the health services away from a reactive under-resourced hospital infrastructural model. As high technology intervention for the most sick becomes the norm, demand will inevitably drive its provision, leading to an ethical and values discussion in Irish society (as in countries everywhere) about what level of care is appropriate for whom. Ageist definitions of care delivery are inappropriate but the opportunity cost of intensive intervention without clear benefit is considerable also. Initiatives such as the UK's National Institute for Health and Clinical Excellence (see www.nice.org.uk) have been established to set out standards of good practice in public health, health technologies and clinical practice.

The kind of comprehensive policy approach needed for this country has not materialised. Health Minister Mary Harney's documented policy interest since taking office in 2004 has been on the acute hospital sector and with tackling vested interests of the health professionals, particularly medical practitioners. She also sought to separate public from private care, not by creating a common waiting list, but by introducing private hospital construction plans for public hospital sites and the creation of three types of consultant contract: purely public, purely private and mixed provision contracts. Whatever about delivering on consultant practice, such contracts inherently bolster the two-tier system unless it is envisaged that private practice would rapidly become just that, a system completely separated from the existing public system. Such a strategy may be missing the point, in that a purely private service could not deliver on the scale that the subsidised system does at present for the one-half of the population who are health insurance subscribers but are also entitled as taxpayers to public care, and it runs the risk in the short term of overloading a public hospital service to which everyone is entitled, free of charge, at present.

It is to some degree a matter of ideology what the financial underpinning of the health service in Ireland should be and again, as Tussing and Wren (2006) point out, the solutions, whether through universal health insurance, through a comprehensive tax-funded health service or through some form of private health insurance, all have their proponents. What seems clear in any of these models is that equity of access at point of delivery across both primary and acute care is the only means of ensuring seamless delivery. Until that is delivered upon, the Irish healthcare system will continue to be relatively inefficient, particularly for the least affluent. More seriously troubling is its ineffectiveness, in that the drivers of health determinants are being met in too downstream a manner. Primary care remains inaccessible and under-developed for the majority of the population and the health burden will increase as the population ages unless a more proactive approach is taken.

Conclusions and recommendations

What do we know about the health status of the contemporary Irish population? In common with every country the social gradient has been established to exist and the worst health profiles are in the most economically deprived areas as urbanisation spreads. As the economy has strengthened, we have replaced a traditional pattern of fairly universal disadvantage with a widening health inequality. The inverse care law of inadequate provision for the most needy remains true. However, and this is the policy question that is slow to be grasped, it is often amenities and services outside the health sector that are likely to make the difference, making health impact assessment across public policies necessary.

The shift from a past of rural deprivation, but with mixed, well-integrated communities and supports, to a more polarised and urbanised society may be expected to translate into ever-widening inequalities if corrective action is not taken at policy level to plan new communities adequately. The provision of affordable and mixed housing (observed in the breach in the main) is a case in point of well-intentioned public policy not being implemented in practice. The need to address the ageing population means a shift towards primary care and step-down policies will be crucial in the next decade, but there is no public debate around this question. And ironically it seems, given the controversy generated by Noel Browne's proposals at the time, it is mother and child services, as in proper pregnancy and parenting support and early-life education, that will best address the future equity questions in Irish society. We therefore have the mother and father of a dilemma. The health of present and future generations requires constant and concerted input and we need to tackle not just the present-day health needs of the sick and infirm, but policies that are investments for Ireland's future generations, now just being born.

It is recommended that the following actions are taken:

- Implement health impact assessments for all public policies, to ensure that major developments in areas such as transport, housing and education provision are appropriate and serve to promote, rather than demote, the health of the population as a whole. This is an inter-sectoral challenge, deserving high-level national and local government attention

- Introduce comprehensive mother and child services across health, education and social welfare sectors, including non-means-tested primary care eligibility until children reach the age of eighteen. This is justified by the mounting scientific literature on life-course influences on long-term health and may be the best means of ensuring an equitable start from the beginning

- Remove the two-tier structure from both primary and acute hospital care by ensuring equity of access at point of delivery across both primary and acute care. This can be addressed irrespective of the form of payment for services. It is critical to address the primary care sector in conjunction with the hospital sector as the total perspective is required to ensure the best outcome for all. The policy debate is too upstream, at hospital level, at this point

- Implement the primary care team network nationwide. This is rolling out on a graduated basis at present and should be accelerated as a policy priority

- Develop a major primary-care-led health service for older people programme, running the spectrum from health promotion and social support through to acute hospital and pastoral care. The demographic and health status data indicate that careful needs assessment planning will be required into the future.

References

Barker, D. (2003), 'The Midwife, the Coincidence and the Hypothesis', *British Medical Journal*, vol. 327, pp. 1428–1430

Barrington, R. (1987), *Health, Medicine and Politics in Ireland 1900–1970*, Dublin: Institute of Public Administration

Ben-Shlomo, Y. and Kuh, D. (2002), 'A Life Course Approach to Chronic Disease Epidemiology: Conceptual Models, Empirical Challenges and Interdisciplinary Perspectives', *International Journal of Epidemiology*, vol. 31, no. 2, pp. 481–482

Boilson, A., Craven, F., Fitzsimon, N., O'Mahony, D., Staines, S. and Kelleher, C. C. (2007), *Findings of the Health Service Executive Consumer Satisfaction Survey 2007*, Naas: Health Service Executive

CPA (2006), *Poverty in Ireland – The Facts: 2004*, Dublin: Combat Poverty Agency

CSO (2004), *Health Statistics of the Irish Population*, Dublin: Central Statistics Office

CSO (2007), *Census 2006. Principal Demographic Results*, Dublin: Central Statistics Office

Davey Smith, G., Hart, C., Blane, D. and Hole, D. (1998), 'Adverse Socio-Economic Conditions in Childhood and Cause-Specific Adult Mortality: Prospective Observational Study', *British Medical Journal*, vol. 316, pp. 1631–1635

DOH (1986), *Health, the Wider Dimensions*, Dublin: Department of Health

DOHC (2001a), *Primary Care – A New Direction*, Dublin: Department of Health and Children

DOHC (2001b), *Quality and Fairness. A Health System for You*, Dublin: Department of Health and Children

DOHC (2003), *Report of the National Task Force on Medical Staffing*, Dublin: Department of Health and Children [Hanly Report]

DOHC (2005), *Obesity: The Policy Challenges, Report of the National Taskforce on Obesity*, Dublin: Department of Health and Children

DOHC (2006a), *Medical Education in Ireland: A New Direction, Report of the Working Group on Undergraduate Medical Education and Training*, Dublin: Department of Health and Children [Fottrell Report]

DOHC (2006b), *Preparing Ireland's Doctors to Meet the Health Needs of the 21st Century, Report of the Postgraduate Medical Education and Training Group*, Dublin: Department of Health and Children [Buttimer Report]

Eriksson, J. G. (2005), 'The Fetal Origins Hypothesis – 10 Years On', *British Medical Journal*, vol. 330, pp. 1096–1097

Eriksson, J. G., Forsen, T., Tuomilehto, J., Osmond, C. and Barker, D. J. (2003), 'Early Adiposity Rebound in Childhood and Risk of Type 2 Diabetes in Adult Life', *Diabetologia*, vol. 46, pp. 190–194

Friel, S., Walsh, O. and McCarthy, D. (2004), *Cost of Healthy Eating in the Republic of Ireland*, Dublin: Combat Poverty Agency

Gambling, L. and McArdle, H. J. (2004), 'Iron, Copper and Fetal Development', *Proceedings of the Nutrition Society*, vol. 63, pp. 553–562

Gladwell, M. (2000), *The Tipping Point: How Little Things Can Make a Big Difference*, New York: Little Brown

HSE (2007), *Health Service Executive Emergency Departments. Patient Profiles, Experiences and Perceptions, Summary Report of a National Survey Among People Who Attended During 2006*, Naas: HSE

Institute of Public Health in Ireland (2001), *Inequalities in Mortality 1989–1998*, Dublin: The Institute of Public Health in Ireland

Institute of Public Health in Ireland (2007), *Unequal at Birth. Inequalities in the Occurrence of Low Birthweight Babies in Ireland*, Dublin: The Institute of Public Health in Ireland

Kabir, Z., Bennett, K., Critchley, J. A. and Capewell, S. (2007), 'Can Future Changes in Cardiovascular Risk Factors Predict Large Future Reductions in Coronary Heart Disease Mortality in Ireland?, *European Journal of Epidemiology*, vol. 22, no. 2, pp. 83–89

Kelleher, C. C., Friel, S., Nic Gabhainn, S. and Tay, J. B. (2003a), 'Socio-Demographic Predictors of Self-Rated Health in the Republic of Ireland: Findings from the National Survey on Lifestyle, Attitudes and Nutrition, SLÁN', *Social Science Medicine*, vol. 57, no. 3, pp. 477–486

Kelleher, C. C., Harrington, J. and Friel, S. (2002), 'Measures of Self-Reported Morbidity According to Age, Gender and General Medical Services Eligibility in the National Survey of Lifestyles, Attitudes and Nutrition', *Irish Journal of Medical Science*, vol. 171, no. 3, pp. 134–138

Kelleher, C. C., Lynch, J. W., Daly, L., Harper, S., Fitz-Simon, N., Bimpeh, Y., Daly, E. and Ulmer, H. (2006), 'The "Americanisation" of Migrants: Evidence for the Contribution of Ethnicity, Social Deprivation, Lifestyle and Life-Course Processes to the Mid-20th-Century Coronary Heart Disease Epidemic in the US', *Social Science Medicine*, vol. 63, no. 2, pp. 465–484

Kelleher, C. C., Lynch, J., Harper, S., Tay, J. B. and Nolan, G. (2004), 'Hurling Alone? How Social Capital Failed to Save the Irish from Cardiovascular Disease in the United States', *American Journal of Public Health*, vol. 94, no. 12, pp. 2162–2169

Kelleher, C. C., Nic Gabhainn, S., Friel, S., Corrigan, H., Nolan, G., Sixsmith, J., Walsh, O. and Cooke, M. (2003b), *Results of the National Health and Lifestyle Surveys*, Galway: Centre for Health Promotion Studies

Kim, D. and Kawachi, I. (2007), 'U.S. State-Level Social Capital and Health-Related Quality of Life: Multilevel Evidence of Main, Mediating and Modifying Effects', *Annals of Epidemiology*, vol. 17, no. 4, pp. 258–269

Lee, A. (2006), *Community Development: Current Issues and Challenges*, Dublin: Combat Poverty Agency

Marmot, M. and Wilkinson, R. G. (2001), 'Psychosocial and Material Pathways in the Relation Between Income and Health: A Response to Lynch *et al.*', *British Medical Journal*, vol. 322(7296), pp. 1233–1236

Muntaner, C., Lynch, J. W., Hillemeier, M., Lee, J. H., David, R., Benach, J. and Borrell, C. (2002), 'Economic Inequality, Working-Class Power, Social Capital, and Cause-Specific Mortality in Wealthy Countries', *International Journal of Health Service*, vol. 32, no. 4, pp. 629–656

NESF (2003), *The Policy Implications of Social Capital*, Forum Report no. 28, Dublin: National Economic and Social Forum

O'Kelly, K. P. (2006), *The Evaluation of Mainstreaming Social Inclusion in Europe*, Dublin: Combat Poverty Agency

Perlmann, J. (1988), *Ethnic Differences, Schooling and Social Structure Among the Irish, Italians, Jews and Blacks in an American City 1880–1935*, New York: Cambridge University Press

Putnam, R. (2000), *Bowling Alone: The Collapse and Revival of American Community*, New York: Simon & Schuster

Rogers, E. M. (1995), *Diffusion of Innovations*, 4th edn, New York: The Free Press

Shelley, F., Daly, L., Collins, C., Christie, M., Conroy, R., Gibney, M., Hickey, N., Kelleher, C., Kilcoyne, D., Lee, P., Mulcahy, R., Murray, P., O'Dwyer, T., Radic, A. and Graham, I. (1995), 'Cardiovascular Risk Factor Changes in the Kilkenny Health Project, a Community Health Promotion Programme', *European Heart Journal*, vol. 16, pp. 752–760

Stansfield, S. A. and Marmot, M. G. (eds.) (2002), *Stress and the Heart*, London: BMJ Books

Taskforce on Active Citizenship (2007), *Report of the Taskforce on Active Citizenship*, Dublin: Secretariat of the Taskforce on Active Citizenship

Tay, J. B., Kelleher, C. C., Hope, A., Barry, M., Nic Gabhainn, S. N. and Sixsmith, J. (2004), 'Influence of Sociodemographic and Neighbourhood Factors on Self-Rated Health and Quality of Life in Rural Communities: Findings from the Agriproject in the Republic of Ireland', *Journal of Epidemiology and Community Health*, vol. 11, pp. 904–911

Tussing, A. D. and Wren, M. A. (2006), *How Ireland Cares. The Case for Health Care Reform*, Dublin: New Island

Ulmer, H., Kelleher, C. C., Fitz-Simon, N., Diem, G. and Concin, C. (2007), 'Secular Trends in Cardiovascular Risk Factors: An Age-Period Cohort Analysis of 698,954 Health Examinations in 181,350 Austrian Men and Women', *Journal of International Medicine*, vol. 261, no. 6, pp. 566–576

WHC and NCR (2006), *Women and Cancer in Ireland 1994–2001*, Dublin: Women's Health Council and National Cancer Registry

Wilkinson, R. (1996), *Unhealthy Societies: The Affliction of Inequality*, London: Routledge

Chapter 8

Disability and poverty

Eithne Fitzgerald

Introduction

People with disabilities or long-term health conditions are one of the groups in Irish society at highest risk of poverty. These high poverty levels are linked to a very low rate of participation in employment. There is a two-way link between disability and poverty. Not only are disabled people more likely to be poor, but also, in Ireland as elsewhere, people who are poor are more likely to become disabled or to develop a long-term illness. This reflects the well-established link between income or social class and poorer health.

While the sustained period of economic growth in Ireland from the mid-1990s has led to significant reductions in economic risk for other groups, people with disabilities have remained highly vulnerable to poverty and their employment rates have not risen in spite of the jobs boom. People with disabilities are also disproportionately likely to experience social exclusion in other areas of life. They have significantly lower participation than others in areas such as education, employment, marital status, car ownership, physical access to the environment and social life. People with disabilities, whatever their age, have on average lower educational qualifications, which reduce their prospects of being in work and lower their earning capacity if in a job. So lower educational attainment increases the likelihood of poverty.

For three out of four disabled people, those whose impairment or long-term illness restricts them in their day-to-day activities, disability status adds to the degree of poverty and social exclusion they would experience because they are older or less educated than the average. For one in four disabled people, those whose impairment does not restrict them in their day-to-day activities, the higher degree of poverty they experience reflects the fact that they are drawn from an older, less educated population than the average.

The Commission on the Status of People with Disabilities (1996) drew attention to the high incidence of poverty among those out of work due to illness or disability and recommended enhanced welfare support, a cost of disability payment and actions to raise employment rates. The increased focus on disability subsequent to the Commission's report led to a number of legislative and other initiatives, culminating in the announcement in 2004 of a national disability strategy to address the exclusion of people with disabilities through a range of joined-up measures.

This chapter sets out the facts and figures on the poverty and social exclusion of people with disabilities and long-term health conditions; documents the links between poverty, low levels of education and absence from the labour market; traces the evolution of public policy on disability and social exclusion; and examines how disability has been addressed in successive national strategy documents on poverty.

Profile of disability

While the 2002 Census showed 8.3 per cent of the population had a disability, the incidence of disability is much lower among younger people and rises significantly with age (see Table 8.1). Over 40 per cent of people with disabilities are aged 65 years and over. This age profile is one of the reasons behind the low labour market participation and high dependence on welfare incomes of people with disabilities.

Table 8.1: Disability and age

Age	% with a disability
15	3.1
20	3.2
30	4.2
40	6.0
50	9.0
60	14.8
70	20.0
80	42.0
80+	58.8

Source: Census 2002

Most school-leavers with a disability have had their condition from birth or early childhood. However, for most disabled people of working age, the onset of disability occurred in adult life.

Learning/intellectual disability is the most prevalent type of disability among children, with other forms of disability becoming more frequent as people age.

Among the under 20s, boys are more likely than girls to have a disability; in the 55–70 age range, male disability is again

higher; above the age of 70, disability levels become higher
for women (see Figure 8.1).

Figure 8.1: Age profile of disability in Ireland by gender, 2002

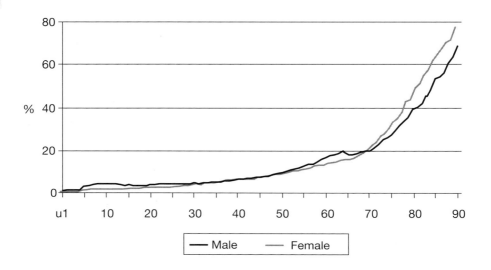

Source: Census 2002

More details of the profile of disability in Ireland will emerge
when the results of the National Disability Survey conducted
in autumn 2006 become available.

Poverty and disability – facts and figures

While different survey methods and questions produce
different figures, there is a consistent association of disability
or long-term illness with a very high risk of poverty.
However, changes in definitions between successive surveys
mean only very limited comparisons can be made over
time.

The most comprehensive picture of poverty and disability comes from the Living in Ireland Surveys conducted between 1994 and 2001, covering adults aged 16 years and over, and which refer to people with a 'chronic physical or mental health problem, illness or disability'. Detailed analyses of the relationships between disability and social exclusion have been conducted by Gannon and Nolan (2004, 2005, 2007) using these data. The results show that people with chronic illness or disability are about twice as likely to be at risk of poverty, twice as likely to experience basic deprivation and twice as likely to be consistently poor as those who are not ill or disabled. The degree of poverty is even higher for people of working age unable to work because of their illness or disability – in 2001, members of this group were about four times as likely to be at risk of poverty and about seven times as likely to be in consistent poverty as those who were not ill or disabled (see Table 8.2). The onset of disability results on average in a 15 per cent fall in household income, after accounting for other personal and household characteristics (Gannon and Nolan, 2007).

Table 8.2: Poverty and illness/disability among adults, 2001

	Risk of poverty* (%)	Experiencing basic deprivation (%)	Consistently poor (%)
Not ill/disabled	16.7	7.4	2.9
Ill/disabled, all	37.5	13.2	7.4
Labour force status is ill/disabled**	66.5	n.a.	22.5

* Risk-of-poverty income threshold: 60 per cent of median income
** This classification excludes disabled people who identify their main economic status as in education, in employment, on home duties, unemployed or retired
n.a. Data not available
Sources: Gannon and Nolan, 2005 and Whelan et al., 2003

Restriction in daily activities

Three out of every four people with a disability are hampered in day-to-day activities by their impairment. The higher the degree of restriction experienced, the greater the likelihood of being in poverty or socially excluded in other ways. In 2001, about one in four of those severely hampered in daily activities experienced basic deprivation – that is going without basics because of lack of money, or running into debt on day-to-day living expenses (Gannon and Nolan, 2005). This may reflect the extra costs of living associated with having a restrictive disability.

Strong link between poverty and joblessness

Employment figures from Census 2002 show 26 per cent of disabled people of working age have a job compared to a 70 per cent employment rate for non-disabled people. In 2001, over 80 per cent of chronically ill or disabled people at risk of poverty were living in households where no one had a job. Being out of work, or living in a household where no one works, is one of the principal explanations for the higher poverty rate experienced by people with disabilities. Living in a working household lifts people out of poverty – three-quarters of ill or disabled people above the risk-of-poverty line live in homes where there are one or more people in work (Gannon and Nolan, 2005).[1] The association between persistent disability and a higher likelihood of being poor is also significantly linked to the absence of a job (Gannon and Nolan, 2007).[2] A history of employment, as evidenced by having an occupational pension, also led to reduced poverty

---

[1]   This finding is similar to that of Burchardt (2003) for the UK.
[2]   Where persistent disability refers to people recorded with a chronic illness or disability in each year from 1995 to 2001.

risk (Gannon and Nolan, 2005).[3] This evidence shows that raising employment rates must be an important part of the strategy to reduce poverty among people of working age with disabilities.

People who are already out of work are somewhat more likely to experience the onset of a chronic illness or disability. Such onset is associated with a drop of about 20 per cent in employment participation rates (Gannon and Nolan, 2007).

Education gap

There is a consistent pattern of lower levels of education achieved by people with disabilities compared to others of their generation (NDA, 2005b). This gap is larger for younger generations. Chronic illness or disability in childhood can treble the risk of leaving school with no qualifications, that is without having attained at least a Junior Certificate or equivalent, once the impact of age, gender and region on education are separated out. The probability that someone severely hampered by illness or disability left school with no qualification is 60 per cent compared to 20 per cent for a non-disabled person (Gannon and Nolan, 2005).

There are strong links between low qualifications and the employment prospects of people with disabilities. For example, the employment rate in 2002 of disabled men aged

---

[3] Gannon and Nolan (2005) find that 67 per cent of those ill/disabled but not at risk of poverty rely mainly on incomes from work, while 13.7 per cent rely mainly on private pensions. 86.5 per cent of ill/disabled at poverty risk rely mainly on social welfare incomes. Econometric analysis, taking other background factors into account, shows that having a job reduces the likelihood of being below the 60 per cent of median income line by 23 percentage points and of being consistently poor by about 5 percentage points.

25 to 34 years with a Junior Certificate was 37 per cent, compared to 51 per cent for those with a Leaving Certificate and 71 per cent for those with a degree.[4] Moving up the qualifications ladder is one way to increase employment, and reduce poverty, among people with disabilities.

However, disabled people with similar levels of qualification are less likely to be in a job than their non-disabled counterparts, as Table 8.3 shows. This disability gap in employment rates is on roughly the same scale for men and for women.

Table 8.3: Employment rates for the 25–34 age group by education level, gender and disability status

| | Leaving Certificate | | Degree | |
	Male (%)	Female (%)	Male (%)	Female (%)
Disabled	51	34	71	65
Non-disabled	92	74	94	90

Source: Census 2002

Left behind by the economic boom
The second half of the 1990s was a sustained period of economic growth, which saw incomes rise and consistent poverty rates fall for the general population. However, incomes of people with disabilities disimproved over this period relative to the rest of society.

As Table 8.4 illustrates, the proportion of people with disabilities whose incomes fell well below the average – those

---

4   Census 2002, special tabulation – see NDA (2005b).

termed at risk of poverty – grew significantly between 1995 and 2001, while for the rest of the population, relative poverty remained static over this period. Meanwhile consistent poverty halved for non-disabled people between 1995 and 2001, but there was only a marginal decline in consistent poverty among people with disabilities.

Table 8.4: Poverty and illness/disability among adults, 1995 and 2001

	Risk of poverty (%)	Experiencing basic deprivation (%)	Consistently poor (%)
Ill/disabled			
1995	21.2	26.0	7.8
2001	37.5	13.2	7.4
Not ill/disabled			
1995	16.7	15.7	6.0
2001	16.7	7.4	2.9

Source: Gannon and Nolan, 2005, using data from the Living in Ireland Surveys 1995 and 2001

Figures for 2003 to 2005 from the European Union Survey of Income and Living Conditions (EU-SILC) suggest some modest reduction in poverty in this more recent period (see Table 8.5). This change is likely to reflect improved incomes from welfare rather than more people at work, given that the proportion of disabled people in a job if anything fell over this period.[5] The 2003 to 2005 figures were compiled on a different basis to those for 1995 to 2001, and the information

---

[5] The Quarterly National Household Survey 2002 found 40.1 per cent of long-term ill or disabled people aged 15 to 64 years in work in 2002, and a corresponding rate of 37.1 per cent in 2004. Some of the fall may reflect sampling error.

on disability status is limited to people whose labour force status is ill/disabled.

Table 8.5: Proportion of labour force status 'ill/disabled' in poverty, 2003–2005

	2003 (%)	2004 (%)	2005 (%)
Risk of poverty (60% line)			
All	19.7	19.4	18.5
Labour force status ill/disabled	51.7	47.3	40.6
Consistent poverty			
All	8.8	6.8	7.0
Labour force status ill/disabled	22.4	21.7	17.4

Source: EU-SILC

Gender, disability and poverty

While disabled women, like other women, are less likely to hold a job than their male counterparts, the employment gap between disabled and other women is similar to that between disabled and other men (NDA, 2005a). Both the 2001 data, and the 2003 to 2005 EU-SILC data, albeit compiled on a different basis, suggest a slightly lower incidence of poverty among disabled women than among disabled men (Gannon and Nolan, 2005).

International comparisons are difficult

It is extremely difficult to conduct any international comparisons of levels of disability and poverty because of the effect of cultural differences on how identical questions on disability are answered. For example, in 1998, in an EU-wide survey, the self-reported incidence of long-term illness or disability among people of working age ranged from 9.3 per cent in Italy to 37.9 per cent in Sweden (Gannon and Nolan,

2004). That means that cross-country differences in poverty rates may be attributable to how people describe their disability status and not necessarily to underlying differences in poverty rates across countries.

Wider exclusion

Low employment levels and a higher risk of poverty are just two aspects of the higher risk of social exclusion faced by people with disabilities across widespread aspects of their lives (NDA, 2005b). Compared to non-disabled people, people with disabilities are:

- Less likely to have achieved any qualifications

- Earning less on average in a job

- Less likely to marry, and more likely to be separated or divorced

- More likely to experience poor health

- Less likely to be physically active

- More likely to live with their parents well into adulthood

- Less likely to have a car

- More likely to have difficulty with public transport

- Less likely to have a computer or Internet connection

- More restricted in socialising outside the home

- Less likely to have an annual holiday.

In the light of this multidimensional picture of exclusion, it is important that public policy to tackle it is equally broad ranging. The next section traces how disability policy in Ireland has evolved towards a wider focus on inclusion.

The evolution of disability policy

Historically, disability policy in Ireland developed within a medical model, characterised by provision of care in large segregated institutions. Until the mid-1960s, the state engaged in little strategic thinking or planning for disability services, with new services largely emerging only where the voluntary sector had taken an initiative. It was a laissez-faire approach, where the state neither undertook the duty to provide services nor acknowledged the rights of individuals with disabilities. Even when the state began to take a more active role in the planning and funding of services, for example following the report of the Commission of Inquiry on Mental Handicap (1965), the emphasis initially remained on separate provision, dependence and inability.

International developments

In the last decades of the twentieth century, an increased international focus on disability was marked by a shift in policy away from segregation and dependence towards promoting inclusion, equality and independence. Leading disability thinkers argued for replacing the medical model of disability with a social model (Oliver, 1989). Years of activism by people with disabilities, including Vietnam War veterans, led to the US's path-breaking Americans with Disabilities Act in 1990.

The UN's World Programme of Action on Disability in 1982 was followed by a Decade of Disabled Persons (1983–1992) and the UN Standard Rules on the Equalization of Opportunities for Persons with Disabilities in 1993. As well as the traditional areas of care and rehabilitation, these Rules covered accessibility, education, employment, incomes, social security, family life, culture, recreation, sport and religion. This work culminated in the adoption of the UN Convention on the Rights of Persons with Disabilities, which was signed by eighty-eight countries, including Ireland, when the process for ratification opened in spring 2007.[6] A key feature of the drafting of this Convention was the involvement of people with disabilities and their representative organisations.

In Ireland as elsewhere, people with disabilities and their families have increasingly found their voice, putting disability issues on the public agenda. As Quin and Redmond (2005, p. 144) note: 'The concept of rights has been of central importance in switching the focus from the individual's "inability" to perform a range of physical and intellectual tasks to a society which takes little or no account of such differences, organising itself in such a way that those who need to do things differently from the norm are hampered'.

In 1993, the Department of Equality and Law Reform was set up (from 1997 it was merged into the Department of Justice, Equality and Law Reform) and took over strategic policy on disability from the Department of Health, marking an explicit break with the medical model, and a new focus on disability as an equality issue. One of the first acts of the new department was to establish the Commission on the Status of People with Disabilities, which had a majority of members consisting of people with disabilities or their immediate families.

The Commission's landmark 1996 report *A Strategy for Equality* has guided Ireland's changed approach to disability

---

[6] The two-stage process for adoption of the convention is signature followed by ratification.

policy. The key principles set out in the Commission's report are:

- Equality – that people with disabilities should be recognised and treated as having equal status with all other citizens
- Participation – that people with disabilities have the right to participate in Irish life to the fullest extent
- Independence and choice – that people with disabilities have the right to be able to achieve their full potential, make their own decisions and choices.

Legislation outlawing discrimination in the provision of goods and services and in employment on grounds of disability (among other grounds) followed: the Employment Equality Act 1998, the Equal Status Act 2000 and the Equality Act 2004.

From June 2000, it became official policy to incorporate policies and services for people with disabilities into the mainstream work of government departments and public bodies. This was given legal effect in the Disability Act 2005. As an example of the move from specialist to mainstream provision, the specialist state disability agency – the National Rehabilitation Board – was dissolved, its employment services were re-assigned to FÁS and its role in advising individuals on entitlements went to Comhairle (now the Citizens Information Board).

National disability strategy
The national disability strategy announced in autumn 2004 comprises new laws on services and supports, statutory action plans on disability (entitled sectoral plans) in six key

government departments, a personal advocacy service to assist the most vulnerable people to access the services they require and a multi-annual investment programme for disability support services. A monitoring mechanism – involving senior officials across key departments together with disability stakeholders and the National Disability Authority (NDA) – has been set up to oversee coherence and delivery and to report to the Cabinet Committee on Social Inclusion.

The key legislative elements of the strategy are the Disability Act 2005, the Education for Persons with Special Educational Needs Act 2004 and the Citizens Information Act 2007. The Disability Act provides for independent statutory assessment of disability service needs, and for delivery of services to meet those needs, subject to resource constraints. A commitment to €18.8 billion for disability services needs was made in the National Development Plan 2007–2013 (Ireland, 2007b). The Education for Persons with Special Education Needs Act provides for a parallel system of assessment of children's education needs and for allocation of resources to meet these. The emphasis is on integrated education where appropriate.

The Disability Act obliges public bodies to cater for people with disabilities alongside other service users, supported by accessible information and premises and procurement of accessible goods and services. The Act gives legal effect to the public sector employment target (first set in 1977) that people with disabilities should make up at least 3 per cent of the total staff.

Sectoral plans

One of the most innovative features of the Disability Act is the requirement for special disability action plans – entitled sectoral plans – from six of the key government departments.

Covering communications, employment, environment and housing, health, social welfare and transport, the first plans were adopted by the Oireachtas in October 2006. Disability action plans across a range of government agencies are also a feature of the Australian[7] and New Zealand disability strategies, but Ireland is unique in giving such plans the status of statutory endorsement by parliament.

Each sectoral plan provides for an internal complaints mechanism and appeal to the Ombudsman. There is a statutory requirement for cross-departmental cooperation in three key interfaces: between social welfare, health and employment; between housing authorities and the health service; and between transport and the environment.

The sectoral plans set out targets and timetables for accessible streets, parks and public sector offices; accessible public transport; subtitled television broadcasts; employment and social welfare; and for independent assessment of disability service and care needs. As people with disabilities experience social exclusion which goes well beyond material poverty, a broad-ranging and joined-up approach of this kind is essential if the multiple causes and aspects of social exclusion are to be satisfactorily addressed.

The Department of Enterprise, Trade and Employment's sectoral plan 2006 promises a comprehensive employment strategy for people with disabilities and sets a target for an extra 7,000 people with disabilities in work by 2010. The Department of Social and Family Affairs sectoral plan 2006

---

[7]   Originally, Australian government departments adopted separate annual disability action plans; now these plans are integrated into departments' strategy statements and business plans.

proposes a systematic programme of engagement with people on disability payments to encourage maximum participation in society. This is in line with the NESC's *The Developmental Welfare State* (2005), which advocates a shift from passive income support to pathways for participation.

The sectoral plans also propose to address benefit traps which inhibit entry to the workforce. Research suggests that the key issue in this area for people with disabilities is the retention of the medical card (Workway, 2005).

Towards 2016

The social partnership agreement *Towards 2016* (Ireland, 2006) is built around a lifecycle framework, with policies addressed at children, working-aged adults, elderly people and people with disabilities. On disability, the agreement sets out long-term goals for the ten years to 2016:

- Every person with a disability will have access to an income which is sufficient to sustain an acceptable standard of living

- Every person with a disability will, in conformity with their needs and abilities, have access to appropriate care, health, education, employment, training and social services

- Every person with a disability will have access to public spaces, buildings, transport, information, advocacy and other public services and appropriate housing

- Every person with a disability will be supported to enable them, as far as possible, to lead full and independent lives, to participate in work and in society and to maximise their potential

- Carers will be acknowledged and supported in their caring role.

These goals harmonise with the approach to rights set out in the Disability Legislation Consultative Group's *Equal Citizens* (2003, p. 10): 'A key issue is that a rights-based approach positions the individual person with disabilities at the centre of service provision, and through needs assessment and service coordination resources are attached to the person him/herself'.

Strategic approaches to disability and poverty

In line with an increasing focus on disability issues in public policy generally, the emphasis on disability issues in the *National Action Plan for Social Inclusion 2007–2016* (Ireland, 2007a) is significantly greater than in its predecessors.

National Anti-Poverty Strategy 1997

Ireland's first anti-poverty strategy document *Sharing in Progress* (Ireland, 1997) touched on disability, but its main focus was on preventing and providing pathways out of long-term unemployment. Many of the proposals on disability identified by the Working Group on Long-term Unemployment which fed into the *National Anti-Poverty Strategy*, such as action on job retention, an income support payment for people who wish to take up employment and initiatives to promote workplace redesign, did not make it into the final core strategy. Those actions on disability which were included centred on strengthening the 3 per cent employment target for people with disabilities throughout the wider public service and ensuring a continuum of provision in special education.

Building an Inclusive Society 2002

Ireland's second anti-poverty strategy (2002) contained few targets on disability and poverty, citing the lack of data. It proposed raising the proportion of people with disabilities in third level education to 1.35 per cent in 2003 and 1.9 per cent by 2006. Improved respite care arrangements were also promised.

National Action Plan for Social Inclusion 2007–2016

One of the high-level goals of the latest anti-poverty strategy document, the *National Action Plan for Social Inclusion 2007–2016* (Ireland, 2007a), is to raise employment rates of people with disabilities. Its chapter on disability issues incorporates commitments made in the sectoral plans, *Towards 2016* and the National Development Plan 2007–2013, including commitments on improved accessibility of the environment, transport and housing. The action plan sets the goal of reducing consistent poverty to between 2 and 4 per cent by 2012, but it does not set any separate targets for reducing poverty rates among people with disabilities.

Focus on employment

There is now a growing emphasis in official policy on employment as a strategy to reduce poverty among people with disabilities.

The Commission on the Status of People with Disabilities (1996) set modest targets for measures to expand employment of people with disabilities – an extra 500 places in sheltered employment, 500 equipment adaptation grants to be paid each year and 500 places on the employment support scheme. As data on the scale of the employment gap have become available, the NDA (2005a) shows that if employment rates of those disabled people who are able to work were to rise to that of their non-disabled peers, it would mean an extra 14,000 people at work.

Drawing on the experience of reintegrating other marginalised groups into employment, the NDA (2006) recommends a comprehensive five-point strategy for employment of people with disabilities, which in summary is to:

- Remove benefit traps and make work pay
- Equip people with disabilities for today's labour market through effective education, training and work experience
- Achieve leadership from private and public sectors in offering jobs
- Stem the flow into inactivity by focusing on job retention and reducing the numbers leaving school early without qualifications
- Develop a systematic process of engagement with people with disabilities around their employment aspirations.

This work has informed the targets set in the 2006 sectoral plan on employment and its commitment to develop a comprehensive employment strategy for people with disabilities.

Social welfare

Over the years, income support through the social welfare system has been the main tool used to address poverty issues for people with disabilities. It will remain central to offering decent incomes to older people with disabilities and others who are unable to earn their living.

Social welfare provision

In 2005, almost 250,000 people were receiving social welfare payments each week relating to illness, disability or caring. About 133,000 of these were social insurance payments, payable to people with a history of employment and without a means test. 81,000 were means-tested payments in respect of long-term disability and 26,000 were carers' payments. The Commission on Social Welfare (1986) argued for improvements in the basic rates of all social welfare payments rather than higher rates for payments related to disability. The Commission's approach to raising and harmonising benefit levels has informed social welfare policy in the intervening years. The Social Welfare Benchmarking and Indexation Group (DSFA, 2001), established under the *Programme for Prosperity and Fairness* (Ireland, 1999), recommended targets for welfare payment rates as a percentage of gross average industrial earnings. Adherence to this approach has retained a relationship between welfare incomes and incomes elsewhere in the community.

Commission on the Status of People with Disabilities

The Commission on the Status of People with Disabilities (1996) recommended the introduction of a disability pension, a cost of disability payment and a carer's allowance for all carers. It recommended the disability pension be set at the invalidity pension level, payable to all who qualified, including people living in residential care, without a means test.

Of the Commission's recommendations, disability allowance has been extended since 1999 to people entering residential care, and from 2007 to all people with disabilities already living in residential care, most of whom had previously no entitlement to an independent social welfare income.

However people in long-term residential care are now subject to statutory maintenance charges. Separate schemes of insurance-based invalidity pension and a means-tested disability allowance remain.

From passive welfare payments towards promoting participation

The Developmental Welfare State (NESC, 2005) highlights the largely passive nature of the Irish income support system and argues for tailored progression pathways to be the rule rather than the exception for welfare recipients of working age. This report's strategic thinking informs the sectoral plan on social welfare and underpins the *Towards 2016* social partnership agreement. Specifically, the report draws attention to the steady growth in dependence on disability payment transfers. In the decade to 2005, the numbers receiving these payments grew by about 100,000. In common with the *Expenditure Review on Illness and Disability Payment Schemes* (DSFA, 2003), the NESC argued for a more flexible system offering income support to people who would be partially incapable of work. Informed by research highlighting the practical impact of the benefits trap, the earnings limit for people engaged in rehabilitative employment was relaxed, from June 2006, to allow a tapered retention of disability allowance and secondary benefits where earnings are below €350 per week.

Towards 2016

Towards 2016 sets out the following commitment in relation to income support (Ireland, 2006, p. 68):

> In terms of ensuring adequate levels of income for people with disabilities, we will work for the continued enhancement and integration of supports in line with

overall social welfare commitments and targets. This will include a rationalisation of existing allowances for people with disabilities in the context of the Government's policy of mainstreaming and the proposed transfer of functions from the Health Service Executive to the Department of Social and Family Affairs. Other issues around cost of disability will be considered following the development of a needs assessment system provided for under Part 2 of the Disability Act, 2005.

Cost of disability

The Commission on the Status of People with Disabilities (1996) identified the extra costs of living for people with a disability in respect of additional equipment, medical, transport, communication, daily living and care costs. Both national and international studies show considerable variation in what those costs are for individuals.[8] The Commission called for a variable cost of disability payment to be introduced where these extra costs were not being met in other ways, such a payment would be linked into a needs assessment process and paid independent of employment status.

People on long-term disability-type payments (disability allowance and invalidity pension) qualify for free travel and for the household benefits package in the same way as

---

[8] Indecon (2004) gathered together national and international evidence on the extra costs of living associated with disability. Using a methodology similar to that used to derive equivalence scales for large and small households, this study tried to quantify the scale of additional costs which might be involved, however these estimates are subject to considerable sampling error given the degree of variation involved.

pensioners. The blind welfare allowance is a form of cost of disability payment, but limited to this particular impairment only. The *Expenditure Review of Illness and Disability Payment Schemes* (DSFA, 2003, p. 53) recommends that the additional costs of disability be met through a separate payment: 'Needs arising from the additional costs of disability should be addressed separately rather than through higher basic income maintenance payments, which would not be targeted at those individuals whose needs are greatest. The additional costs of disability are best met in ways that are less dependent on the person's labour force status'.

The NDA (2004) also recommends introduction of a cost of disability payment and estimates that a payment ranging in scale from €10 to €40 a week would cost about €170 million per year. The sectoral plans and *Towards 2016* social partnership agreement commit to further consideration of the cost of disability issue when the needs assessment process provided for in Part 2 of the Disability Act is in place.

Conclusions

People with disabilities are among the groups at highest risk of poverty, with those whose labour force status is 'unable to work' and those whose disabilities severely restrict everyday life the most vulnerable of all to poverty. While employment has boomed in Celtic Tiger Ireland, the number of people relying on social welfare disability payments has grown by over two-thirds and the employment rates of people with disabilities have fallen. If, in the face of the boom years, employment of people with disabilities remained static or fell, it is clear there is a need for a change in the strategic direction of employment policy.

There must be a comprehensive approach which addresses systemic issues such as the benefits trap and the passive nature of income support, which stems the outflow from employment by promoting retention and re-employment of people who acquire a disability in adult life and which engages both private and public sector employers in this task. Official thinking, as evidenced in the sectoral plans, *Towards 2016* and the *National Action Plan on Social Inclusion 2007–2016*, is moving in this direction. Setting numerical targets for improving employment numbers and rates provides the impetus to carry through with the changed policies to achieve those targets.

However many people with disabilities take up work, there will always be considerable numbers who remain outside the workforce, such as the 40 per cent of people with disabilities over pension age as well as those whose illness or impairment restricts their capacity to earn a living. Adequate levels of welfare payments, which track other incomes in society, will remain the cornerstone of anti-poverty policies for this group.

There is now widespread recognition that the extra costs of disability need to be addressed. The cost of disability is a key issue on the anti-poverty as well as the equality agenda, as the evidence shows that people with disabilities are significantly more likely than others in our society to be going without basic essentials because they cannot afford them. While there are significant practical issues to be addressed in coming up with a fair and workable scheme, early consideration of these practicalities is desirable.

The signing by Ireland of the UN Convention on the Rights of People with Disabilities (2006) should lend a further impetus to the disability policy developments of recent years (see Appendix). Tackling poverty needs to remain central to that disability agenda.

References

Burchardt, T. (2003), *Being and Becoming: Social Exclusion and the Onset of Disability*, Centre for Analysis of Social Exclusion Report no. 21, London: London School of Economics

Commission of Inquiry on Mental Handicap (1965), *Report*, Dublin: Stationery Office

Commission on Social Welfare (1986), *Report*, Dublin: Stationery Office

Commission on the Status of People with Disabilities (1996), *A Strategy for Equality*, Dublin: Stationery Office

Disability Legislation Consultative Group (2003), *Equal Citizens: Proposals for Core Elements of Disability Legislation*, Dublin: National Disability Authority

DSFA (2001), *Interim Report of the Social Welfare Benchmarking and Indexation Group*, Dublin: Department of Social and Family Affairs

DSFA (2003), *Expenditure Review of Illness and Disability Payment Schemes*, Dublin: Department of Social and Family Affairs

Gannon, B. and Nolan, B. (2004), *Disability and Labour Market Participation*, Dublin: Equality Authority

Gannon, B. and Nolan, B. (2005), *Disability and Social Inclusion in Ireland*, Dublin: Equality Authority and National Disability Authority

Gannon, B. and Nolan, B. (2007), *The Dynamics of Disability and Social Inclusion*, Dublin: Equality Authority and National Disability Authority

Indecon (2004), *Disability and the Cost of Living*, Dublin: National Disability Authority

Ireland (1997), *Sharing in Progress: National Anti-Poverty Strategy*, Dublin: Stationery Office

Ireland (1999), *Programme for Prosperity and Fairness*, Dublin: Stationery Office

Ireland (2002), *Building an Inclusive Society*, Dublin: Stationery Office

Ireland (2006), *Towards 2016: Ten-Year Framework Social Partnership Agreement 2007–2016*, Dublin: Stationery Office

Ireland (2007a), *National Action Plan for Social Inclusion 2007–2016*, Dublin: Stationery Office

Ireland (2007b), *Transforming Ireland: A Better Quality of Life for All*, National Development Plan 2007–2013, Dublin: Stationery Office

NDA (2004), 'Foreword', *Disability and the Cost of Living*, Dublin: National Disability Authority

NDA (2005a), *Disability and Work – The Picture We Learn from Official Statistics*, Dublin: National Disability Authority

NDA (2005b), *How Far Towards Equality?*, Dublin: National Disability Authority

NDA (2006), *A Strategy of Engagement – Towards a Comprehensive Employment Strategy for People With Disabilities*, Dublin: National Disability Authority

NESC (2005), *The Developmental Welfare State*, Dublin: National Economic and Social Council

Oliver, M. (1989), 'The Social Model of Disability: Current Reflections', in Jeffs, T. and Smith, M. (eds.), *Social Work and Social Welfare Year Book One*, Milton Keynes: Open University Press

Quin, S. and Redmond, B. (2005), 'Disability and Social Policy', in Quin, S., Kennedy, P., Matthews, A. and Kiely, G. (eds.), *Contemporary Irish Social Policy*, Dublin: UCD Press

UN (2006), *Convention on the Rights of Persons with Disabilities*, New York: United Nations

Whelan, C. T., Layte, R., Maître, B., Gannon, B., Nolan, B., Watson, D. and Williams, J. (2003), *Monitoring Poverty Trends in Ireland: Results from the 2001 Living in Ireland Survey*, Dublin: ESRI

Workway (2005), *The Way Ahead: Workway Policy Paper*, Dublin: Workway:
www.workway.ie/article/index.php?cat_id=708&item_id=19252

Appendix

UN Convention on the Rights of Persons with Disabilities, Article 28 – Adequate Standard of Living and Social Protection

1. States Parties recognize the right of persons with disabilities to an adequate standard of living for themselves and their families, including adequate food, clothing and housing, and to the continuous improvement of living conditions, and shall take appropriate steps to safeguard and promote the realization of this right without discrimination on the basis of disability.

2. States Parties recognize the right of persons with disabilities to social protection and to the enjoyment of that right without discrimination on the basis of disability, and shall take appropriate steps to safeguard and promote the realization of this right, including measures:

   (a) To ensure equal access by persons with disabilities to clean water services, and to ensure access to appropriate and affordable services, devices and other assistance for disability-related needs;

   (b) To ensure access by persons with disabilities, in particular women and girls with disabilities and older persons with disabilities, to social protection programmes and poverty reduction programmes;

   (c) To ensure access by persons with disabilities and their families living in situations of poverty to assistance from the State with disability-related expenses, including adequate training, counselling, financial assistance and respite care;

(d) To ensure access by persons with disabilities to public housing programmes;

(e) To ensure equal access by persons with disabilities to retirement benefits and programmes.

Chapter 9

Migration and social inclusion policy

Jane Pillinger

Introduction

Many migrants living in Ireland today experience exclusion, marginalisation and poverty. Compared to other groups in the population their inclusion and belonging is mediated by their access to rights and entitlements associated with immigration status, and therefore to the conditions that facilitate inclusion, such as work and access to services. Until recently, limited attention has been given to issues that address social exclusion, poverty, access to services and migrants' integration into Irish society. Whilst migration was not a subject of the original or revised national anti-poverty strategies, in recent years there has been a recognition of the need to prioritise the integration of migrants within a broad framework of poverty and social inclusion policy in Ireland (Ireland, 2006; IOM, 2006; NESC, 2006).

This chapter discusses why migration has significant implications for Irish policy on poverty and social inclusion. It argues that the full integration and inclusion of migrants in Irish society requires investment in resources and an understanding of how racism and other barriers to participation in society can be overcome. This includes addressing the interrelated areas of inclusion in work, inclusion in community and civil life and inclusion with respect to how mainstream institutions can meet individual and societal needs in areas such as education, health, employment, social care and housing.

In this context, the scope of social policy in meeting the needs of migrants must be addressed through the provision of culturally appropriate, responsive and accessible services that promote their rights, inclusion and autonomy. Access to social inclusion is affected by restrictions that are imposed on some groups in their access to social rights and access to certain services. Discrimination and racism also impact negatively on inclusion by reducing opportunities and by perpetuating institutional or systemic forms of discrimination that result in poor access to rights and services, for example because of language barriers or because of a lack of understanding of a person's culture or religion.

Most migrants are young and in work and make few demands on services; whereas asylum seekers have different needs by virtue of the restrictions imposed on their participation in work and education and also because they may experience unique health and support needs that may place additional demands on services.

Migration has affected Ireland's economy in positive ways. Evidence from Ireland, the UK and the US shows that there is a fiscal gain from immigrants and that migrants are also important sources of labour in the social care and health services by helping to alleviate labour shortages (IOM, 2006; Ruhs, 2005; Minns, 2005). However, many migrants are working below their potential in jobs that do not utilise their skills fully (MRCI, 2007; Pillinger, 2006b).

The 2006 Census shows that immigration to Ireland has accounted for the majority of Ireland's recent population growth, with 420,000 foreign nationals living in Ireland in 2006 (compared to 224,000 in 2002) (CSO, 2007). Fuelled by the booming economy and a relatively open policy on immigration, Ireland's population of non-Irish migrant workers is one of the highest in the EU and currently stands at 10 per cent of the population. This trend is likely to continue and CSO projections suggest that the population will continue to grow in a buoyant economy and that the immigration of up to 300,000 new migrants will take place between 2006 and 2016. Migration growth is likely to account for one-half of Ireland's population growth between 2006 and 2020 (NESC, 2006). This growth is seen to be particularly important if Ireland is to cope with the care needs associated with an ageing population.

Although there is relatively limited data on migrants in Ireland, non-Irish nationals have higher rates of consistent poverty (13.1 per cent) compared to Irish nationals (6.6 per cent) (Ireland, 2007a). There is a higher employment rate amongst migrants (71 per cent of non-Irish nationals compared to 60 per cent of Irish nationals) (CSO, 2007). Non-Irish nationals have higher levels of education than Irish nationals, with many working significantly below their potential. Twice as many non-Irish nationals have second level educational qualifications compared to Irish nationals (54 per cent of non-Irish nationals) (Barrett et al., 2006). In particular, women migrant workers experience higher levels of exclusion and poverty (IOM, 2006; Pillinger, 2006b).

Anti-poverty and social inclusion policy context

Anti-poverty and social inclusion measures are not only important to promoting inclusion and integration, but also to preventing racism and addressing access to services in areas such as health, childcare, training and employment. Underpinning much of the recent development of Irish policy has been the progression of a multifaceted approach to equality covering both employment equality and equality in the provision of services. The Equal Status Acts 2000 and 2004 play an important role in improving access to healthcare, welfare, education, employment, housing and other services.

The *National Anti-Poverty Strategy* (Ireland, 1997), *Building an Inclusive Society* (Ireland, 2002a) and the *National Action Plan against Poverty and Social Exclusion 2001–2003* (Ireland, 2002b) were focused on reducing poverty by 2010. Targets were developed in the areas of unemployment, income adequacy, educational disadvantage, health, housing and disadvantaged rural and urban areas. They included new and emerging groups such as ethnic minorities along with other groups at risk of poverty, although no specific reference to migrants was made. The 2005 discussion paper on immigration and residence in Ireland (DJELR, 2005a) reinforces the need for a better integration of public policy relating to immigration, including the impact on services such as education, health and housing.

National Action Plan for Social Inclusion 2007–2016

Both the *National Action Plan for Social Inclusion 2007–2016* (NAPinclusion) and the National Development Plan 2007–2013, *Transforming Ireland: A Better Quality of Life for All*, highlight high-level goals for reducing poverty and social exclusion (Ireland 2007a, 2007b). The NAPinclusion acknowledges that migrants, amongst other disadvantaged groups, have not benefited equally from the booming economy and are at risk of poverty and exclusion. The integration of migrants is one of the NAPinclusion's high-level goals, which are designed to 'mobilise resources to address long-standing and serious deficits' (Ireland, 2007, p. 21).

The focus of the goal is on the integration of migrants into Irish society, to be achieved through the provision of language support services in the education sector and measures to improve access to other public services to 'develop a strategy aimed at achieving the integration of newcomers in our society. As an initial action, resources for the provision of 550 teachers for language supports in the education sector will be provided by 2009 and access to other public services through translation of information and supports will be improved' (p. 15). Between 2007 and 2013, €36 million is committed 'to facilitate coordination initiatives and generally promote integration' (p. 15) through the provision of interpretation services in the local offices of the Department of Social and Family Affairs (DSFA) and the provision of web-based information guides about the schemes and services provided by the DSFA in eight languages (Arabic, Chinese, French, Polish, Portuguese, Romanian, Russian and Spanish). Other initiatives are those contained under the *National Action Plan against Racism 2005–2008* (see below).

Other commitments concern broad priorities to improve access to employment opportunities, second chance education and quality health services for migrants and other minority ethnic groups. However, there is no specific reference to asylum seekers and refugees in the NAPinclusion, and no reference to the provision of accommodation through direct provision.

National Action Plan against Racism 2005–2008

Planning for Diversity: The National Action Plan against Racism 2005–2008 (NPAR) is a broad-ranging approach containing some specific strategic social policy developments (DJELR, 2005b). However, the NPAR has no statutory basis nor is a specific budget allocated for the implementation of the actions it contains. It identifies a framework for the development of 'a more inclusive, intercultural society in Ireland ... based on policies that promote interaction, equality of opportunity, understanding and respect' (p. 27). The intercultural framework includes a range of measures that focus on the integration of migrants within equality policy, anti-poverty policy and public service modernisation. The five underpinning objectives have particularly important implications for social policy developments:

- Protection: effective protection and redress against racism

- Inclusion: economic inclusion and equality of opportunity

- Provision: accommodating diversity in service provision

- Recognition: recognition and awareness of diversity

- Participation: full participation in Irish society.

The methods to be used to achieve the aims of the framework are as follows:

- Mainstreaming an intercultural approach into policy-making processes and into all relevant policy areas, with reference to Ireland's commitments to equality and human rights

- Targeting of specific strategies to overcome the inequalities experienced by specific groups informed by an evidence-based approach to policy-making

- Benchmarking progress through targets and timescales and the development of statistical strategies to provide the necessary data to measure such progress

- Engagement of key stakeholders and drivers to support the implementation of the NPAR, including policy-makers, specialised and expert bodies, the social partners and local communities, which include groups representing cultural and ethnic minorities.

The plan calls for the reasonable accommodation of diversity and positive action in the design and implementation of policies, programmes and organisational practices. Although it has no resources attached to it, it has provided a framework for engaging policy-makers and raising awareness of social and economic issues facing migrants in Ireland. It has raised the need to address the planning of services as well as mainstream and targeted policy initiatives. In the area of policy development there are specific mechanisms to integrate the needs of migrants into macroeconomic and social policy planning, although, concerning migrant workers, this is to be 'consistent with the requirements of policy on immigration, employment and equality' (p. 31).

European and international policy frameworks
National developments are also informed by international and European policy frameworks. There are basic social standards established in the United Nation's Convention on the Protection of the Rights of All Migrant Workers and Members of Their Families (not ratified by Ireland). Under Article 28, migrant workers and members of their families shall enjoy the same treatment granted to nationals, this includes the right to receive any medical care that is urgently required; and Article 30 provides for the basic right of access

to education based on the principle of equality of treatment with nationals. The ILO (2004) has drawn up a non-binding multilateral framework for a rights-based approach to labour migration with guidelines and principles for policies based on best practice and international standards. The NCCRI (2004) argues that even if these conventions are not ratified and implemented they should still underpin minimum standards in Irish policy.

The EU's social policy framework includes reference to the need to integrate migrants into work and society. The European Commission's (2006) *Green Paper on an EU Approach to Managing Economic Migration* addresses some core social policy issues, there is a Commission Communication on 'A Common Agenda for Integration: Framework for the Integration of Third-Country Nationals in the European Union' (2005a), and the Justice and Home Affairs Council (2004) has drawn up *Common Basic Principles on Integration* (discussed below). Other specific provisions are found in the Directive on Family Reunification (2003/86/EC of 22 September 2003), which seeks to protect migrant families and family life in accordance with principles of international law.

Integration: A new framework for social inclusion?

In recent years the debate about the social inclusion of migrants has focused on integration. Balancing the recognition of a diversity of cultures and backgrounds and an increasingly multicultural society with the common values, social cohesion and identity of the host country is a challenge for policy-makers and service-providers. Integration debates have not been without their difficulties and have been contested. This has ranged from the need for broad-based measures to promote the social inclusion of immigrants (Spencer, 2004; MRCI, 2006) and that recognise integration as equal treatment and the prohibition of discrimination (UN, 2006) to measures required to foster integration through the provision of language and introductory courses to promote civic participation and community activity (Healy, 2007). At the other end of the spectrum are more limited integration measures that focus on how migrants can be assimilated into one society (Healy, 2007; Brubaker, 2001).

As Spencer argues, 'Integration is not simply about access to the labour market and services, or about changing attitudes of civic engagement; it is a two-way process of adaptation by migrant *and* host society at all of those levels' (2004, p. 24). Therefore, if integration is to work as a reciprocal process it requires there to be a balance between granting rights and entitlements to migrants and a willingness to adapt to the norms of the host country. The objective should be that integration impacts positively on migrants through 'the process of learning a new culture, acquiring rights and obligations, gaining access to positions and social status, building personal relationships with members of the host society and forming a feeling of belonging to, and identification with, that society' (p. 24). Integration also benefits the host society by 'opening up institutions and granting equal opportunities to immigrants' (Bosswick and Heckmann, 2006, p. 5).

Integration is increasingly part of the language of policy-makers in Ireland. It has been linked to participation in society and cultural identity (Interdepartmental Working Group on the Integration of Refugees in Ireland, 1999), mutual obligations (DJELR, 2005a), active citizenship and interculturalism (Department of Education and Science, 2000). The

Immigration, Residence and Protection Bill recommends the establishment of an immigrant integration unit with the remit to 'promote and coordinate social and organisational measures' (DJELR, 2005a, p. 5).

In the EU the *Common Basic Principles on Integration* include the promotion of basic knowledge of the receiving society's language, history and institutions, as well as 'normative adaptation'. Integration is defined as a two-way process, with integration policies covering work, social inclusion and the engagement of civil society, all of which are areas that will be important for the planning of future social policies. However, in practice, EU policies have been developed within a framework of restricted conditionality that, according to Carrera (2005, p. 1), 'may negatively affect social cohesion and inclusion, and undermine the fundamental rights of immigrants'. With this in mind, integration strategies need to be focused on the goal of inclusion with a process that guarantees equality of treatment and full access to social, economic and political rights.

As the experience from other European countries suggests, along with anecdotal evidence in Ireland, many of the new migrants to Ireland are not temporary migrants, but are here to stay for the long term, with many aspiring to Irish citizenship and long-term residency. This suggests that there is a need for long-term planning for the integration and inclusion of migrants as a feature of Irish society, particularly to avoid some of the experiences of exclusion and ghettoisation of migrants in other countries. Improving access to public services in areas such as health, education, employment and housing, along with access to English language and orientation programmes, can be critical to long-term integration and participation. However, prevailing policy assumptions are that migration is temporary, whilst political discourse is often focused on limiting migrants' rights in order to prevent public hostility, often for short-term political gain.

This results in significant policy gaps which if addressed could enhance integration and reduce the risks of exclusion and marginalisation. There are important lessons from other countries of the need to invest in policies and programmes for those migrants that choose to stay. This can be seen in the higher levels of disadvantage, poverty and exclusion that are manifest in under-representation in democratic institutions and policy-making, poorer health, higher unemployment, educational under-achievement and poorer housing experienced by second and third generation migrants.

Migrants who are vulnerable to poverty and exclusion

The social inclusion and equality of migrants is mediated by their legal status which in turn influences their social rights and entitlements, including access to social, health, employment and other services. There are different entitlements for different groups of migrant workers (depending on whether they hold a work authorisation/working visa/work permit, are citizens of the new EU member states or are working students) and refugees and asylum seekers. There are some groups that are particularly vulnerable and at risk of social exclusion by virtue of their status, including asylum seekers, unaccompanied minors, victims of human trafficking and dependent spouses of work permit holders.

Migrant workers

There is a growing body of evidence of the impact of low pay, exploitation and poor working conditions on the exclusion of some migrant workers (MRCI, 2006, 2004; ICI, 2005; NESC, 2006; IOM, 2006). However, there are differences in status between migrant workers holding work permits (which the employer has to apply for) and those holding work authorisation visas/working visas, regarding family reunification, access to services and legal status. The working visa and work authorisation scheme introduced in 2000 and the Employment Permits Act 2006 extended entitlements to highly skilled workers, including settlement and family reunification, two-year visas and quicker routes to gaining residency. In contrast, work permit employers have to apply for work permits on behalf of their employees for one year. Since the enactment of the Employment Permits Act, the work permit is held by the employee. Work permits are normally issued to lower skilled occupations in the horticultural, construction, social care and service sectors of the economy. There are no rights to family reunification or for spouses to work.

Access to the labour market was granted to citizens from the ten new EU member states in May 2004 and this resulted in a corresponding reduction in the number of work permits issued to non-EU migrants. Between May 2004 and February 2006, approximately 186,000 migrants from the new member states (aged 15 years or over) arrived in the country. By mid-2006, approximately 10,000 people from these countries were applying for personal public service numbers each month (the majority of whom were from Poland, Lithuania, Latvia and Slovakia). A more restrictive attitude to EU migration can be seen in the 2006 enlargement of the EU to include Romania and Bulgaria, which has not resulted in free access to the Irish labour market for Romanian and Bulgarian citizens.

Refugees and asylum seekers

Although global political insecurities and human displacement will continue in the future, there has been a reduction in the numbers of asylum seekers entering Ireland. Under the 1951 Geneva Convention, Ireland accepts an agreed number of programme refugees as part of its international obligations to protect people fleeing persecution and by responding to asylum seekers applying to be recognised as refugees. Asylum seekers receive more limited entitlements to social supports and are unable to work, although refugee status brings with it similar rights to those held by Irish citizens, and refugees have the right to apply for citizenship. Government policy can be found in *Integration: A Two Way Process* (Interdepartmental Working Group on the Integration of Refugees in Ireland, 1999) and support for asylum seekers is covered under a policy of dispersal and direct provision.

The social inclusion of refugees and asylum seekers has been the subject of concern (Cáirde, 2006; Irish Refugee Council, 2004) and refugee support groups highlight the concerns about the exclusion resulting from social isolation, not having the right to work or to participate in education and training, and the limited supports for women asylum seekers with children. In particular, the Irish policy of dispersal and direct provision has raised a number of social policy challenges concerning access to social networks, healthcare, language classes, interpretation services, childcare and other supports. Specific problems have been highlighted about the negative impact of direct provision on mental and physical health and wellbeing.

The Reception and Integration Agency operates around seventy accommodation centres across the country for asylum seekers, who are provided with full board and accommodation and a weekly allowance of €19.10 (2006). Many live in reception centres, often in poor quality and overcrowded accommodation, for as long as five years whilst waiting for a decision on their status. Asylum seekers are entitled to schooling for children between the ages of 6 and 16, English language and literacy supports provided within an adult education context, medical cards and access to healthcare. There are also measures to include asylum seekers in local community and cultural activities.

Asylum seekers living in direct provision frequently report poor living conditions. In most cases asylum seekers are living in hostels where meals are provided; there is also a limited provision of self-catering accommodation. Between April 2000 and November 2006 there were 50,793 applications for asylum, with an overall decline in those seeking asylum in recent years. At the end of 2006, 4,861 people seeking asylum were being accommodated in direct provision with a further 489 people accommodated in self-catering facilities. There is a young age profile of people in direct provision, with 2,559 of the total of 5,350 people accommodated via this system in 2006 being below 25 years, 1,436 of whom were under 12 years of age. Legal restrictions on rent allowances to pay for private rented accommodation were introduced to reduce the incentive for asylum seekers to move out of accommodation provided by the Reception and Integration Agency, thereby reducing the opportunities for asylum seekers to avail of subsidised private accommodation.

Asylum seekers and refugees experience many of the crises that are recognised factors in contributing to social exclusion, poor housing and homelessness. The Irish Refugee Council (2000, 2001) states that extended stays in direct provisions contribute to the institutionalisation and deskilling of asylum seekers, whilst social exclusion is a direct effect of restrictions on education and training and prohibitions on engaging in paid employment while awaiting decision on their application. The health impacts of living in direct provision have been documented in the HSE's consultations for the *Intercultural Strategy in Health* (2007a) and by organisations representing minority ethnic groups (Cáirde, 2006). Difficulties arise for those who get refugee status in finding accommodation and in obtaining information about how to live independently and access accommodation, training and employment.

The right to citizenship as a result of being an Irish-born child ended with the citizenship referendum in 2003 and the provision allowing parents to have access to residency by virtue of an Irish citizen child was also ended following a decision of the Supreme Court the following year. These provisions impact on both parents and children regarding access to social rights associated with residency and citizenship.

Additional social supports were recommended under the NPAR and service-providers in the health and education sectors have put in place additional services and supports for asylum seekers and their children. One example of this has been the development of national performance indicators on asylum seekers which require the HSE to report to the Department of Health and Children on the provision of services.

Unaccompanied minors

Specific concerns have been expressed about the care and support needs of unaccompanied minors. Around 300 unaccompanied minors have gone missing in the state and some of them could be at risk of labour and sexual abuse and exploitation (Conroy, 2003). Unaccompanied minors are largely housed in private hostels that are not subject to inspection by the Irish Social Services Inspectorate, in contrast to services for cared for Irish children. Once these children reach the age of eighteen their 'cared for' status ends (when they become known as 'aged out minors') and their only option is to enter the asylum process. Many of these children are not eligible for residency and are treated as refugees under the asylum process, many are subsequently deported to countries that they have never lived in and with few supports.

Victims of human trafficking

Although at a level that is lower than other countries there has been a recent and worrying increase in human trafficking, the majority of which is of the sexual exploitation of women and children. According to the Report of the Department of Justice, Equality and Law Reform and An Garda Síochána Working Group on Trafficking in Human Beings (DJELR, 2006, p. 8), 'Ireland is at risk from the same threats as those facing its EU partners and, in particular, our nearest neighbours. Garda operations have uncovered a small number of trafficking cases'.

In Ireland there has been an absence of a policy framework on human trafficking, particularly regarding the support, security, health and care needs of victims of trafficking. Ireland has not signed up to the two main international conventions on human trafficking – the UN's Palermo Protocol and the Council of Europe's Convention on Human Trafficking[1] – which include guidance on the support and security needs of victims. The health, accommodation and support needs of victims of trafficking have yet to be addressed in policy and have been largely left to community-based organisations such as Ruhama.

Women migrants

The concerns and challenges that are unique to the experience of women migrants are often overlooked. Whilst migration can benefit the women involved by giving them access to higher incomes and possibilities of sending remittances to family members, they are also open to an increased risk of gender-specific forms of abuse and exploitation (Migration Policy Institute, 2003). There are different situations and conditions faced by immigrant women and men in the integration process, including double discrimination faced by immigrant women in the labour market, poor working conditions and exploitation. In some areas of work, such as domestic service and contract cleaning, where women are isolated and do not have access to trade unions, there is a greater vulnerability to exploitation (MRCI, 2004; Pillinger, 2006b). The European Commission (2005b) highlights the need for a gender mainstreaming

---

[1] The UN Convention against Transnational Organised Crime includes a comprehensive approach to addressing trafficking in human beings: its Protocol to Prevent, Suppress and Punish Trafficking in Persons, Especially Women and Children (Palermo Protocol, 2000, Supplanting the UN Convention against Transnational Organised Crime). The Council of Europe Convention on Action against Trafficking in Human Beings was agreed by the Committee of Ministers on 3 May 2005 (signing in Warsaw opened on 16 May 2005).

approach in order to integrate a gender perspective into immigration and integration policies. This is particularly important because the increasing feminisation of migration shapes channels of entry and access to services, benefits, work, asylum and family reunification.

There are also many gendered assumptions underlying family reunification policies which are often embedded in assumptions of women's dependence in the family, whilst in practice the majority of migrant women migrate alone. Although the law does not provide a right to family reunification, migrants granted long-term residency or permission to remain are permitted to have their family members live with them. However, the decision to grant family reunification is at the discretion of the Minister for Justice and applicants have to prove sufficient resources to support family members. This is a difficult situation for many migrants, especially women, who may not be granted the right to work in Ireland or whose incomes are very low. As the National Women's Council of Ireland (2005, p. 2) states, 'Family reunification is of immense importance to many migrants and in particular to migrant women who have been forced to leave their children and families behind when they emigrate to Ireland. This puts huge strains particularly on mothers of young children as well as on the children themselves'.

Immigrant women represent a larger proportion of full-time workers than Irish women (39.8 per cent of those in full-time employment compared to 31.1 per cent of Irish women) and are a lower proportion of part-time workers and those economically inactive. They also tend to be of a younger working age, with an average age of 30, an age when women are likely to be engaged in childbirth and childrearing.

Although immigrant women have higher educational qualifications than Irish women, many of these women are over-represented in the lower skilled jobs compared to both Irish women and Irish men. They predominate in highly feminised sectors such as catering, domestic work, care and health services. Women migrant workers are often the poorest in the community and many work in low-paid, exploitative and invisible employment.

Many women migrate alone and large numbers do so to send money home to their families and the number of women that are engaged in transnational parenting has grown significantly in recent years. Social isolation is enhanced because of the sectors that women work in and because many women migrants do not have family networks to help them with childcare (MRCI, 2006; Pillinger, 2006b).

In other cases, women who migrate with spouses who are work permit holders are not allowed to work. This reinforces dependence on their husbands/partners and an environment based on dependence and inequality can in some cases lead to abuse and domestic violence. This has implications for support systems for women who experience domestic violence, pregnancy or social isolation. As a result, organisations such as Women's Aid have called for greater legal protection – for women who experience domestic violence to be given independent legal status and the right to remain in Ireland. This situation is worsened by the fact that the Habitual Residence Condition (see below) enhances their social exclusion, leaving them without access to social welfare and other core services.

There is a need for a gender-based analysis of approaches to migration policy, which could be modelled on the Canadian approach which resulted in the assessment of gender-specific impacts in migration policy and implementation and has included proposals to increase the age of dependence from 18 to 22, aimed at dependent daughters who in some cultures may stay at home until marriage or after divorce. In particular, a more flexible migration system is needed so that spouses of migrant workers can work and have access to social welfare benefits and domestic violence services.

Access to services

Health services

The social impacts of migration are only just beginning to be considered in Irish health policy planning and reporting. There is no mention of migration as a specific issue in the government's health strategy *Quality and Fairness*, nor in other policy documents that have recently underpinned the development of services, such as the primary healthcare strategy, and the health promotion strategy (DOHC, 2000, 2001a, 2001b). In some respects this is not surprising since these policy documents pre-date migration into Ireland. In 2006, the Health Service Executive (HSE, 2007a) drew up an *Intercultural Strategy in Health*, after an extensive consultation process with staff working in the HSE and with service-users from minority ethnic communities and migrant community-based organisations. The strategy has highlighted the need for:

- An improved evidence base and data on the utilisation of services by different minority ethnic groups and migrants to inform the provision of appropriate health and social care services so that they take full account of minority ethnic people's diverse health needs

- A better understanding of the barriers experienced by different migrant communities, including better access to information about accessing health services, and improved access to culturally appropriate services, in particular GP, maternity and mental health services

- Improved training for staff in the provision of cultural competence services

- Enhanced access to services for those migrant groups that do not access services or that are not aware of how the 'system' works

- A community development model as an effective and sustainable approach to the provision of culturally appropriate health services.

Service-users and community organisations identified issues such as access to information, interpretation and translation, and the importance of resourcing community development and community-based approaches to health (HSE, 2007b). Barriers identified in accessing health services include a person's culture, religion, language and legal status, communications and information barriers and significant problems in understanding the links between inequality and mental health difficulty experienced by some groups, particularly refugees and asylum seekers. Specific health issues are raised by asylum seekers and refugees concerning the impact on social isolation and health and wellbeing of living in direct provision hostels, as well as trauma and post-migration stress, racism, fear of deportation, lack of understanding of services and language barriers (HSE, 2007b).

There has been a growth of peer-led and community development approaches to the social inclusion of migrants.

Examples of this are a support organisation for asylum seekers provided by Spirasi, which offers a health information programme through a peer-led project that trains groups of asylum seekers and refugees in health issues and resources, using visual, multilingual and audio communication aids. Another example is the community-based organisation Cáirde, which provides support, training and community-based programmes to minority ethnic leaders, with specific programmes for women.

The Habitual Residence Condition and access to social welfare benefits

Following the enlargement of the EU in 2004, Ireland provided general access to the labour market for workers of the ten new member states, but put in place a number of restrictions regarding access to welfare benefits and other forms of social assistance through the Habitual Residence Condition (HRC).[2] This restricts access to welfare benefits for all EU and European Economic Area citizens and is intended to prevent 'welfare tourism'. An applicant for social welfare has to demonstrate that he or she is habitually resident in the state. However, because of the extreme hardship experienced by some migrant workers, community welfare officers have used the discretionary powers to provide exceptional and urgent needs payments. Although the European Commission did make some criticisms of the operation of the HRC in the UK in that it was against the principle of free movement of labour, they do not appear to have pursued these and the European

---

[2] Introduced under Section 17 of the Social Welfare (Miscellaneous Provisions) Act 2004 and Schedule 1 to the Act, see now the Social Welfare (Consolidation) Act 2005. See Department of Social and Family Affairs (2005).

Court of Justice has upheld the UK HRC as long as it is applied in a proportionate manner. A review of the HRC was initiated by the Department of Social and Family Affairs in 2005 with a view to ending confusion about access to emergency support through supplementary welfare for all migrant workers.

Housing and accommodation

Low wages are a reality for a large number of immigrants in Ireland; many are living in poor quality and overcrowded accommodation – with migrants reporting renting properties that are dirty, damp, infested with rodents and without proper heating – or in substandard accommodation provided by their employers (ICI, 2004). Research by the Homeless Agency (TSA, 2006; Pillinger, 2006a) has revealed growing numbers of people from the new EU member states who are principally homeless because of income and work-related problems, including exploitative work situations, poor information concerning work opportunities and the high cost of living in Dublin in particular. It was estimated that at any one time between thirty-five and eighty-five nationals of the 2004 EU accession states were accessing homeless services in Dublin in September 2005, although this was considered an under-estimation of the problem (TSA, 2006).

The HRC has been applied to the funding of homeless and domestic violence services and this means that migrants who do not fulfil the conditions are unable to avail of these services, including refuges for women who experience domestic violence. Reports of homelessness among migrants, including a high-profile story concerning a young Ukrainian worker who had her legs amputated after being found homeless and suffering from frostbite, underline the links between migrants' social and working environments and their health status.

Education

Access to education for children and adults of all ages is critical for the integration and inclusion of migrants. As the NESC states, 'the challenge for diversity will be acutely felt in the education system since education is central to the success of integration' (2006, p. 199). In particular, the provision of English language courses is generally viewed as a key element of the integration into work and of accessing services, rights, entitlements and information (European Commission, 2005; Healy, 2006). Whilst this provision remains very limited, a number of community organisations have gained funding for the provision of language classes and language tuition has been introduced into the classroom for children.

A working group on interculturalism has been established by the Department of Education and Science and the National Council for Curriculum and Assessment has reviewed national curricula to ensure the promotion of intercultural education. The NPAR sets out a number of recommendations including the development of a national intercultural education strategy, an inclusive and intercultural school environment and curriculum, specific issues covering youth work and enhancing participation in education for unaccompanied minors and refugee and asylum seekers up to 18 years old, and for those with leave to remain to have improved access to further and higher education (DJELR, 2005b).

Information

Many migrants experience problems in accessing information because of language barriers or unfamiliarity with the 'system'. For example, Ireland's network of citizen's information services report on the poor use made of information and advice provision by migrant groups. Guidelines have been developed to improve the accessibility of information for those groups that experience the greatest barriers, including refugees and asylum seekers and migrant workers (Comhairle, 2005) and grants for information and advocacy projects have been funded through Comhairle (now the Citizens Information Board). A number of organisations have produced specialist information about specific groups, for example the Immigration Council of Ireland's *Handbook on Immigrants' Rights and Entitlements in Ireland* (ICI, 2003). In recent years there has been a significant increase in support organisations for migrants. Many of these organisations are migrant-led and provide accessible information, advice, advocacy and community development programmes. Examples include the Polish Information and Advice Centre, the Migrant Rights Centre Ireland and Akida (for African women).

Conclusions and recommendations

Many migrant groups, especially low-skilled migrants, face social exclusion because of language barriers and many are vulnerable in the labour market to exploitation and social isolation. Immigrants with an undocumented or indeterminate status, low-paid and socially isolated migrant workers, women migrants and young migrants are particularly vulnerable to poverty, poor housing conditions, poor access to services and exclusion from society (IOM, 2006).

According to the NESC, the challenge for integration policy and social policy is to respond effectively to the scale and diversity of migration by improving capacity and service developments: 'These include improving the collection and use of data, enhancing the ability of staff to deal with a diversity of users, understanding the vulnerabilities of women in the migration-integration process and providing the public

with better information on service entitlements and standards'
(2006, p. xvi).

This chapter has shown that some migrants living and
working in Ireland experience poverty, poor living conditions,
social exclusion, racism and poor access to employment,
particularly well-paid and secure employment. The
vulnerability of certain groups, for example asylum seekers,
unaccompanied minors, victims of trafficking, spouses of
work permit holders, low-paid migrant workers and migrant
workers who do not fulfil the Habitual Residence Condition,
raise important challenges for Irish social policy.

Migration is still relatively new to Ireland and there are many
opportunities to develop the best frameworks on integration,
multiculturalism and social inclusion, whilst adapting and
creating inclusive and culturally competent services. This can
help avoid problems – such as institutional racism, social
isolation and disadvantage, as well as hostility and
resentment from Irish citizens – being replicated in the future,
whilst also ensuring that migration contributes equally to
Ireland's economic and social development. The issue is that
improving access to social rights and to quality services for
migrants can also help to improve rights and access to
quality services for the whole population.

Research and data

The limited knowledge and data about migrants' education,
social welfare, employment and healthcare needs have
implications for policy and planning. Improved data is needed
to inform policies on settlement, social inclusion and
integration. More detailed evidence-based research needs to
be put in place to inform policy developments and service
planning. This should highlight the experiences of migrants in

areas such as family reunification, access to core services and social benefits in particular communities and their impact on settlement and integration.

Planning of services
Attention will need to be given to the long-term planning of services that reflect increased numbers of migrants and the diversity of the community, particularly since it is likely that many migrants may wish to settle in Ireland. The impact of these patterns on social policy planning in education, health, social welfare and housing will need to be considered and the planning, delivery and monitoring of services proofed for their impact on specific migrant groups and communities.

Engagement, involvement and participation of migrant communities
A key factor will be to enhance the engagement of migrant communities themselves, particularly through peer-led and community development approaches. The provision of resources for migrant-led and community organisations will need to increase if there is to be a wider engagement with migrant communities in the future. There should be support for the involvement and participation of people from, and organisations representing, migrant communities in the planning, delivery, monitoring and evaluation of health, education, housing, social welfare and other services.

The social inclusion of the most vulnerable groups
There needs to be more attention given to the vulnerability of those migrants living and working in Ireland who experience poverty, poor living conditions, social exclusion, racism and poor access to employment, particularly well-paid and secure employment. In particular, the vulnerability of unaccompanied

minors, spouses of work permit holders and migrant workers who do not fulfil the Habitual Residence Condition raises important challenges for Irish social policy.

Rights and entitlements
More efforts need to be made to ensure that migrants are fully aware of their rights and entitlements. There needs to be more information about rights, entitlements and the structure of health, social care, education, housing and other services, particularly in orientating people when they first arrive in Ireland. Some of this preparation could take place before migrants leave their home country.

Social welfare and the Habitual Residence Condition
The review of the Habitual Residence Condition should be carried out with a view to establishing an equitable system for providing welfare rights to excluded migrant workers.

Policy on integration
It will be important for future policy developments in the area of integration to be broad ranging and to cover economic, social, political and cultural rights that impact on work, social inclusion and the engagement of civil society. It will therefore be important to ensure that integration policy is based on a comprehensive strategy for inclusion and equality, with sufficient resources for mainstream and targeted actions. This should be progressed through the framework for the integration of migrants outlined in the NPAR.

Cross-cutting mechanism
There should be a high-level cross-cutting mechanism on migration introduced so that relevant government departments develop more effective actions that help to

integrate migrants into work and community life. This could be formed under the remit of the Cabinet Committee on Social Inclusion.

Integrating the impact of policies on migrants
The emerging framework on equality and social inclusion in Ireland has resulted in a method for equality and poverty proofing. This system could be further developed to identify the impact of social policies on all categories of migrants, particularly those that are the most excluded and vulnerable. In this context it will be particularly important for the social impacts of migration to be highlighted and reflected in policy discussions.

A more flexible migration system
There is a need for a more flexible migration system so that spouses of migrant workers can work and that there are possibilities for migrant workers to have permanence and access to social benefits.

Family reunification
Rights to family reunification should be established in law and should recognise the constitutional right given to the family. Migrant workers, who pay taxes in the same way as all other workers, should have an equal right to family reunification, education, housing and social welfare. Spouses of all migrant workers should have the right to work.

Gender perspective
A gender perspective should be included in all policy developments concerning migration policy and the integration and inclusion of migrants in Ireland. In particular, women experiencing domestic violence and women and children who

have experienced trafficking for sexual exploitation should be given temporary leave to remain in the state and have full access to social welfare and other benefits for their children. Specific targeted support and outreach programmes should be funded for voluntary organisations working with women migrant workers, particularly women who are socially isolated and at risk of abuse or violence.

References

Barrett, A., Bergin, A. and Duffy, D. (2006), 'The Labour Market Characteristics and Labour Market Impact of Immigrants in Ireland', *The Economic and Social Review*, vol. 37, no. 1, pp. 1–26

Bosswick, W. and Heckmann, F. (2006), *Social Integration of Immigrants: Contribution of Local and Regional Authorities*, Dublin: European Foundation for the Improvement of Living and Working Conditions

Brubaker, R. (2001), 'The Return of Assimilation? Changing Perspectives on Immigration and Its Sequels in France, Germany and the United States', *Ethnic and Racial Studies*, vol. 24, no. 4, pp. 531–548

Cáirde (2006), *Assessing the Health and Related Needs of Minority Ethnic Groups in Dublin's North Inner City*, Dublin: Cáirde

Carrera, S. (2005), 'Integration as a Process of Inclusion for Migrants? The Case of Long-Term Residents in the EU', Centre for European Policy Studies Working Document no. 219, 1 March

Comhairle (2005), *Access to Information for All*, Dublin: Comhairle

Conroy, P. (2003), *Trafficking in Unaccompanied Minors in the European Union Member States – Ireland: Research Summary*, Dublin: International Organisation for Migration

CSO (2007), *Census 2006. Principal Demographic Results*, Dublin: Central Statistics Office

DES (2000), *Learning for Life: White Paper on Adult Education*, Dublin: Stationery Office

DOHC (2000), *National Health Promotion Strategy 2000–2005*, Dublin: Department of Health and Children

DOHC (2001a), *Primary Care – A New Direction*, Dublin: Department of Health and Children

DOHC (2001b), *Quality and Fairness: A Health System for You*, Dublin: Department of Health and Children

DJELR (2005a), *Immigration and Residence in Ireland: Outline Policy Proposals for an Immigration and Residence Bill – A Discussion Document*, Dublin: Department of Justice, Equality and Law Reform

DJELR (2005b), *Planning for Diversity: The National Action Plan against Racism 2005–2008*, Department of Justice, Equality and Law Reform, Dublin: Stationery Office

DJELR (2006), *Report of the Department of Justice, Equality and Law Reform and An Garda Síochána Working Group on Trafficking in Human Beings*, Dublin: Department of Justice, Equality and Law Reform

DSFA (2005), *Habitual Residence Condition*, Dublin: Department of Social and Family Affairs

European Commission (2005a), 'A Common Agenda for Integration: Framework for the Integration of Third-Country Nationals in the European Union', Communication from the Commission to the Council, the European Parliament, the European Economic and Social Committee and the Committee of the Regions, Brussels, Com(2005) 389 final

European Commission (2005b), *Report from the Commission to the Council, the European Parliament, the European Economic and Social Committee and the Committee of the Regions on Equality between Women and Men*, Brussels, Com(2005) 44 final

European Commission (2006), *Green Paper on an EU Approach to Managing Economic Migration*, Brussels, Com(2004) 811 final

Healy, C. (2007, forthcoming), *On Speaking Terms: Language, Integration and the New Irish*, Dublin: Immigrant Council of Ireland

HSE (2007a), *Intercultural Strategy in Health*, Dublin: Health Service Executive

HSE (2007b), *Report of the Consultations: Intercultural Strategy in Health*, Dublin: Health Service Executive

ICI (2003), *Handbook on Immigrants' Rights and Entitlements in Ireland*, Dublin: Immigrant Council of Ireland

ICI (2004), *Voices of Immigrants: The Challenges of Inclusion*, Report by Kelleher Associates, Dublin: Immigrant Council of Ireland

ICI (2005), *Summary Analysis and Initial Response to the Government's Proposals for an Immigration and Residency Bill*, Dublin: Immigrant Council of Ireland

ILO (2004), *Non-Binding Multilateral Framework for a Rights-Based Approach to Labour Migration*, Geneva: International Labour Organization

Interdepartmental Working Group on the Integration of Refugees in Ireland (1999), *Integration: A Two Way Process*, Dublin: Department of Justice, Equality and Law Reform

IOM (2006), *Managing Migration in Ireland: A Social and Economic Analysis, Report of the International Organization for Migration for the National Economic and Social Council of Ireland*, Dublin: NESC

Ireland (1997), *Sharing in Progress: National Anti-Poverty Strategy*, Dublin: Stationery Office

Ireland (2002a), *Building an Inclusive Society*, Dublin: Stationery Office

Ireland (2002b), *National Action Plan against Poverty and Social Exclusion 2001–2003*, Dublin: Stationery Office

Ireland (2006), *National Report for Ireland on Strategies for Social Protection and Social Inclusion, 2006–2008*, Dublin: Stationery Office

Ireland (2007a), *National Action Plan for Social Inclusion 2007–2016*, Dublin: Stationery Office

Ireland (2007b), *Transforming Ireland: A Better Quality of Life for All*, National Development Plan 2007–2013, Dublin: Stationery Office

Irish Refugee Council (2000), *Asylum Seekers and the Right to Work in Ireland*, Dublin: Irish Refugee Council

Irish Refugee Council (2001), *Direct Provision and Dispersal – 18 Months On*, Dublin: Irish Refugee Council

Irish Refugee Council (2004), *Reflections by the Irish Refugee Council on World Refugee Day*, Dublin: Irish Refugee Council

Justice and Home Affairs Council (2004), *Common Basic Principles on Integration*, Brussels: Council of the European Union

Migration Policy Institute (2003), *The Feminization of International Migration: Issues of Labor, Health, and Family Coping Strategies*, Washington DC: Migration Policy Institute

Minns, C. (2005), *Immigration Policy and the Skills of Irish Immigrants: Evidence and Implications*, Discussion Paper Series, Dublin: The Institute for International Integration Studies

MRCI (2004), *Private Homes, A Public Concern: The Experience of Twenty Migrant Women Employed in the Home in Ireland*, Dublin: Migrant Rights Centre Ireland

MRCI (2006), *Realising Integration: Creating the Conditions for Economic, Social, Political and Cultural Inclusion of Migrant Workers and Their Families in Ireland*, Dublin: Migrant Rights Centre Ireland

MRCI (2007), *No Way Forward, No Going Back: Identifying the Problem of Trafficking for Forced Labour in Ireland*, Dublin: Migrant's Rights Centre Ireland

National Women's Council of Ireland (2005), 'Immigration and Residence in Ireland', discussion document, Dublin: National Women's Council of Ireland

NCCRI (2004), 'Proposed Changes in the Social Welfare Code Arising from EU Enlargement', submission from the National Consultative Committee on Racism and Interculturalism (NCCRI) to the Department of Social and Family Affairs

NESC (2006), *Migration Policy,* Dublin: National Economic and Social Council

Pillinger, J. (2006a), *Preventing Homelessness: A Comprehensive Strategy to Prevent Homelessness in Dublin, 2005–2010,* Dublin: Homeless Agency

Pillinger, J. (2006b), *An Introduction to the Situation and Experience of Women Migrant Workers in Ireland*, Dublin: Equality Authority

Ruhs, M. (2005), *Managing the Immigration and Employment of Non-EU Nationals in Ireland*, Studies in Public Policy, no. 19, Dublin: The Policy Institute

Spencer, S. (2004), 'Achieving the Social Inclusion of Migrants', presentation to the Irish Presidency Conference on Reconciling Mobility and Social Inclusion – The Role of Employment and Social Policy, Dublin, 1 and 2 April

TSA (2006), *Away from Home. Homeless Quantification and Profile of EU 10 Nationals Using Homeless Services and Recommendations to Address Their Needs,* Dublin: Homeless Agency

UN (2006), *International Migration and Development: Report of the Secretary-General*, New York: United Nations General Assembly

Chapter 10

Developing an inclusive society: The way forward

Mel Cousins

The objective of this book is to provide an overview and analysis of key issues concerning public policy and poverty and social inclusion in Ireland and to draw policy lessons for the future. The individual chapters have reviewed policy developments in a number of areas which are central to developing an inclusive society. This chapter rehearses some of the main findings of previous chapters and identifies key challenges and possible options from a public policy perspective.

What have we achieved and what remains to be achieved?

Major progress has been achieved
This book highlights the striking progress which has been made in Ireland in many areas over the past twenty years. The number of people employed doubled from 1.1 million in 1987 to 2.2 million in 2007, unemployment fell from 17 per cent to 4 per cent and overall living standards improved enormously. Research has also found a substantial upgrading

of the class structure and increased levels of social mobility (Whelan and Layte, 2006). Perhaps the best indicator of the dramatic change that has occurred, however, is the turnaround in migration from a situation in the 1980s when up to 200,000 people left Ireland to look for work abroad to the situation when over 60,000 people came to Ireland in 2006 alone to take advantage of the opportunities that now exist here.[1]

But major challenges remain

Despite the dramatic progress made in many aspects of the Irish economy and Irish society, as shown in this book, major challenges remain.

Ireland still has one of the highest risk-of-poverty rates in the EU. As discussed in Chapter 2, this rate has shown little change over the period for which comparable data is available. In fact, the situation has, if anything, got worse in relative terms: while our high level of poverty was in line with our relatively low GDP per capita in the 1980s, our high level of poverty is now completely out of line with our national prosperity. Even in terms of the consistent poverty measure (combining income and deprivation) which has been the focus of official targets since 1997, Ireland has a higher rate of poverty than many of our European neighbours at the same level of economic development.

As the detailed studies of children, older people, migrants and people with disabilities have shown, large proportions of our population are still facing very limited opportunities and are effectively excluded from playing their full role in Irish

---

[1] Data refer to net migration.

society. The chapters on health and education indicate the extent to which our health and education systems still lead to highly unequal outcomes – despite considerable investment and despite many positive measures which seek to assist the more disadvantaged sections of our population.

Why have we not done better?

The studies in this book suggest that the main problem is that public policy has yet to adopt and implement a coherent anti-poverty approach. It is not the case that policy is clearly focused on delivering anti-poverty outcomes but that its implementation is faulty. Rather, as we can see in the chapters on health and education, the system is structured in such a way that unequal outcomes are the likely result.

There is no doubt that poverty and social inclusion have been seen by successive governments as important policy issues with the establishment of the first *National Anti-Poverty Strategy* (NAPS) in 1997 (in advance of EU moves in this area) leading to the 2007 *National Action Plan on Social Inclusion* (NAPinclusion). Issues relating to poverty and social inclusion have also featured in a number of national agreements – including the current social partnership agreement *Towards 2016.* Nonetheless, the evidence points to the fact that general statements, objectives and even specific targets on poverty have not been translated into actual policy measures let alone poverty outcomes.

It is, for example, regrettable to note that there is little indication in this review of welfare policy that the detailed targets set in the initial and revised NAPS have had a major impact on policy. Some targets have been met, some have not and in other cases the non-availability of data means that

progress cannot be assessed. However, even where targets
have been met, there is little indication that policies adopted
as part of the NAPS process – as opposed to broader
economic and political developments – were a major
contributor.[2]

One might suggest that the rapid nature of our economic
turnaround and the tendency towards policy convergence
amongst political parties has meant that we have not had the
debates about the appropriate direction for public policy (as it
relates to poverty) which took place in many of the countries
in which anti-poverty policy is more strongly located at the
centre of public policy (see O'Kelly, 2007). Policies which
were focused on providing basic standards of welfare, health
and education services – which may have been appropriate in
the relatively poor Ireland up to the 1980s – now lead to
significantly different outcomes and can contribute to social
exclusion (rather than countering it as originally intended).

Connolly's (2007) examination of the extent to which anti-
poverty policy has been institutionalised in social partnership
suggests that the place of anti-poverty policy over this period
is that of a residual policy category, shaped primarily by the
needs of macroeconomic policy. She argues that the 'policy
frame evident in the social partnership process has proven to
be a barrier to developing anti-poverty policy beyond the
parameters laid down in the early agreements' (p. 38). The

[2] It might be argued that the achievement of the income adequacy target
in the NAPS (€150 in 2002 terms by 2007) disproves this assertion.
However, the meaning of the specific commitment is, at best, opaque
and could have been 'achieved' in a number of different ways. This
suggests that it was broader policy and political factors which led to
the very significant increases in welfare rates in recent years.

implication of these factors, Connolly claims, are that 'incremental change will not significantly alter the place of anti-poverty policy within Irish public policy and it will require a reworking of the fundamental ideas that underpin this institutionally embedded policy regime to produce an effective response to the poverty and inequality in Irish society' (p. 38). The findings of this book are generally consistent with that analysis in relation to overall public policy.

A developmental welfare state and poverty policy

As seen in Chapter 1 (and in many of the other chapters), the role of a *developmental* welfare state has recently been highlighted by the NESC (2005a). The NESC's study is important from a poverty perspective for two main reasons. First, it identifies the need for a new approach to welfare policy if we are to address the challenges of poverty and social exclusion. Second, it provides a coherent rationale for seeing social policy as a central concern of government and as a vital contributor to our economic progress rather than as a residual issue subsidiary to the (more) important economic policy issues. The NESC stresses that economic and social policy are closely interrelated. Thus, on the one hand, 'the development of a dynamic, knowledge-based economy has inherent social implications that can serve social justice and a more egalitarian society' and, on the other, a move to a developmental welfare state is integral to sustaining the dynamism and flexibility of Ireland's economy (p. xxiii).

Building a developmental welfare state?
But, accepting the importance of the NESC's contribution to the debate, to what extent has its vision of a developmental

welfare state been implemented in practice? The NESC holds an important position in the Irish policy-making constellation and includes members of all the key social partners. However, the social partners do not always prioritise in social partnership agreements the more general statements of policy they agree to in the context of the NESC. Nor is it entirely clear that the NESC's vision influenced politicians in the formulation of policy positions in the 2007 general election campaign.

Looking at subsequent policy statements such as *Towards 2016* and the *National Action Plan on Social Inclusion*, we might suggest that the NESC's vision has been imperfectly implemented to date.

Towards 2016 does state that 'The Social Partners subscribe to the NESC vision of Ireland in the future, the key foundations of which are: a dynamic, internationalised, and participatory society and economy, with a strong commitment to social justice, where economic development is environmentally sustainable, and internationally competitive' (Ireland, 2006b). *Towards 2016* also adopts a lifecycle framework, as set out by the NESC in *The Developmental Welfare State* (DWS), which the agreement describes as one of its key innovative features.

The NAPinclusion 2007–2016 refers on a number of occasions to the NESC's report. For example, it states that, in line with the DWS approach, there is now a greater emphasis on services and activation (rather than income measures) as a means of tackling social exclusion (Ireland, 2007). It also agrees with the NESC that access to a wide set of services is essential to underpin the economy, to maintain social cohesion and to combat social exclusion. As with *Towards*

2016, the NAPinclusion uses a lifecycle approach. Within each lifecycle area it also reflects the NESC's emphasis on income support, services and innovative measures.

The impact of the NESC's approach appears to have been greatest in terms of the lifecycle approach. The NESC states that 'a feature of the DWS [is] that differentiated thinking is brought to bear on income supports for individuals at different stages in the lifecycle' (2005a, p. xx) – although it does not, in fact, use the term 'lifecycle approach'. However, one might wonder whether this was the most fundamental aspect of the report or rather a means to an end.

The second area in which the NESC appears to have had an impact is in relation to its proposals for people of working age. This is, perhaps, unsurprising, as the application of the NESC's approach is most fully worked out in this area. However, in the critical area of services, the NAPinclusion is rather lacking any fundamental reappraisal along the lines recommended by the NESC (see below). Indeed, in the area of education, it repeats a target concerning completion of second level education that was originally set in the first NAPS in 1997 (and unachieved since) while very specific and challenging health targets set in the revised NAPS (Ireland, 2002) have disappeared from the current NAPinclusion.[3]

While it might be unfair to suggest that the impact of the NESC's report has been mainly in terms of how the issues are presented, it is far from clear that its central message has

---

[3]   For example, the revised NAPS set a target to reduce the gap in premature mortality between the lowest and highest socio-economic groups by at least 10 per cent for circulatory diseases, for cancers and for injuries and poisonings by 2007 (Ireland, 2002).

been taken on board in recent policy agreements and strategies.

Key policy areas

Examining some of the key issues which need to be addressed if we are to achieve a more inclusive society, this section draws on the analysis contained in the NESC's report and looks, in particular, at the provision of services and income supports from an anti-poverty perspective.[4]

Services

As we have seen, the NESC (2005a) identifies access to a wide set of services (including education, health, childcare, eldercare, transport and employment services) as 'essential to attaining the workforce quality that underpins a competitive, knowledge-based economy, to maintaining social cohesion and combating social exclusion' (p. xix). The NESC regards 'the radical development of services as the single most important route to improving social protection' (p. xix). It sees the first public policy challenge as being to ensure that every member of Irish society has access to the level and quality of service she or he needs, with quality and equity being assured.

Chapters 6 and 7 in this book highlight the inequality in educational and health outcomes in Irish society and suggest that, despite the important work carried out and the recent reforms, quality and equity are still fundamentally lacking in both areas.

---

4 Space does not allow a consideration of the third area identified by the NESC, that of 'activist measures'.

Education

Tormey (Chapter 6) shows that those from poor and working-class backgrounds fare worst within our education system. To give some examples:

- Young people in schools in disadvantaged areas have a greater risk of having significant reading difficulties

- Absenteeism is notably higher in schools in highly disadvantaged areas

- Young people from poor backgrounds leave school earlier and with fewer qualifications

- Even where young people finish school, students from working-class backgrounds take fewer honours subjects at Leaving Certificate and achieve fewer points than those from middle-class backgrounds.

This is particularly important for future life outcomes as research in Ireland has identified a link between low levels of educational qualifications and unemployment, between educational attainment and rates of pay, and that the gap in income and job security between those with educational qualifications and those without widens over time. In fact, Tormey points out that the link between education and future life chances may even be stronger in Ireland than in many other industrialised countries. Tormey highlights the need for systemic reform of the education system in order to address those aspects which are contributing to inequality. He suggests a number of measures, including:

- A centralised or regional applications and allocations system for primary and secondary education to counter market forces and to de-segregate the school system

- Addressing school practices associated with inequality (such as streaming or banding)

- In-career teacher development to promote more appropriate pedagogic models.

Health

Kelleher (Chapter 7) points out that by comparison with international neighbours Ireland's contemporary health status (based on measures such as life expectancy) is still poor. There is also evidence of a class differential, with an appreciable mortality difference between the highest and lowest occupational classes, for example a 300 per cent difference for circulatory diseases and a 600 per cent difference for injuries, poisonings and respiratory diseases. Kelleher emphasises the need to ensure universal equity of access to healthcare in both primary and hospital care facilities and proposes a range of measures including:

- The implementation of health impact assessments for all public policies to ensure that major developments in areas such as transport, housing and education provision are appropriate

- Introducing comprehensive mother and child services across health, education and social welfare sectors, including non-means-tested primary care eligibility until children reach the age of eighteen

- Removing the two-tier structure from both primary and acute hospital care

- Implementing the primary care team network nationwide

- Implementing consultant-directed acute hospital services without re-creating a two-tier public–private infrastructure

- Developing a major primary-care-led health service for older people running the spectrum from health promotion and social support through to acute hospital and pastoral care.

Disability

Fitzgerald (Chapter 8) discusses the major challenges that people with disabilities in Ireland face in playing their full role in society. However, one encouraging sign from this review of welfare policy and poverty is the extent to which the national disability strategy is an attempt, not simply to address some of the inequalities facing people with disabilities, but rather to place disability issues right at the centre of the policy-making process through a coordinated programme of legislation (Disability Act, Education for Persons with Special Education Needs Act and Citizens Information Act), a multi-annual investment programme and departmental sectoral plans.

There has been considerable debate over whether disability services should be rights-based, however Nolan (2003) points out that it may be possible to make progress incrementally in improving the position of people with disabilities without having to resolve the issue as to the appropriate legal basis for such services. As Nolan argues, it would be a significant advance if:

- The state, through the relevant authorities, set out clearly what level of service provision the current level of resources is intended to underpin

- People with disabilities not only knew what this level of service provision was at an individual level, but had an entitlement to those services with associated enforcement mechanisms

- It was set out in concrete terms how services are to be improved over time as more resources become available.

The national disability strategy holds out the possibility that disability issues can be placed at the centre of the policy-making process, leading to the important improvements in services to which Nolan refers. The key issue will be, of course, the extent to which the promise of the strategy is translated into a reality for people with disabilities in Ireland.

Immigration

Pillinger (Chapter 9) shows that migrants are another group who face important challenges in integrating into Irish society. This is an entirely new challenge for Irish society. On the one hand, research indicates that migrants tend to be quite highly educated with migrant workers having significantly higher educational qualifications than the workforce as a whole. On the other hand, research also indicates that, controlling for education and work experience, immigrants earn 18 per cent less than native workers and immigrants from non-English speaking countries are at a 31 per cent wage disadvantage compared to native workers (Barrett and McCarthy, 2006).[5]

Pillinger also shows the difficulties facing migrants in other aspects of their lives – in particular asylum seekers,

---

[5] It should be noted that initial low pay for immigrants would not be unexpected. It has been argued that immigrants may initially lack location-specific human capital (such as language). This analysis would expect immigrants' earnings to converge with those of Irish people over time. However, whether this thesis is correct and whether convergence will occur in practice remains to be seen and may very much depend on the adoption of appropriate policies of support.

unaccompanied minors, victims of trafficking, spouses of work permit holders, low-paid migrant workers and migrant workers who do not fulfil the Habitual Residence Condition. This highlights the importance of a societal response to ensure that migrants and their families are enabled to have access to the full range of services which they require and that they are supported in integrating into Irish society.

Pillinger sets out a range of recommendations including:

- The need for long-term planning of services to reflect increased numbers and the diversity of the community

- A high-level cross-cutting mechanism on migration so that relevant government departments develop more effective actions that help to integrate migrants into work and community life

- The engagement of migrant communities themselves, particularly through peer-led and community development approaches

- Particular attention given to the vulnerability of those migrants living and working in Ireland who experience poverty, poor living conditions, social exclusion, racism and poor access to employment

- More information about rights, entitlements and the structure of health, social care, education, housing and other services

- A more flexible migration and family reunification system.

She argues that future policy developments in the area of integration should be broad ranging and cover economic, social, political and cultural rights that impact on work, social inclusion and the engagement of civil society.

Income

This section reviews the issues concerning income support over the lifecycle.

Working-aged

As Murphy (Chapter 4) shows, a focus on the concept of the working-aged is a recent development in Irish social policy, reflecting the dramatic rise in the employment rate. Previously, the main emphasis had been on the unemployed and those on sickness benefits, with lone parents and people on long-term disability payments being seen as outside the labour market. The NESC (2005a) highlights the importance of looking at the proportion of people of working age on welfare – rather than the now outdated focus on the live register. It envisages the development of a more inclusive labour market with higher employment rates which would, in turn, place social protection on a sounder footing. An integral part of this is a move away from a 'passive' approach to those of working age on welfare, extending the type of approach to unemployed claimants seen under the national employment action plan to broader groups. The NESC recommends that tailored progression pathways should become the norm for working-aged claimants.

One of the working-aged areas highlighted by the NESC is that of lone parents. Here the numbers have grown very significantly in recent years albeit that this, in large part, reflects demographic trends and a broadening of the scope of the schemes for lone parents in the 1990s. The more activist approach has already been reflected in a government discussion paper on reform of income supports for lone parents and low-income parents (Ireland, 2006a). This recommends a quite radical change in approach to support in this area. It identifies the problems with the existing schemes, including the fact that child poverty remains quite high in Ireland, that the conditions of the scheme deter family formation and joint custody and that there is no structured or systematic engagement with the claimants from a labour market perspective.

Having considered a number of different options for reform, the discussion paper recommends the establishment of a new parental allowance for low-income families with young children. This would replace the current one-parent family payment and qualified adult allowance (for social assistance payments). The new payment would be time-limited: payable to families where the youngest child is under a specified age (the report recommends seven years). There would be no employment-related conditions until the youngest child reached five years. When the youngest child was between the ages of five and seven, more active and compulsory engagement would take place involving attending meetings with a job facilitator to provide information and advice on education, training or employment options. Payment of the allowance would be conditional on participation in this process. When the child reached the cut-off age, payment of the allowance would cease and, if the parent was not in employment, the person could apply for any other appropriate social welfare payment such as jobseeker's allowance or the back to work allowance.[6]

The proposal is quite a radical one and aims to achieve a number of different objectives largely in line with the proposals of the NESC. It would ensure a more active and participation-based approach, moving away from the contingency-based approach which arguably traps lone parents on one-parent family payment, and would involve a move towards partial individualisation of payments.

This activist approach to lone parents is continued in the NAPinclusion (although the status of the specific proposals remains somewhat unclear). The NAPinclusion proposes that an active case management approach will be introduced to support those on long-term social welfare into education, training and employment. It sets a target to support 50,000 such people, including lone parents and the long-term unemployed, with an overall aim of reducing by 20 per cent the number of those whose total income is derived from long-term social welfare payments by 2016 (Ireland, 2007).

While the NESC's analysis of what needs to be done in the area of the working-aged population is very clear, there

---

6   The discussion paper recommends that those in receipt of the parental allowance should be allowed to retain earnings (up to a certain level) without affecting the payment. It recommends the abolition of the existing cohabitation rule (which applies to lone-parent payments) and the abolition of the limitation on the amount of welfare payable to a couple where both are in receipt of a means-tested payment. This would mean that if a person in receipt of the new parental allowance lived with someone in receipt of jobseeker's allowance or another means-tested payment, he or she would continue to receive the full payment in their own right.

remains a lot of work to do to implement it. And there is a need to prioritise the most important steps to take to achieve its objectives. Arguably the most important measure which should be taken is the immediate engagement with people on payments such as one-parent family payment and disability allowance which can be done (and has been done on a pilot basis) without any change in the law. Whether any changes are necessary to make engagement compulsory (as recommended by the NESC) might best be decided after an initial voluntary approach. However, politicians and administrators appear to have been reluctant to attempt such an approach without a change in the underlying legislation.

The role (if any) of in-work benefits requires further consideration. The NESC has taken a somewhat inconsistent approach in this area. It recommends, on the one hand, uprating disregards of earned income (that is, increasing the amount of income a person can earn without affecting their welfare payment); and on the other hand, reducing the duration which people spend on benefits. But the increase in disregards may well lead to people staying on benefits as long or longer and combining work and welfare income.

The UK and US have been pioneers of in-work benefits and have distinguished clearly between 'bad' welfare benefits and 'good' in-work payments (operating now in both countries through the income tax system). This approach at least allows a clear focus on both reducing benefit duration and supporting work. But in-work benefits, even in this developed form, are not without problems. As Iversen (2005) points out, a focus on in-work benefits can provide a disincentive to workers to acquire skills, may discourage low-skilled workers from improving their skills through additional formal education and may give rise to increased fiscal costs if a rise in low pay and inequality is to be avoided. Such benefits are dependent on a healthy economy and an over-emphasis on such an approach could lead to pro-cyclical cuts in spending in a downturn as low-wage workers lose both jobs and benefits.

Ireland has the advantage that in-work benefits are currently quite small and we can therefore decide whether this is an appropriate path before rather than after we increase spending. Further research might usefully be carried out on the international experience in this area.

Children

Recent research by the OECD indicates that policies to reduce poverty amongst children 'should not be seen as choosing between either work or benefits, but require a balanced approach that encourages increased employment among parents and also increases the reward of paid work at the same time' (Whiteford and Adema, 2007, p. 36). Thus they will involve both child support measures and working-aged policies.

As Sweeney (Chapter 3) describes, the primary focus of support for children over the past decade has been child benefit. Beginning in 1994 under the Rainbow coalition government, child dependant allowances (additional payments directly linked to social welfare payments intended to provide support for child dependants) were frozen in level and resources directed instead towards the universal child benefit. However, for a number of years there was no consistent approach to the appropriate level of child benefit. In 2000, the Fianna Fáil-led government took a very significant step in this area announcing a major programme of investment in child benefit over a three-year period to almost triple the payment. However, after two years of significant increases, the implementation of this policy was slowed down[7] and the emphasis altered, insofar as coverage of childcare was concerned, in Budget 2006 with the announcement of a new childcare payment for children under six years.

Given the considerable cost of child benefit increases, the NESC was tasked in *Sustaining Progress* (Ireland, 2003) with carrying out a study on whether a new child support payment could be established, replacing child dependant allowances and the current in-work payment (family income supplement). The report arising from this study has not yet been published, presumably due to disagreements amongst the social partners.[8] However, Sweeney highlights a number of findings from the study – for example the costly nature of child benefit and the limited extent to which it is focused on people on low incomes – and explores the possibility of introducing a targeted second-tier child support payment which would channel support to children in low-income families.

The NESC argues that the current high rates of child poverty 'represent a very poor return' for the significant increases in child benefit in recent years (2005b, p. 155). However an alternative perspective would suggest, firstly, that the

---

[7] The original target was eventually 'reached' in 2006 but this obviously does not have regard to changes in earnings and the cost of living in the interim period.

[8] This is perhaps an area where it would be preferable, in line with the earlier practice of the NESC, to commission an independent study of the options upon which the Council could then comment rather than attempting to obtain agreement amongst all the social partners in relation to such a complex issue.

objective of child benefit is not only to reduce poverty but that it also has a horizontal redistributional component, that is to direct support to families with children. Secondly, focusing solely on the anti-poverty aspect, child benefit does not, it is true, direct significant resources to those in the lowest income deciles but this is because those in those deciles have few children. An alternative comparison would be to look at the distribution of benefits to families (with children). Here studies have shown that those with children (particularly large families) have a very high poverty risk and so a universal payment, such as child benefit, directs resources to such families in a manner which avoids both the employment and household formation problems implicit in any targeted approach. Research by the ESRI confirms that the major increases in child benefit (and the introduction of the early childcare supplement) led to a significant decrease (of 4.2 per cent) in the proportion of children falling below the relative income poverty line (Callan *et al.*, 2006).

One disadvantage of any targeted second-tier payment is withdrawal of benefits as income rises. This can be done sharply, which means that people can actually end up worse off as earned income rises (although this will affect a relatively small group of people). Conversely, one can withdraw support slowly to minimise disincentive effects (although this then affects a much wider group of people). Arguably if one adopts such an approach the best way to do it is through the income tax system (as in the UK) so that tax and welfare supports are coordinated. But why then introduce a new taxable child benefit supplement when the simplest way to introduce greater targeting would be to tax child benefit itself?

Child benefit may be a good example of the paradox of redistribution (Korpi and Palme, 1998), whereby payment of a universal as opposed to a more targeted benefit in fact results in a greater degree of redistribution because of the greater level of political and public support provided to such a cross-class benefit.[9]

Pensions

McCashin (Chapter 5) describes the development of pensions policy and notes that the absence of any earnings-related pension system is one of the key challenges facing policy-makers in Ireland. The Pensions Act 2000 required a review of pension cover to be prepared not later than September 2006. The review was carried out by the Pensions Board (2006a), which re-evaluated the targets, both in relation to the level of pension provided and of pension cover, set out by the National Pensions Policy Initiative (NPPI) in 1998. In addition, the Board considered a range of options in order to meet the targets and enhance pension coverage in Ireland. It generally endorsed the view that a replacement income target of 50 per cent of gross pre-retirement earnings remained appropriate and that the old age contributory pension should be raised to 34 per cent of gross average industrial earnings.[10] It also accepted the NPPI coverage target that 70 per cent of those working who are aged thirty or over should have occupational

---

[9] One of the difficulties with the introduction of any second-tier payment is that the relationship between the universal child benefit and the targeted supplement is unclear. What percentage of total support will the universal payment – as opposed to the targeted supplement – represent?

[10] In the latter case, a number of members believed that a higher minimum pension target is needed. In relation to the sustainability of the first-tier pensions, the Board recommended that persons retiring should be offered the option of deferring their retirement date in exchange for a higher pension.

or personal pension cover. However, although most members agreed that the pension targets would not be met without some change in the present pension system, the Board was unable to agree on a clear policy direction in this regard.

The Board outlined a number of possible options including a significant increase in the first pillar pension, the introduction of an earnings-related state pension and making private provision mandatory.[11] It agreed to recommend specific enhancements to the current voluntary system and many members considered that these enhancements could, over time, achieve significant improvement in coverage and adequacy.[12] However, it must be seriously doubted, based on the evidence in Ireland and other European countries to date, whether these proposals have a realistic chance of increasing pension coverage to the required extent.

When it came to mandatory pension coverage, although some members of the Board believed that a mandatory approach was the only certain way of achieving targets, others believed that the cost of this approach was too great in terms of its potential economic impact. However, then Minister for Social and Family Affairs Séamus Brennan asked the Board to complete its consideration on this aspect of pension policy and, rather than asking whether such a

---

[11] The Board commissioned a number of useful studies in relation to these options which are appended to its report.

[12] Other members of the Board, although not thinking that the proposals would achieve the targets, nonetheless supported them as a means of improving the current situation. Specifically, the Board recommended that the state incentive for Personal Retirement Savings Account (PRSA) pension contributions be granted by means of a matching contribution of €1 for each €1 invested rather than through tax relief, subject to a maximum amount.

pension should be introduced, asked for analysis of what such a pension might look like (Pensions Board, 2006b). Following on from this study, the government committed in *Towards 2016* to publish a green paper on pension policy outlining the major policy choices and challenges in this area and taking into account the views of the social partners.

The position in Ireland is somewhat similar to that in the UK.[13] The options in the UK have been clearly summarised by the Pensions Commission (2006). Given the projected rise in older people as a proportion of the population, these are:

1. Future pensioners will on average be poorer relative to average net incomes than today

2. Taxes/insurance contributions will have to rise to pay for pensions or other public spending will be cut to make room for pensions

3. Each generation will have to save more and be reliant on the next generation also choosing to save more and therefore buying the larger stock of assets accumulated by the prior generation

4. Average retirement ages will have to rise.

---

[13] The key differences are that while Ireland's first-tier pension is largely contributory based, in the UK there is heavy reliance on a means-tested system to achieve adequacy rates; and the UK already has a mandatory second-tier pension.

If, given the fact that very significant numbers of pensioners are on relatively low incomes at present,[14] we rule out option one, this means that policy must involve some combination of options 2, 3 and 4. The Pensions Board (2006a) discussed raising the pension age and it is sometimes suggested that this is necessary to address pension costs. However, many Irish people currently retire well before the statutory pension age. Before addressing the controversial topic of raising the pension age (other than on a voluntary basis), it makes more sense to try to get people to work up to the existing pension age and look at the range of employment and other policies necessary to encourage people to stay at work. As McCashin points out, raising the pension age on its own is a very blunt instrument and does not necessarily ensure that retirement age rises accordingly (as people may seek to use alternative invalidity or disability payments or rely on occupational pensions).

Secondly, some form of greatly increased pension will be necessary to provide a decent retirement income. The introduction of PRSAs has not led to a significant increase in pension take-up and seems unlikely to do so to a sufficient extent. The Pensions Board has now recommended even further and restructured government incentives to take out a pension on a voluntary basis. However, as McCashin argues, tax incentives are already expensive, benefit those on higher incomes most and have been ineffective in raising pension

---

14 As McCashin shows in Chapter 5, the apparent 'fall' in the proportion of older people in poverty after 2001 is due to the fact that the poverty line has only increased marginally, allowing pensions to 'catch up' with it. Pensions increased by 31 per cent between 1998 and 2001 but pensioner poverty rose to 44 per cent. Pensions increased by 17 per cent between 2001 and 2004 but pensioner poverty fell to 27 per cent.

coverage over the period from the 1970s. It is not clear that revised incentives will be more successful but they certainly will be even more costly.

The alternative is some form of mandatory approach, such as higher social welfare pensions, a state earnings-related pension or mandatory (or quasi-mandatory) private pensions (or a combination of these options). McCashin points to the benefits of a development of the current social welfare pensions with a significant increase in the rate of pension to 50 per cent of average industrial earnings.[15] It would appear that the government should make a decision that mandatory coverage is necessary and carry out any necessary further studies as to the appropriate options rather than going further down the road of voluntary approaches which have yet to be shown to work in any country.

Key cross-cutting issues

As identified in Chapter 1, this book examines a number of cross-cutting themes, including, in particular, gender and equality and rights-based policies.

Gender

As Walsh highlights in Chapter 2 (and in a range of previous studies), poverty has a particular gendered impact. At most stages of the lifecycle, women remain much more likely to be in poverty than men. Walsh shows that the risk-of-poverty rate for women has increased over time from a low of 16 per

---

[15] For a discussion of different options see Stewart, 2005; Cousins, 2005; Whelan, 2006; and the studies annexed to the *National Pensions Review* and the subsequent report on mandatory pensions (Pensions Board, 2006a, 2006b).

cent in 1994 to a high of 23 per cent in 2001, before falling back to 18.5 per cent in 2005. This trend is shaped by the pattern for older people, as there is a predominance of women among older people and they are more reliant on welfare payments. The level of consistent poverty for women is also somewhat higher than the male rate. And these adverse findings extend into other policy areas. Kelleher (Chapter 7) shows that, from a health perspective, cancer incidence in women in Ireland is the third highest in Europe and cancer mortality the second highest. Pillinger (Chapter 9) highlights the fact that women migrants often experience particular difficulties including the double discrimination faced by immigrant women in the labour market, poor working conditions and exploitation.

These findings highlight the need for policy-makers to put gender issues at the centre of the policy-making process. In the area of income support, it emphasises the importance of looking at issues such as child income support from a gendered perspective. It also, as Murphy shows in Chapter 4, accentuates the importance of taking account of gender issues (such as the need for family-friendly and childcare measures) in any policy to encourage currently non-employed welfare claimants into employment. Equally important is access to income support for older women, given that older women may be particularly at risk of poverty. This emphasises the importance of ensuring access to adequate pensions, but, as McCashin shows in Chapter 5, the percentage of older men in direct receipt of a state old age pension is significantly higher than the proportion of the female population – 95 per cent in contrast to 80 per cent – and while three-quarters of men receive an insurance pension, among women the figure is much lower.

Equality and rights-based policies

Interestingly, issues concerning rights rarely arose in the chapters dealing with income support. This is clearly because a legal right to payment already exists in these areas with a related right of appeal to the independent Social Welfare Appeals Office. Provision of services is generally much less rights-based. On the one hand, it may be more difficult to adjudicate on issues concerning the right to, for example, health services, which can raise complex medical issues. On the other hand, it can be argued that some of the failings of the existing services, for example the inability of some children to access basic educational services, have been due to the lack of any rights-based approach in practice.[16] Similarly Murphy, in Chapter 4, highlights the need for a rights-based approach in the area of active labour market policies so as to safeguard the right to social inclusion and ensure it is not made contingent solely on economic participation.

In Chapter 9, Pillinger highlights the importance of rights in relation to migration policy at a number of different levels. First, the importance of respect for international human rights such as those set out in the European Convention on Human Rights. Second, the need for a rights-based approach to migration policy so that people can be aware of the reasons for, and be able to challenge, adverse decisions. And third, the importance of ensuring that migrants can enforce rights which do exist to, for example, welfare benefits, where they

---

[16] In fact the Irish Constitution provides an obligation on the state to provide for primary education. However, this right has not been given effect through legislation or administrative practice, which means that, in practice, children either cannot enforce it or, a rare minority, have to take proceedings in the High Court to do so.

may encounter difficulties because of lack of local knowledge or language barriers.

The Disability Act 2005 – while not explicitly rights-based – is an interesting attempt to provide statutory rules as to assessment for and the provision of services and to establish a mechanism to enforce the provision of those services. On the basis of the debates about that legislation, it may be unrealistic to expect that all services will be established on the basis of justiciable rights in the immediate future. Nonetheless, there are a number of steps which can be taken to improve access to services from an anti-poverty perspective. First, where constitutional and statutory rights already exist (as, for example, in relation to aspects of health and education services), measures should be put in place to allow people to enforce those rights (without having to have access to the courts).[17] Second, the potential of the 'quality standards' approach can be tested to examine the contribution which it can make in practice to improving the position of people who are in poverty.[18] The Equal Status Acts 2000 to 2004 and the European Convention on Human Rights are likely to become increasingly important over time both in helping to establish rights and in ensuring that particular groups are not discriminated against in terms of access to services.[19] Finally, information, advice and

---

[17] For example, the Health Acts provide for a statutory appeal system concerning the refusal of a medical card but this has never been brought into force.

[18] Through, for example, the recently established complaints procedure under Part 9 of the Health Act 2004.

[19] The Equal Status Act currently excludes statutory services provided under 'any enactment'. However, this leaves many aspects of public services within the remit of the Act.

advocacy services need to ensure that all people can access the available rights and services.

Conclusions

The key message of this book is that, despite the important progress in many aspects of Irish society, our social development – in terms of poverty levels, health and education outcomes – has not kept pace with our economic development. The studies in this book suggest that the main reason for this is that public policy has yet to adopt and implement a consistent anti-poverty approach as a core policy concern. The NESC's identification of a coherent approach to and rationale for a developmental welfare state is an essential first step in the birth of a new welfare dispensation and the development of a more inclusive society.

A number of recent studies have identified the links between different employment and business structures and the development of welfare states. For example Mares (2003) argues that the presence of skilled workers, firm size and the relative incidence of risk facing a firm can affect employer preferences for social policy developments. In a similar vein, Iversen (2005) argues that employees who have invested in specific skills also tend to favour greater welfare state spending. Insofar as the Irish economy will focus in the future on more internationally traded services and higher skills, this would suggest greater pressure for higher welfare state spending. However, welfare state spending cannot simply be read off the employment or business structure of a particular country. If the developmental welfare state is to be implemented in practice, political decisions will be essential. And while it is an important achievement for the social partners to agree on a theoretical approach in the NESC, it may be unrealistic to expect them to agree to the important changes necessary to implement this approach in practice. Here political initiative will be essential.

We are now at a critical juncture in the development of Irish anti-poverty policy. Demographic pressures are relatively low. Economically, Ireland has moved from being a relatively poor peripheral European country to having a GNP per capita that is one of the highest in the EU. It has long been argued that such economic development is a necessary pre-condition for social policy improvements. We now have the economic resources to invest in social policy. Just as important – as has been argued by the NESC and others – social development is essential both in itself and as a necessary component of future balanced economic growth.

We are now able to make important decisions about the future of Irish society. And the decisions we make (or do not make) now will influence welfare outcomes for the next decades. Public policy has set the goal of developing a participatory society and economy, with a strong commitment to social justice. However, as shown in this book, the focus of policies has been on targeted measures to address poverty and social inclusion rather than on ensuring that policies themselves are designed to achieve equal and equitable outcomes.

If we are to achieve in the area of social development what has been achieved in economic development, it will be essential that policy-makers move the developmental approach to the centre of the policy-making process. This is a challenge and a responsibility for us all.

References

Barrett, A. and McCarthy, Y. (2006), *Immigrants in a Booming Economy: Analysing Their Earnings and Welfare Dependency*, Bonn: IZA

Callan, T., Coleman, K., Nolan, B. and Walsh, J. R. (2006), 'Child Poverty and Child Income Supports: Ireland in Comparative Perspective', in *Budgetary Perspectives 2007*, Dublin: ESRI

Connolly, E. (2007), *The Institutionalization of Anti-Poverty and Social Exclusion Policy in Irish Social Partnership*, Dublin: Combat Poverty Agency

Cousins, M. (2005), *Explaining the Irish Welfare State*, Lewiston: Edwin Mellen

Ireland (1997), *Sharing in Progress: National Anti-Poverty Strategy*, Dublin: Stationery Office

Ireland (2002), *Building an Inclusive Society*, Dublin: Stationery Office

Ireland (2003), *Sustaining Progress: Social Partnership Agreement 2003–2005*, Dublin: Stationery Office

Ireland (2006a), *Government Discussion Paper: Proposals for Supporting Lone Parents*, Dublin: Stationery Office

Ireland (2006b), *Towards 2016: Ten-Year Framework Social Partnership Agreement 2007–2016*, Dublin: Stationery Office

Ireland (2007), *National Action Plan for Social Inclusion 2007–2016*, Dublin: Stationery Office

Iversen, T. (2005), *Capitalism, Democracy and Welfare*, Cambridge: Cambridge University Press

Korpi, W. and Palme, J. (1998), 'The Paradox of Redistribution and Strategies of Equality', *American Sociological Review*, vol. 63, no. 5, pp. 661–687

Mares, I. (2003), *The Politics of Social Risk*, Cambridge: Cambridge University Press

NESC (2005a), *The Developmental Welfare State*, Dublin: National Economic and Social Council

NESC (2005b), *Strategy 2006: People, Productivity and Purpose*, Dublin: National Economic and Social Council.

Nolan, B. (2003), *On Rights-Based Services for People with Disabilities*, Dublin: ESRI

O'Kelly, K. P. (2007), *The Evaluation of Mainstreaming Social Inclusion in Europe*, Dublin: Combat Poverty Agency

Pensions Board (2006a), *National Pensions Review*, Dublin: Pensions Board

Pensions Board (2006b), *Special Savings for Retirement*, Dublin: Pensions Board

Pensions Commission (2006), *A New Pension Settlement for the Twenty-First Century,* London: HMSO

Stewart, J. (ed.) (2005), *For Richer, For Poorer: An Investigation of the Irish Pension System,* Dublin: tasc

Whelan, C. T. and Layte, R. (2006), 'Economic Boom and Social Mobility: The Irish Experience', *Research in Social Stratification and Mobility*, vol. 24, no. 2, pp. 193–208

Whelan, S. (2006), 'A Constructive Critique of Pension Policy in Ireland', 21st Annual Conference of the Foundation for Fiscal Studies, Dublin, 29 March

Whiteford, P. and Adema, W. (2007), *What Works Best in Reducing Child Poverty: A Benefit of Work Strategy?*, Paris: OECD

Glossary

Benchmarking: A point of reference. It is often used in the public sector as a term for comparing the performance in the public sector with the private sector or for comparing systems in Ireland with systems in other countries.

Child dependant: *see* Qualified child.

Community development: The long-term process whereby people who are marginalised or living in poverty work together to identify their needs, create change, exert more influence in the decisions which affect their lives and work to improve the quality of their lives, the communities in which they live and the society of which they are part.

Consistent poverty: A measure of poverty which combines relative income poverty with a measure of deprivation, i.e. the lack of basic items such as a warm coat, sufficient food or adequate heating. The percentage of people living in consistent poverty is the proportion of the total population who are living on a lower than normal income and who lack certain basic essential items thereby experiencing a lower standard of living than the rest of society.

Demographic ageing: Occurs when a relatively higher proportion of the population is made up of ageing or older people, with implications for social spending on pensions, healthcare and other supports.

Direct provision: A support system for asylum seekers whereby all accommodation costs together with the cost of three main meals and snacks, heat, light, laundry, maintenance etc. are paid directly by the state. In addition, asylum seekers in receipt of direct provision are paid €19.10 per adult and €9.60 per child per week.

Economic, social and cultural rights: Refers to the rights of all persons to live a fully human life which meets their physical, emotional, intellectual and social needs. Being deprived of these rights is often symptomatic of living in poverty. *See also* justiciable rights.

Empowerment: The process of transferring decision-making power from influential sectors to poor communities and individuals who have traditionally been excluded from it.

EU-15, EU-25: Refer to the composition of the EU at different stages of enlargement. EU-15 refers to the fifteen member states before the accession of ten new countries in 2004, while EU-25 refers to the position after that accession.

EU-SILC: European Union Survey of Income and Living Conditions conducted by the Central Statistics Office. It replaced the Living in Ireland Survey as the major source of poverty data from 2003.

GDP, GNP: Measures of the total value of goods and services produced by a nation. Gross national product (GNP) is the value of all final goods and services produced within a nation in a given year, plus income earned by its citizens abroad, minus income earned by foreigners from domestic production. In contrast, gross domestic product (GDP) excludes net income from abroad (that is, interest and profits from overseas loans and investments, less payments on foreign debts and investments in the country; and net receipts of workers' wages).

Gini coefficient: A quantitative measure of income inequality ranging from 0 to 1. The higher the coefficient, the higher the inequality of the income distribution.

Income deciles: Measuring and comparing the relative income of different groups by dividing the total population into tenths.

Indexation: A method by which social welfare payments would be increased by a certain amount each year. This amount would relate to a particular factor index in the economy such as inflation, earnings or incomes.

Justiciable rights: Rights provide a claim or entitlement to a particular resource or opportunity, such as the right to housing, the right to an adequate standard of living or the right to vote. Justiciable rights refer to rights that are part of the legal structure and that can be brought by an individual or a group before the courts for judgment on whether the right can be enforced or can be used to ensure the provision of a particular resource.

Lisbon Strategy: An agreement reached by EU heads of government at the Lisbon European Council in 2000 to integrate employment, economic and social policies in order to make the EU the most competitive economy in the world.

Living in Ireland Survey (LIS): A survey carried out by the Economic and Social Research Institute from 1994 to 2001, the primary source of data on poverty and deprivation in Ireland. Replaced by the EU-SILC from 2003.

Marginalisation: The process whereby certain groups suffering deprivation, for example the impoverished, unemployed, single parents and those with limited formal education, are pushed to the edge of society where they have little say in decision-making and are denied the means to improve their position.

Multiculturalism: The status of several different ethnic, racial, religious or cultural groups coexisting in harmony in the same society.

NAPinclusion: National action plan on poverty and social inclusion agreed by each EU member state in order to work towards greater social inclusion through encouraging sustainable economic growth and quality employment for the poorer sectors of society.

National Anti-Poverty Strategy (NAPS): The ten-year plan of the Irish government aimed at tackling poverty, which involves consultation, target setting and poverty proofing. NAPS sought to achieve a better understanding of the structural causes of poverty such as unemployment, low income and educational disadvantage. (Now subsumed into the NAPinclusion.)

National Development Plan (NDP): The Irish government's strategy for allocating EU Structural Funds and other public monies aimed at stimulating long-term growth and a fairer distribution of resources across the whole economy.

Open method of policy coordination: A process whereby EU member states are responsible for national employment and social inclusion policies but are open to evaluation by other member states by submitting national action plans to the European Commission. These are discussed by the Commission and by social affairs ministers at the European Council meeting each spring. Guidelines for the plans are set at EU level and include specific timetables for achieving goals set, the establishment of indicators to compare best practice, translating the European guidelines into national and regional policies and periodic monitoring and review.

Poverty: People are said to be living in poverty if their income and resources are so inadequate as to preclude them from having a standard of living considered acceptable in Irish society. Because of their poverty they may experience multiple disadvantage through unemployment, low income, poor housing, inadequate healthcare and barriers to education. They are often marginalised and excluded from participating in activities that are the norm for other people. *See also* consistent poverty, relative income poverty.

Poverty lines: From a base of average household income, poverty lines show the number of households and families falling below a certain income level and how far below that level they are. Poverty lines are usually set at 40 per cent, 50 per cent or 60 per cent of the average or median income.

Poverty proofing: The process by which government departments, local authorities and state agencies assess policies and programmes at design and review stages in relation to the likely impact that they will have, or have had, on poverty and on inequalities that are likely to lead to poverty, with a view to poverty reduction.

PRSA (Personal retirement savings account): A new form of personal pension in Ireland. It is intended to be more 'user-friendly' than existing pensions and to help increase the uptake of personal pension cover.

PRSI (Pay-related social insurance): The social insurance contribution paid by employees, employers and the self-employed to fund certain social welfare benefits.

Qualified adult: A person (normally a spouse or a partner of the opposite sex) in respect of whom an increase in a social welfare payment is paid (formerly known as adult dependant).

Qualified child: A child in respect of whom an increase in a social welfare payment is paid (formerly known as child dependant).

Quarterly National Household Survey (QNHS): Conducted by the Central Statistics Office every three months, the

QNHS provides the official measure of employment and unemployment.

Redistribution: Individuals and groups on higher incomes or wealth distributing to those on lower incomes or wealth. Redistribution by government is usually through transfers, regulation or provision of public services. Transfers involve the collection of money from people through the tax system and the payment of income to people through payments such as unemployment assistance or subsidies such as mortgage interest relief. The minimum wage or rent controls are examples of regulation. Public transport and local authority housing are examples of the state provision of services.

Relative income poverty: Relative income poverty is having an income that is less than that regarded as the norm in society, giving a lower than normal standard of living. It is 'relative' because it is measured by how much less it is relative to the income of the majority of people. It is usually expressed as a percentage, for example the 60 per cent relative income poverty line is 60 per cent of the average or median disposable household income. *See also* consistent poverty, risk of poverty.

Rights: *see* Economic, social and cultural rights.

Risk of poverty: The proportion of people living in households where their disposable income is below the threshold of 60 per cent of the national average disposable income. The EU measure of risk of poverty is defined as the proportion of persons with an equivalent total net income below 60 per cent of national average income.

Schools designated with disadvantaged status: A number of primary schools are designated as disadvantaged in Ireland. This means that they get a greater level of support in terms of pupil–teacher ratios, special grants etc.

Social capital: Networks, understanding and values that shape the way we relate to each other and participate in social activities.

Social cohesion: Bringing together, in an integrated way, economic, social, health and educational policies to facilitate the participation of citizens in societal life.

Social exclusion: The process whereby certain groups are pushed to the margins of society and prevented from participating fully by virtue of their poverty, low education or inadequate life skills. This distances them from employment, income and education opportunities as well as social and community networks. They have little access to power and decision-making bodies, little chance of influencing decisions or policies that affect them and little chance of bettering their standard of living.

Social inclusion: Ensuring the marginalised and those living in poverty have greater participation in decision-making which affects their lives, allowing them to improve their living standards and their overall wellbeing.

Social partnership: The process where government, employers, trade unions, farmers and the community and voluntary sector devise economic and social agreements for a set timeframe.

Sustainable economic and social development: The type of broad-based, long-term human growth which encourages the continual development of skills, capacities and talents to the fullest possible extent as a means of challenging <u>poverty</u> and <u>social exclusion</u>.

Index